Checking the Courts

SUNY series in American Constitutionalism

Robert J. Spitzer, editor

Checking the Courts

Law, Ideology, and Contingent Discretion

Kirk A. Randazzo

and

Richard W. Waterman

SUNY
PRESS

Published by State University of New York Press, Albany

© 2014 State University of New York

For information, contact State University of New York Press, Albany, NY
www.sunypress.edu

Production by Diane Ganeles
Marketing by Anne M. Valentine

Library of Congress Cataloging-in-Publication Data

Randazzo, Kirk A., author.
  Checking the courts : law, ideology, and contingent discretion / Kirk A. Randazzo and Richard W. Waterman.
       pages cm. — (SUNY series in American constitutionalism)
  Includes bibliographical references and index.
  ISBN 978-1-4384-5287-6 (hardcover : alk. paper)
  ISBN 978-1-4384 5288-3 (pbk.: alk. paper)
  1. Courts—United States.   2. Judicial process—United States.   3. Political questions and judicial power—United States.   4. Constitutional law—United States.   I. Waterman, Richard W., author.   II. Title.

  KF8700.R36 2014
  347.73'12—dc23   2013040987

10 9 8 7 6 5 4 3 2 1

Contents

List of Illustrations   vii
Acknowledgments   xi

1   Introduction   1

     Anecdotal Evidence of Statutory Influence on Judges   3
     Systematic Statutory Influences on Judicial Behavior   5
     Measuring Legal Factors   7
     Organization of the Book   9

2   Theoretical Foundations   11

     Approaches to Interpretation and the Canons of
          Statutory Construction   12
     Separation of Powers Models   17
     Influence of Law and Ideology on Judicial Behavior   21
     Placing Judicial Decision Making into a Broader
          Theoretical Context   25
     The Model of Contingent Discretion   28
     Operationalization of Statutory Discretion   37
     Conclusions   38

3   U.S. Courts of Appeals   41

     Historical Development of the Federal Appellate Courts   42
     Anecdotal Evidence from Appeals Court Judges   44
     Empirical Analysis of Statutory Influence   47
     Circuit-Specific Analyses of Statutory Influence   57
     An Alternative Specification   58
     Conclusions   62

4   The U.S. Supreme Court   63

     Historical Development of the Supreme Court   65
     Anecdotal Evidence from Supreme Court Justices   66
     Empirical Evidence Analysis of Statutory Influence   71
     Justice-Specific Analyses of Statutory Influence   85
     An Alternative Specification   87
     Examination of Statutes Under Judicial Review   89
     Corollary Analysis of Statutes and Unanimous Decisions   92
     Conclusions   94

5   State Supreme Courts   97

     Influence of Law and Ideology on State Supreme Courts   98
     Anecdotal Evidence from State Court Judges   100
     Empirical Analysis of Statutory Influence   103
     Corollary Analysis of Statutes and Judicial
        Elections/Appointments   113
     Conclusions   116

6   Temporal Analysis of Supreme Court Behavior   119

     The Temporal Nature of the Law   120
     Evolution of Congressional Statutory Language   124
     Empirical Analysis of Statutory Influence versus
        Judicial Annotations   129
     Corollary Analysis of Statutes and Unanimous Decisions 135
     Conclusions   137

7   Toward a New Paradigm   141

     Summary of Empirical Evidence   143
     Theoretical and Substantive Implications   145
     Important Caveats   152
     Remaining Questions   153

Appendix   155
Notes   179
References   189
Index   199

Illustrations

Figures

2.1. General Separation of Powers Model A   18

2.2. General Separation of Powers Model B   18

2.3. General Separation of Powers Model C   20

3.1. Impact of Statutory Detail on Sincere Voting in Criminal Cases   54

3.2. Impact of Statutes on Sincere Voting in Individual Liberties Cases   57

3.3. Impact of Statutory Detail Across Circuits   59

4.1. Impact of Constraint and Ideology in *Non-Civil Rights* Cases   84

4.2. Impact of Statutory Detail Across Individual Justices   86

4.3. Influence of Statute Length on Unanimous Decisions   93

5.1. Impact of Constraint on Sincere Voting in Criminal Cases   109

6.1. Changes in Statute Length over Time   125

6.2. Changes in Criminal Statutes over Time   126

6.3. Changes in Civil Liberties Statutes over Time   126

6.4. Changes in Economic Statutes over Time   127

6.5. Changes in Judicial Annotations over Time   128

6.6. Impact of Judicial Annotations on Sincere Voting   135

6.7. Influence of Statute Length on Unanimous Decisions   136

6.8. Influence of Judicial Annotations on Unanimous
     Decisions   137

7.1. Individual Decision Making Under Multiple Influence
     Scenario A   146

7.2. Individual Decision Making Under Multiple Influence
     Scenario B   147

7.3. Individual Decision Making Under Multiple Influence
     Scenario C   148

7.4. Individual Decision Making Under Multiple Influence
     Scenario D   149

7.5. Ideological Decision Making   150

7.6. Ideological Decision Making with Statutory Influences   150

7.7. Ideological Decision Making with Statutory and
     Temporal Influences   151

Tables

3.1. The Nature of Congressional Statutes Under Review   50

3.2. Congressional Statutes Under Review by Issue Area   51

3.3. Probit Analysis of Appellate Decisions   53

3.4. Probit Analysis of Appellate Decisions   55

3.5. An Alternative Specification for Criminal Cases   61

4.1. The Nature of Congressional Statutes Under Review   74

4.2. Congressional Statutes Under Review by Issue Area   75

4.3. Appeals Courts—Supreme Court Comparison   77

4.4. Probit Analysis of Supreme Court Decisions   78

4.5. Probit Analysis of More Specific Categories   82

4.6. An Alternative Specification for Criminal Cases   88

4.7. Questioning the Constitutionality of
     Congressional Statutes   90

4.8. Probit Analysis of Statutes Under Judicial Review   91

5.1. Multilevel Model of Statutory Influence   108

5.2. Multilevel Model of Statutory Constraint in Death
     Penalty Cases   111

5.3. Fixed Effects Model of Statutory Constraint in
     Discrimination Cases   112

5.4. Determinants of the Level of Detail in State Statutes 115

6.1. The Interplay of Statutes and Annotations in
     Criminal Cases   131

6.2. The Interplay of Statutes and Annotations in
     Non-Civil Rights Cases   134

Acknowledgments

As with any project of this magnitude, its completion would not be possible without the generous support and assistance from several individuals and sources. First, we are extremely grateful to the National Science Foundation for providing a grant (SES-0719328) to support substantial portions of this research. Second, we appreciate the research assistance provided by Jeffrey Fine, Michael Fix, and S. Andrew Martin. Third, we would like to thank the numerous departments, associations, and institutions who listened to presentations of the research. Previous versions of this manuscript were presented at annual meetings of the American Political Science Association (2004, 2005, 2006, 2007, and 2009), the University of Kentucky School of Law (2007), the Conference on the Seventh Circuit Court of Appeals at Southern Illinois University–Carbondale School of Law (2008), the annual meeting of the Southern Political Science Association (2009), the Empirical Implications of Theoretical Models Institute (EITM) at the University of Michigan (2009), the University of South Carolina's Department of Political Science (2011), the University of Alabama's Department of Political Science (2011), and the EITM Alumni Conference at the annual meeting of the Midwest Political Science Association (2012). We also wish to thank Michael Rinella, Senior Acquisitions Editor at SUNY Press, for all of his support and advice.

Additionally, we appreciate the many individuals who offered comments throughout the development of this research. Our sincere thanks to John Aldrich, Chris Bonneau, Bradley Canon, David Darmofal, Charles Finocchiaro, Richard Fording, Matthew Gabel, Elizabeth Gerber, Douglas Gibler, Robert Howard, Mark Hurwitz, Arthur "Skip" Lupia, Mark Peffley, Reginald Sheehan, Harold Spaeth, Donald Songer, Lee Walker, and Neal Woods. Though these individuals all contributed to the completion of this book, any errors or omissions are solely the responsibility of the authors.

Portions of this book have appeared in various journals, and we thank the editors for their gracious permission to reprint some of the text here. In particular, portions of this research have appeared in the *Journal of Politics, Political Research Quarterly*, the *Justice System Journal*, and the *Southern Illinois University Law Review*. More specifically, portions of the introduction in Chapter 1 and the theoretical argument articulated in Chapter 2 appear in all of the journals. Additionally, portions of the empirical analyses in Chapter 3 appear in the *Journal of Politics* and the *Southern Illinois University Law Review*; a portion of the empirical analyses in Chapter 4 appears in the *Justice System Journal*; and, portions of the analyses in Chapter 5 appear in *Political Research Quarterly*.

Finally, Randazzo wishes to thank the Departments of Political Science at the University of South Carolina and the University of Kentucky for their support and encouragement throughout the project. He also wishes to thank his wife, Carol, and two children, Samuel and Anna, for their continued love and support. They constantly remind him of what is truly important and their smiles always brighten any day.

Richard Waterman thanks the University of Kentucky for its support. He also thanks his partner Sendil Nathan.

1

Introduction

> Whoever hath an absolute authority to interpret any written or spoken laws, it is he who is truly the lawgiver, to all intents and purposes, and not the person who first spoke or wrote them.
>
> —Benjamin Hoadly, quoted in Carter and Burke (2002, 68)

This quotation raises an important and fundamental question concerning the development of law in the United States: from where does the law emerge? Benjamin Hoadly's statement indicates that the answer lies with courts and judges, since they possess the authority to interpret the law. Yet, the Constitution provides Congress with the authority to make the law. This overlapping Constitutional authority consequently creates an "invitation to struggle" (Corwin 1957, 171) between the legislature and the judiciary over who makes the law—the Congress that writes statutes, or the courts that interpret them.[1] Chief Justice John Marshall recognized this "invitation to struggle" when he wrote the opinion of the Court in *Marbury v. Madison.*[2] While this case is often cited as the foundation of the Supreme Court's power of judicial review—the ability to examine a legislative statute in reference to the Constitution—it is worth noting that Marshall concluded the opinion by stating that "the framers of the constitution contemplated that instrument [the Constitution] as a rule for government of courts, as well as of the legislature."[3] Fisher (2011, 18) builds upon Marshall's logic when he explains that "the Constitution is often protected when political interests triumph. Political interests have successfully prevailed over judicial opinions in such areas as commerce, race, women's rights, child labor, religion, and privacy." Bailey and Maltzman (2011, 3) agree with Fisher when they note that "the legislative [branch] may be able to push the Court in favored directions with threats and persuasion, thereby attenuating the danger that

1

the Court becomes a policymaker divorced from public will." Thus, from the earliest days of the United States through more recent years the question about the development of the law has perplexed legal experts and generated tension between the legislative and judicial branches.

In the last decade, this "invitation to struggle" became apparent during the confirmation hearing of John Roberts to replace the late William Rehnquist as Chief Justice of the U.S. Supreme Court. On the first day, Senator Arlen Specter (Chair of the Judiciary Committee) included the following statement in his opening remarks: "I'm very much concerned about what I conceive to be an imbalance in the separation of powers between the Congress and the court. I am concerned about what I bluntly say is the denigration by the court of congressional authority."[4] In his opening comments, John Roberts remarked that "judges and justices are servants of the law, not the other way around. Judges are like umpires. Umpires don't make the rules; they apply them. The roles of an umpire and a judge are critical. They make sure everybody plays by the rules. But it is a limited role. Nobody ever went to a ball game to see the umpire."[5] John Roberts was confirmed as Chief Justice of the Supreme Court, in part, because these comments indicated to the U.S. Senate that he viewed a judge's role as an applier of the rules and not as a legislator in judge's robes. Stated another way, the statutes passed by Congress should receive substantial deference from judges and justices because those statutes are the law.

Similar to the Roberts confirmation, the question of "who makes the law" was a prominent issue during the confirmation hearing of Sonia Sotomayor to replace David Souter as an Associate Justice on the U.S. Supreme Court. During her opening remarks Judge Sotomayor stated, "In the past month, many senators have asked me about my judicial philosophy. Simple: fidelity to the law. The task of a judge is not to make the law. It is to apply the law."[6] Throughout her confirmation hearing, Judge Sotomayor was asked repeatedly to elaborate on this comment and to discuss her opinions regarding the separation of powers between Congress and the courts on the meaning of law. On day three of the hearings, Senator Benjamin Cardin stated, "One of my concerns is that we are seeing judicial activism in restricting the clear intent of Congress in moving forward on fundamental protections . . . During your testimony yesterday . . . you made it clear that judges apply the laws enacted . . . with deference to the intent of Congress. Yet we've seen in recent decisions of the Supreme Court . . . that they reject long-standing legal interpretations in the federal [statutes]."[7] As part of her response, Judge Sotomayor stated that the Court must make decisions "with a recognition of the deference it owes to the elected branches in terms of setting policy and making law."[8] Similar to the comments made by John Roberts during his confirmation hearing, Sonia Sotomayor repeatedly indicated that Congress was the branch constitutionally responsible for making the law, while the judiciary simply applied those rules to particular cases.

Anecdotal Evidence of Statutory Influence on Judges

The examples of the Roberts and Sotomayor confirmation hearings serve to illustrate the inherent tension between Congress and the courts over the law. Indeed, defining the lawmaking responsibilities of the legislative and judicial branches is "a highly dynamic process sometimes overlooked" by scholars of these institutions (Campbell and Stack 2001, xiii). Fisher (2001, 21) notes that "although it is conventional to view the judiciary—and especially the Supreme Court—as the ultimate and final arbiter of constitutional law, numerous examples over two centuries suggest a more dynamic and less hierarchical model." This dynamic process is also observed by Paschal (1992) when he notes that there is a "continuing colloquy" between the legislative and judicial branches over the meaning of the law. This ongoing dialogue raises important questions for scholars of the judiciary. To what extent do legal factors (such as legislative statutes) influence the behavior of judges and justices?

Briefly examining a few specific cases serves to illustrate how legislative statutes affect judicial behavior, and also highlights the tension between the legislative and judicial branches over statutory interpretation and the law. For example, in the case of *Burlington Industries, Inc. v. Ellerth*, a civil rights case heard before the Rehnquist Court in 1998,[9] the Supreme Court voted 7–2 in favor of the respondent, who had been sexually harassed by her boss, a vice-president at Burlington Industries. After 15 months she quit her job, and later sued Burlington Industries, claiming they were liable to pay civil damages because the company was negligent in addressing the circumstance and was therefore liable under the Civil Rights Act of 1964. The Court held that even if the employee had no adverse job-related consequences the company is vicariously liable for supervisors who create hostile work environments, even if said employer is not directly responsible for the supervisor's behavior (42 U.S.C. § 2000e is a subsection of Title VII of the Civil Rights Act). This subsection contains a list of legal definitions, which include very specific instructions for judges about how to define vague terms such as "employer," "employment agency," and "labor organization." In the Court's opinion, Justice Anthony Kennedy, a moderate Republican appointee, cited detailed language in 42 U.S.C. § 2000e, which defines an employer to include any agent of the employer. Because the vice-president was an agent of the Burlington Industries, the company was liable and the employee was able to bring suit. This specific language compelled Kennedy, his moderate Republican colleagues Justices O'Connor and Souter, as well as Chief Justice Rehnquist, to vote with the high court's liberal wing (Justices Stevens, Ginsburg, and Breyer).

A second example is found in the case, *Mansell v. Mansell* (1989),[10] which involves an interpretation of the Uniformed Services Former Spouses' Protection Act, where the Supreme Court adjudicated a question concerning retirement pay. Though the justices preferred to rule in favor of the spouse, they were constrained from doing so by the specific language of the Act. In writing for the majority, Justice Thurgood Marshall states:

> We realize that reading the statute literally may inflict economic harm on many former spouses. But we decline to misread the statute in order to reach a sympathetic result when such a reading requires us to do violence to the plain language of the statute and to ignore much of the legislative history. Congress chose the language that requires us to decide as we do, and Congress is free to change it.[11]

A third example comes from the case *Guidry v. Sheet Metal Workers National Pension Fund*.[12] In this case the Supreme Court reviewed a trial court order that placed a constructive trust on an individual's pension benefits pursuant to a guilty plea involving the embezzlement of union funds. The dispute arose, in part, because of a conflict between provisions in the Labor-Management Reporting and Disclosure Act of 1959 and the Employee Retirement Income Security Act of 1974. In ruling on behalf of the petitioner, Guidry, Justice Harold Blackmun commented specifically on the language of the congressional statutes. He stated that "courts should be loath to announce . . . exceptions to legislative requirements or prohibitions that are unqualified by the statutory text . . . The impracticability of defining such [an exception] reinforces our conclusion that the identification of any exception should be left to Congress."[13]

Additionally, it is important to note that these types of examples do not exist solely at the Supreme Court level. Similar discussions occur within the deliberations of state supreme court judges as well. For example, in *Maier v. General Telephone Co.* (2002),[14] the Michigan Supreme Court was asked to review an appeal over the interpretation of the Michigan Worker's Disability Compensation Act. In writing a concurring opinion, Chief Justice Maura D. Corrigan elaborates on aspects of statutory interpretation. She states that "a first principle of statutory interpretation is that *the words expressed in the statute are the law*."[15] She continues to defend this position by claiming that the specific words used in statutes are of paramount importance (rather than the intent of the legislature) because "men may intend what they will; but it is only the laws that they enact which bind us."[16]

Systematic Statutory Influences on Judicial Behavior

While the anecdotal evidence presented above serves as useful illustrations of the tension between legislatures and the judiciary, it does not provide a systematic accounting of the influence of statutory language on judicial behavior. Consequently, in expanding on the "invitation to struggle" between the legislature and the judiciary, one must ask to what extent do legal factors (such as legislative statutes) influence systematically the behavior of judges and justices? On one side of this debate are advocates of the "attitudinal model" who argue that judges are motivated primarily by their personal ideological policy preferences (Segal and Spaeth 1993, 2002). On the other side are legal advocates who contend that the law is of paramount importance (Posner 2001). While numerous analyses exist which empirically demonstrate the influence of ideology,[17] a similar pattern has not emerged for the quantitative analysis of legal influences. Though qualitative research reinforces the conventional wisdom about the influence of law, "the real question is not whether such behavior exists at all, but whether it exists at systematic and substantively meaningful levels" (Spaeth and Segal 1999, 7). Unfortunately, previous quantitative research of legal influences is plagued by inadequate measures. Our book addresses this inadequacy by developing an empirical measure of statutory influence. We then test the measure across decisions in state and federal courts.

To date, the empirical literature on congressional influence over the courts has focused primarily on the nomination process or congressional overrides of judicial decisions. However, these two aspects involve only a small fraction of the interactions between the two branches. Most exchanges between Congress and the judiciary occur after confirmation of judges and before attempts at overrides; namely, over the interpretation of statutes by courts. Yet, statutes have received relatively little attention in the empirical judicial literature, mostly because only rough measures (such as dummy variables) have been available to test their impact. This is unfortunate since, theoretically, statutes are extremely important because *they represent the primary opportunity legislatures have to ensure that those individuals who interpret or implement the law (e.g., judges and bureaucrats) will follow their preferences.* Hence, in those cases where lawmakers have clear policy preferences they can write legislation that encourages judges to strictly interpret the plain meaning of the law, a goal consistent with the legal model of judicial decision making. If legislatures do not write clear legislation, then it leaves open the possibility that judges will make decisions based on their own policy preferences in accord with the tenets of the attitudinal model. Consequently, an important empirical question remains unresolved—*to what extent do legislative statutes exert a systematic influence on judicial behavior?*

"While many (if not most) scholars recognize that the [judges] probably respond to both of these concerns [attitudes and the law], the literature nonetheless tends to present them as competing explanations" (Hansford and Spriggs 2006, 9–10). Consequently, a more robust and dynamic theoretical model is needed that integrates both ideological and legal factors, thereby allowing researchers of the judiciary to fully integrate both Congress and the courts into a single model of judicial behavior. The main reason for this lack of integration is that while scholars possess viable measures of judicial ideology (e.g., Segal and Cover 1989; Martin and Quinn 2002) to support theories of attitudinal voting, similar empirical measures of legal concepts have been less forthcoming. As Segal and Spaeth (2002, 59) argue, "no one [has] systematically demonstrated that [the law] influences the decisions of Supreme Court justices. . . ."

In this book we take up the challenge articulated by Segal and Spaeth and *provide a model that dynamically integrates ideological and legal factors via an empirical measure of the plain meaning of statutes.* The concept of the plain meaning of the law "holds that judges rest their decisions in significant part on the plain meaning of the pertinent language" in statutes and other legal authorities (Segal and Spaeth 2002, 53). However, previous research has been severely hampered in testing this influence. As Segal and Spaeth (2002, 59) declare:

> No proponent has even suggested a falsifiable test for this component of the legal model . . . [This] requires . . . that some method of determining plain meaning in some cases be established *a priori*; corroboration of the model might require . . . that *ceteris paribus*, justices must systematically react positively in some meaningful degree to such arguments. Of this, we have no evidence.

In developing an empirical measure of the plain meaning of statutes, we focus specifically on how much *discretion* Congress (or state legislatures) provides in the statutes it enacts into law. The basic argument is that judges will render decisions according to their ideological preferences *contingent on the level of discretion* afforded by the law. For those statutes containing vague or ambiguous language, judges will possess more discretion to vote according to their individual preferences. However, for statutes containing more detailed language, judges will have less discretion and consequently will be constrained from ideological voting.

Measuring Legal Factors

Our work differs from past research in that scholars most often examine legislative-judicial interactions in terms of a *trade-off* between judicial attitudes and legal constraints (Rowland and Carp 1980; Segal

1997, 1998; Spaeth and Segal 1999; Segal and Spaeth 2002).[18] In so doing, they essentially load the deck by including continuous measures of attitudinal factors, while using less robust measures for legal factors. In fact, "few studies have been undertaken by empirically oriented scholars to examine the effects of traditional legal concepts on case outcomes or judicial votes" (Songer and Haire 1992, 979). In part, this lack of empirical analysis on legal influences arises because of the difficulty inherent in measuring concepts such as plain meaning, legislative intent, and precedent. Some scholars rely on strategies that examine progeny cases from landmark decisions (Songer and Sheehan 1990; Knight and Epstein 1996; Segal and Spaeth 1996; Songer and Lindquist 1996). Other scholars employ a series of dummy variables to capture the presence or absence of specific case facts or legal doctrine (Segal 1984; George and Epstein 1992; Songer and Haire 1992; Songer, Segal and Cameron 1994). Fortunately, more recent studies are now focusing on developing better and more precise ways to measure legal aspects (Gillman 2001; Richards and Kritzer 2002; Friedman 2006; Hansford and Spriggs 2006; Lindquist and Klein 2006; Kahn and Kersch 2006; Black and Owens 2009; Bailey and Maltzman 2011; Geyh 2011, and Corley, Steigerwalt, and Ward 2013).

Yet, there are reasons to believe that statutes are extremely important to consider. For example, in a recent study of the bureaucracy, Huber and Shipan (2002, 31) argue, ". . . legislation is potentially the most definitive set of instructions that can be given to bureaucrats with respect to the actions they must take during policy implementation. In some cases legislatures provide very detailed blueprints that allow little room for other actors . . . to create policy on their own. In other cases, legislatures take a different approach and write statutes that provide only the broad outlines of policy, which gives bureaucrats the opportunity to design and implement policy" (2002, 76). Clearly, judges are not the same as bureaucrats, whose role is to administer or implement the law. Bureaucrats do not have the authority to determine which laws are constitutional, nor can they strike down specific provisions within statutes. Yet, we argue that the key concept captured by Huber and Shipan, the *level of discretion* provided by legislative statutes, is relevant to judges because it embodies an important aspect of the law.

The question we address in this book is whether discretion influences the decisions of federal and state judges. To do so, we develop and test a model of contingent discretion, which posits that *judicial decision making is contingent on the level of discretion afforded by the law*. Consequently, we expect to observe judges voting according to their ideological preferences when they interpret vague or ambiguous statutes that provide high levels of discretion. Conversely, when courts encounter statutes that prescribe more detailed outcomes, and therefore reduce the level of discretion, then we expect the ability of judges to decide cases attitudinally will be constrained. Stated this way, our model of contingent discretion is formulated as a tradeoff between ideology and the law. Yet, we should not expect all judges to encounter similar constraints from any particular statute; and, our findings demonstrate that an additional dimension exists to the model of contingent discretion. Not only can legal factors constrain ideological decision making, they can also enhance and support attitudinal outcomes. That is, the law can actually facilitate the expression of ideology. While this may seem counterintuitive initially, further reflection should reveal that this proposition is extremely compelling. If the law prescribes a particular ideological outcome or policy, then individual judges whose ideological preferences converge with that policy have an opportunity to vote attitudinally without seeming to appear ideological or partisan. Therefore, as we argue throughout the book, the model of contingent discretion is more than a tradeoff model. It captures a vibrant and *dynamic interaction between law and ideology* in its influence on judicial behavior.

Organization of the Book

Chapter 2 explores the theoretical foundations of the analysis. In particular we define our theoretical model—the *model of contingent discretion*—and provide a discussion of how this theoretical model operates on judicial behavior. We then provide a detailed discussion of how the *model of contingent discretion* is operationalized, borrowing from the literatures on bureaucratic politics, judicial politics, and law. We conclude this chapter by stating a testable hypothesis and discussing how this hypothesis could be confirmed or falsified.

Chapter 3 provides the initial test of the *model of contingent discretion*. This empirical analysis expands upon our article (coauthored with Jeffrey Fine) in the *Journal of Politics* (2006) and focuses on the behavior of judges serving on the U.S. Courts of Appeals (from 1960 to 2002). In addition to providing an empirical assessment of all appellate judges, we also analyze the circuits separately to determine whether the influence of statutory language operates consistently across all circuits.

Chapter 4 turns the analysis to the justices of the U.S. Supreme Court (from 1953 to 2007) and expands on our article in the *Justice System Journal* (2011). We begin this chapter by discussing how the unique institutional structure of the Supreme Court—namely the discretionary control of its docket—should mitigate against finding empirical support for statutory influences. We then present the results of several statistical models and demonstrate that justices are constrained by statutes in some instances and in other situations rely on statutory language to facilitate their ideological voting.

Chapter 5 focuses on the effects of statutory language for justices of state supreme courts (from 1994 to 1998), and further develops our article (co-authored with Michael P. Fix) in *Political Research Quarterly* (2011). We begin this chapter with a discussion of the multiple institutional environments encountered by state court judges, and how this institutional variation potentially affects statutory influence. We then present the results of several empirical models to demonstrate the conditions under which state judges are influenced by statutory language. Finally, we provide a corollary analysis that indicates which states employ detailed statutes. The results of this corollary analysis demonstrate that states in which the supreme court justices are directly elected by the public, significantly pass more detailed statutes—presumably to control judges over whom the legislature has no direct influence.

Chapter 6 examines the effects of statutory language on the U.S. Supreme Court from a temporal perspective. We begin the chapter discussing the temporal nature of the law and examining the evolution of statutory language from Congress. We provide several empirical analyses demonstrating the conditions under which statutes have evolved over time, and how this evolution has affected judicial behavior.

Finally, Chapter 7 offers several conclusions concerning the theoretical *model of contingent discretion* and the empirical measure of statutory influence. Additionally, we identify several unanswered questions and argue that these deserve more attention from scholars in future research.

2

Theoretical Foundations

A text . . . helps tether discretion.

—Justice William Brennan (1989, 432)

In the previous chapter we introduce the notion that the Constitution creates an "invitation to struggle" between the legislative and judicial branches over the development of law in the United States. Again, it is important to note that this tension exists at both the federal and state levels of government. That is, the U.S. Constitution creates an "invitation to struggle" between Congress and the federal courts, and state constitutions create similar "invitations" between their legislatures and state courts. Consequently, we believe it is incumbent to examine how these constitutional "invitations" manifest and determine whether they exert a systematic influence on the behaviors and decisions of judges.

Before we develop a robust theoretical model examining the influence of statutory language on judicial behavior, we first examine several distinct literatures; each of which offers important insights concerning specific aspects of legislative—judicial interactions. In particular, we examine the legal literature concerning the approaches to statutory interpretation; the interdisciplinary literature examining the separation-of-powers literature related to the dynamics of inter-branch relations; and the judicial politics literature concerning the systematic influences of law and ideology on judicial behavior. Additionally, we situate our theoretical argument into a larger context by demonstrating its applicability to principal-agent models.

Our discussion of these separate literatures focuses on how each contributes to a robust theoretical model of judicial decision making. We then build upon this foundation by developing our own theoretical argument—the *Model of Contingent Discretion*—and explain the

11

rationales supporting each of its provisions. In the final section of this chapter we then focus on the particular operationalizations employed throughout the remainder of the book to empirically test the *Model of Contingent Discretion* across multiple institutional and contextual scenarios.

Approaches to Interpretation and the Canons of Statutory Construction

From the earliest days of the United States, during the ratification period of the Constitution, the Framers recognized the importance of legislative statutes and the potential conflict between the legislature and the judiciary over the interpretation of laws. In *Federalist* No. 37, Madison notes:

> All new laws, though penned with the greatest technical skill, and passed on the fullest and most mature deliberation, are considered as more or less obscure and equivocal, until their meaning be liquidated and ascertained by a series of particular discussions and adjudications . . . Perspicuity therefore requires not only that ideas should be distinctly formed, but that they should be expressed by words distinct and exclusively appropriated to them. But no language is so copious as to supply words and phrases for every complex idea, or so correct as not to include many equivocally devoted different ideas. Hence, it must happen, that however accurately objects may be discriminated in themselves, and however accurately the discrimination may be considered, the definition of them may be rendered inaccurate by the inaccuracy of the terms in which it is delivered. And this unavoidable inaccuracy must be greater or less, according to the complexity and novelty of the objects defined.

In this passage, Madison speaks about the ambiguity of language as it relates to legislative statutes. Though Congress may work diligently to draft well-worded legislation, the limits of language introduce a degree of subjectivity into every law. This subjectivity becomes the basis upon which interpretations are formed, which in turn leads to the question of whether suitable methods exist for the interpretation of statutes.

Generally speaking there are several approaches developed by legal scholars and practitioners to assist individuals with statutory interpretation. Though these approaches exist, it is important to note that "the hard truth of the matter is that American courts have no intelligible, generally accepted, and consistently applied theory of statutory interpretation" (Rosenkranz 2002, 2086).[1] Consequently, it is useful to examine some of the suggested guidelines that judges should employ when interpreting statutes. Initially, legal scholars and judges relied on particular *canons of statutory construction* to determine the meaning of statutes. These canons were a series of written maxims that served to guide individuals and their interpretations. One of the earliest articulations occurred in 1584 through an opinion written by Sir Edward Coke in *Heydon's Case.* Coke asserted that four aspects should be considered in the interpretation of all statutes: first, what was the common law before the making of the Act; second, what was the mischief and defect for which the common law did not provide; third, what was the remedy provided by Parliament to address the issue; and finally, "the true reason of the remedy; and then the office of all the Judges is always to make such construction as shall suppress the mischief, and advance the remedy, and to suppress subtle inventions and evasions for continuance of the mischief."[2]

After this articulation by Sir Edward Coke, other legal scholars, such as William Blackstone, offered additional articulations that developed into new canons. However, in the early twentieth century, with the evolution of the Legal Realists, scholars began criticizing the use of canons. One of the most influential Legal Realists was Karl Llewellyn. His argument was relatively simple: for every thrust of one canon there was an equally influential parry from another canon leading to an opposite conclusion.[3] He recommended that judges "give up that foolish pretense [that] there must be a set of mutually contradictory correct rules on how to construe statutes" (1950, 399). Judge Posner (1983) has taken Llewellyn's argument one step further and argued that if two contradictory canons exist for any specific question of construction, then judges can simply pick the one that reinforces his or her ideological preferences. Consequently, many individuals[4] recognize that there are no strict rules of interpretation by which judges must abide. Rather, there are relatively broad approaches of interpretation—not more specific canons such as the maxim "*expression unius est exclusion alterius*—the expression of one thing is the exclusion of another" (Rosenkranz 2002, 2086). Thus, our primary interest is to explore the general paradigms of interpretation utilized by judges or codified in legal texts.

In examining statutory interpretation it is also important to note from the outset that legislatures are not single-minded entities possessing a solitary purpose. As Shepsle (1992) argues, Congress (and all legislatures by extension) is a "They" not an "It." Consequently, many statutes are designed with a certain amount of ambiguity so that "legislators with opposing views can then claim that they have prevailed in the legislative arena" (Grundfest and Pritchard 2002, 628). To further complicate matters, as Judge Mikva (1987, 380) notes, within Congress, "those 535 people . . . are going to find it difficult to agree on an agenda, let alone on the words to describe whatever consensus they reach." Faced with these constraints (and without treading into the robust debate about the necessity of using legislative intent during statutory interpretation), judges must offer a legal opinion on the statute. Given these sources of variation, it is therefore remarkable that Justice Holmes remarked, "We do not inquire what the legislature meant; we only ask what the statute means."[5]

Textualism

One of the primary approaches used by judges to interpret legislation is the concept of textualism, which focuses on the actual language of the statute to determine its "plain meaning." Relying on this approach requires judges to examine the actual words of the law because, "of course the words of a statute are always relevant, often decisive, and usually the most important evidence of what the statute was meant to accomplish" (Posner 1983, 808). In the case *Caminetti v. United States* (1917),[6] the Supreme Court stated that "it is elementary that the meaning of a statute must, in the first instance, be sought in the language in which the act is framed, and if that is plain . . . the sole function of the courts is to enforce it according to its terms." It is therefore the specific language of the law, and not other extraneous influences (such as the intent of the legislature), that is of paramount importance.

Perhaps the most visible and vocal advocate of the textualist approach is Justice Antonin Scalia.[7] In several of his opinions, Justice Scalia states explicitly his belief that courts should only rely on the text of the statute to determine meaning. He acknowledges that "every canon of statutory construction supports the conclusion that the court should start from the text of the statute. If the statutory text supplies an answer to the issue, the judge need not delve further into the legislative record . . . And even if the judge finds a clear conflict between the legislative history and statutory language, common precepts of statutory construction would require her to ignore the legislative history in interpreting the statute" (Stock 1990, 161).

For example, in his concurring opinion in the case *H. J., Inc. v. Northwestern Bell Telephone* Scalia rebukes the majority opinion for "elevating to the level of statutory text a phrase taken from the legislative history" (492 U.S. 229 (1989) at 252). Additionally, Scalia writes in his concurring opinion in *United States v. Taylor* that "the text is so unambiguous on these points that it must be assumed that what the Members of the House and the Senators thought they were voting for, and what the President thought he was approving when he signed the bill, was what the text plainly said, rather than what a few Representatives, or even a Committee, said it said" (487 U.S. 326 (1988) at 345).

According to Stock (1990), Scalia's primary justification for adopting a textualist approach is that the Constitution demands a specific procedure for the passage of legislation—one that focuses only on the language of the statute. "The process of creating statutes must include votes by both legislative branches on bills with identical wording and a presidential signature (or the override of a veto) . . . Accordingly, the legislative history, which has not been subjected to review by the other house and the President is not part of the law" (1990, 166).

Dynamic Statutory Interpretation

Somewhat in contrast to the strict textualist approach advocated by Justice Scalia is the notion of dynamic statutory interpretation. Advocates of this approach contend that judges should interpret statutes based not just on the actual language of the law (and the intent of the legislature when the statute was passed) but also on the contemporary environment in which the statute is questioned. Thus, statutes passed fifty or one hundred years prior can receive new interpretations and understandings based on current norms, practices, and traditions.

It is important to note that this approach is not completely antithetical to textualism since both begin with the actual language of the statute. "When the statutory text clearly answers the interpretive question . . . it normally will be the most important consideration . . . The historical perspective is the next most important interpretive consideration; given the traditional assumptions that the legislature is the supreme lawmaking body in a democracy . . ." (Eskridge 1987, 1483). Yet, when the statutory text and legislative history are not clear, then judges may find it useful to incorporate current policies or social understandings into the interpretive process.

One can observe an example of the dynamic statutory interpretation approach in the case *Smith v. Wade*, 461 U.S. 30 (1983). Here, the Supreme Court granted *certiorari* to examine a lawsuit between a prison inmate and a guard that involved an interpretation of the Civil Rights Act of 1871 (which was later codified into the statute 42 U.S.C. § 1983 in 1982). While the majority opinion (written by Justice William Brennan) and the primary dissent (written by Justice William Rehnquist) focused on a statutory interpretation based on the year 1871, Justice O'Connor's dissent argued for a more contemporary understanding of the law. As she states, "although I agree with the result reached in Justice Rehnquist's dissent, I write separately because I cannot agree with the approach taken by either the Court or Justice Rehnquist. Both opinions engage in exhaustive, but ultimately unilluminating, exegesis of the common law of the availability of punitive damages in 1871" (461 U.S. at 92). O'Connor continues to explain "once it is established that the common law of 1871 provides us with no real guidance, we should turn to the policies [of the contemporary statute] to determine which rule best accords with those policies" (461 U.S. at 93).

Regardless of whether one subscribes to Justice Scalia's argument favoring textualism, or a more dynamic method of statutory interpretation, it is difficult to deny the importance of a statute's actual wording. The "meaning of the law" begins first and foremost with the language of the bill under consideration. With this in mind, it therefore becomes incumbent upon scholars of the judiciary to explore whether legislative statutes have an effect on observed judicial behavior. As Eskridge (1999, 671) argues, "there should be little quarrel with the proposition that theories of statutory interpretation should be subjected to empirical testing." Additionally, in designing specific empirical tests, one should recognize that "falsifiable hypotheses should be about something of consequence. At least some significant part [of which] comes from within the law itself" (Friedman 2006, 263).

Separation of Powers Models

When judges make decisions regarding the interpretation of the law they may also consider the preferences of other institutional actors. This occurs because legal interpretation is not a static process that necessarily terminates with a particular judicial decision. Instead, decisions may lead to subsequent legal action prompted by legislative attempts to reconcile court decisions by passing new laws.

Separation of powers (SOP) models examine these interbranch relationships, influences, or effects on the decision-making process. More specifically, SOP models focus on whether one particular branch of government (often the judiciary) will defer to the ideological preferences of another branch (most often the legislative) in order to avoid having a specific decision overturned at a later stage; thereby resulting in a worse policy outcome. This area of research gained popularity after Brian Marks (1988) examined the Supreme Court's decision in *Grove City College v. Bell*[8] and the subsequent attempts in Congress to overturn that ruling.

Following this seminal examination by Marks, scholars increasingly incorporated SOP models in their research (for example see Eskridge 1991a, 1991b; Ferejohn and Weingast 1992; Shepsle 1992; Spiller and Gely 1992; McNollgast 1995; Segal 1997, 1998; Spiller and Tiller 1997; Martin 2001; Rogers 2001; Sala and Spriggs 2004; and Rogers, Flemming, and Bond 2006). While these models continued to develop increasing levels of theoretical and methodological sophistication, the fundamental premise remained consistent—judges "make choices with the expectation that [their] decisions will affect the interests of actors in other political institutions . . . [Judges] who care about policy outcomes therefore have an incentive to take the preferences of other governmental actors into account in their own deliberations" (Sala and Spriggs 2004, 197).

SQ   C   L

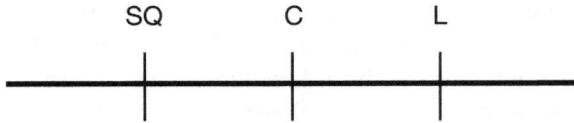

Note: SQ = status quo   C = Court's ideal point   L = Legislature's ideal point

Figure 2.1. General Separation of Powers Model A.

Figure 2.1 provides an illustration of the general approach taken by SOP scholars.[9] In this figure the policy preferences of a Court (C) and a Legislature (L) are arrayed along a unidimensional space. Additionally, the line labeled SQ represents the current status quo, over which the Court must adjudicate a dispute through statutory interpretation. Under the assumption that both actors (C and L) possess perfect and complete information about the preferences of the other actor, we can evaluate how the Court will resolve this dispute. Since its ideal point is on the same side of the status quo as the Legislature, the Court can render a decision at point C without fear of reprisal from the Legislature (since the Legislature prefers point C to the status quo).

In contrast to the first environment, consider Figure 2.2 in which the Court encounters a more difficult decision. Relying on the same assumptions of perfect and complete information and a unidimensional policy space, we see that now the Court's ideal point (C) is

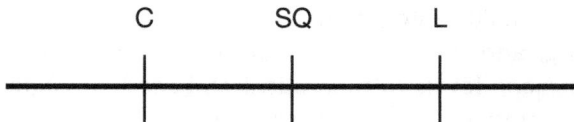

C   SQ   L

Note: SQ = status quo   C = Court's ideal point   L = Legislature's ideal point

Figure 2.2. General Separation of Powers Model B.

located to the left of the status quo whereas the Legislature's ideal point (L) is to the right. In this situation, if the Court chooses to render its decision at point C, it is likely that the Legislature will choose to override this decision and move the policy to point L—which is worse for the Court than to simply affirm the status quo. Consequently, a sophisticatedly thinking and strategically oriented Court will vote to uphold the status quo (SQ) because it cannot achieve a better outcome and could conceivably encounter a worse policy should it attempt to change SQ.

These two examples illustrate the basic approach taken by traditional SOP models, and it is important to recognize that the conclusions generated by this research provide powerful insights into legislative and judicial behavior. Yet, it is also important to recognize that these insights are based entirely on actors' preferences over policy outcomes—they neglect the specific language included in the statute that generates the status quo (SQ) point. And, scholars demonstrate that while "Congress enacts statutes and the courts interpret them, Congress is not always silent on how its actions are to be interpreted" (Ferejohn and Weingast 1992, 567). Consequently, SOP models overlook the range of options available to Congress to specifically describe policy outcomes in the law. As Geyh (2006, 279) notes "if independent judges ignore the rule of law and implement their own policy predilections, judicial independence loses its raison d'être and simply liberates unelected judicial elites to trump the majority's political preferences with their own." Therefore, the SOP models developed by scholars should begin by focusing on the potential options available to legislatures to ensure that other institutions (including courts) adhere to specific policy outcomes. "These details may describe policy outcomes in vague terms, leaving the courts with large amounts of discretion to interpret statutes according to their ideal points; or, the policy outcomes may be the result of extremely specific statutory language which constrains the abilities of judges to alter the status quo points based on their individual ideological preferences" (Randazzo, Waterman, and Fine 2006, 1007).

To illustrate this point, examine Figure 2.3 which presents a refinement to the general SOP model. Instead of representing the status quo as a single point (SQ), it is now portrayed as a range. The size of this range (represented by the distance between α_1 and

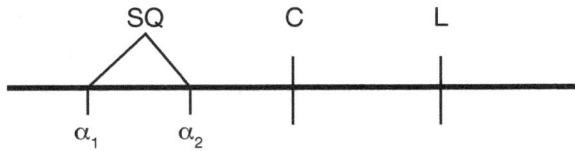

Note: SQ = status quo   C = Court's ideal point   L = Legislature's ideal point

Figure 2.3. General Separation of Powers Model C.

α_2) is determined by the degree of ambiguity written into the legislative statute. Thus, vague statutes—possessing more ambiguous language—will possess wider intervals and more specific statutes (such as the one depicted in Figure 2.3) will possess relatively narrow ranges. Based on this figure, and under the additional assumption that the actual language of the statute exerts an influence, the Court is faced with a dilemma. Though it prefers to render a decision at its ideal point (C), knowing that the Legislature prefers this policy outcome to the status quo range, the Court is constrained by the law. Consequently, we should expect to observe an outcome at α_2 which is the closest point within the statutory range to the Court's ideal point. In such a situation, we might expect to see an invitation from the Court to the Legislature to rewrite the statute (effectively overturning the Court's current decision). As Hausegger and Baum (1999) demonstrate such invitations by the Supreme Court to Congress occur periodically. The opinion by Justice Thurgood Marshall (quoted in Chapter 1) illustrates this dilemma; "we decline to misread the statute in order to reach a sympathetic result when such a reading requires us to do violence to the plain language of the statute . . . Congress chose the language that requires us to decide as we do, and Congress is free to change it."[10]

Our purpose in discussing separation of powers models is not to criticize scholars for relying on pure preference based models. Again, the insights generated from these preference based models help to develop a better understanding of the interbranch relationships between legislatures and courts. Rather, our analyses seek to build upon these SOP conclusions by focusing on an additional and important aspect—the language of the statute. Demonstrating that aspects of the actual statutory wording systematically affect judicial behavior allows us to advance our understanding of traditional SOP models one step further. Rather than assuming that a legislature must wait until after a court makes a decision (and then determine whether to override that decision or not), it can take a more preemptive step by incorporating specific language into a statute that limits the ability of courts to render decisions at (or near) their ideal points. Of course, the reverse is also possible: legislatures may unintentionally constrain courts simply by drafting detailed legislation (without the preemptive consideration) that more clearly dictates how particular policies should be implemented and how the statutes should be interpreted. Regardless of the intent of a legislature, we contend that it is incumbent upon students of the judiciary to determine the extent to which legislatures effectively limit judicial discretion or provide courts with wide leeway to interpret their statutes.

Influence of Law and Ideology on Judicial Behavior

Since SOP models suggest that judges have an incentive to consider legislative preferences, what role does judicial ideology play in the decision making process? Do judges merely interpret the law as written, or do they also make decisions based on their individual attitudes and ideological preferences? A wide-ranging literature examines how these preferences affect judicial decision making.

The literature on judicial behavior is often discussed in terms of a competition or tradeoff between the ideological preferences of individual judges/justices and legal considerations. "While many (if not most) scholars recognize that the justices probably respond to both of these concerns [attitudes and the law], the literature nonetheless tends to present them as competing explanations" (Hansford and Spriggs 2006, 9–10). On one side of this theoretical debate are advocates of the "Attitudinal Model"—who claim that judges are motivated primarily (or in some extreme cases, exclusively) by ideological influences. Perhaps the most noteworthy proponents of this model are Professors Harold J. Spaeth and Jeffrey A. Segal. In their numerous examinations of the Attitudinal Model,[11] they repeatedly argue that judges (specifically the justices of the U.S. Supreme Court) "decide disputes in light of the facts of the case vis-à-vis [their] ideological attitudes and values" (Segal and Spaeth 2002, 86).

Consequently, Justice Antonin Scalia is most likely to cast a conservative vote in a particular case, not because of any legal considerations, but simply because he prefers conservative outcomes more than liberal ones. Conversely, Justice William Brennan is most likely to cast a liberal vote in the same case, not because of the law, but because he prefers liberal outcomes to conservative ones. As Segal and Spaeth (2002, 311) argue at the end of their analysis of legal influences, there is "virtually no evidence for concluding that the justices' decisions are based on legal factors."

On the other side of the theoretical debate are scholars who argue that the "Legal Model" holds sway over the judicial decision-making process. That is to say that judges consider aspects of the plain meaning of statutes, legislative intent, and precedent when adjudicating specific disputes. These examinations often combine a "constellation of contextual, institutional, and attitudinal factors" (Langer 2002, 26) into a single approach rather than focus on the "preoccupation . . . with attitudes and policy preferences of individual justices" (Gillman and Clayton 1999, 1). This more encompassing approach is necessary to examine legal influences on judicial behavior, because "when pressed, no justices or Court scholars really believe that the Court's decisions are mechanically controlled by law, such that political influence is excluded altogether. Still, some [individuals] continue to suggest that such a possibility is realistic and desirable" (Keck 2004, 256).

For example, in addition to the opinions of Justice Scalia about the importance of the law (discussed earlier in this chapter), Justice Clarence Thomas provides an illustrative discussion of how the Supreme Court should adhere to the original interpretation and understanding of the Constitution (and the law, generally speaking). He states that this approach would help "to reduce judicial discretion and to maintain judicial impartiality. [B]y tethering their analysis to the understanding of those who drafted and ratified the text, modern judges [would be] prevented from substituting their own preferences for the Constitution" (quoted in Keck 2004, 258). Justice William Brennan also shared some affinity for this view, though his ideological preferences were generally the opposite of Justice Thomas. Brennan (1989, 432) states the importance of written laws and a written Constitution because "[w]ithout a textual anchor for their decisions, judges

would have to rely on some theory of natural rights, or some alleg-
edly shared standard of the ends and limits of government . . . But
an appeal to normative ideals that lack any mooring in the written
law . . . would in societies like ours be suspect . . . A text . . . helps
tether discretion."

While several individuals have examined the influence of the
law through a qualitative or historical analytic framework (for examples, see Gillman and Clayton 1991; Gillman 1994; Keck 2002; and
Whittington 2005), "few studies have been undertaken by empirically
oriented scholars to examine the effects of traditional legal concepts
on case outcomes or judicial votes" (Songer and Haire 1992, 979). In
part, this lack of empirical analysis on legal influences arises because
of the difficulty inherent in measuring concepts such as plain meaning, legislative intent and precedent. Some scholars rely on strategies that examine progeny cases from landmark decisions (Songer
and Sheehan 1990; Knight and Epstein 1996; Segal and Spaeth 1996;
Songer and Lindquist 1996). Other scholars employ a series of dummy variables to capture the presence or absence of specific case facts
or legal doctrine (Segal 1984; George and Epstein 1992; Songer and
Haire 1992; Songer, Segal and Cameron 1994).

More recent scholarship addresses these limitations by providing more sophisticated systematic analyses of legal influences on
judicial behavior. For example, Hansford and Spriggs (2006; see also
Spriggs and Hansford 2000, 2001, and 2002) examine the Supreme
Court's treatment of precedent and discover that the vitality of a
precedent has a systematic influence on the justices' voting patterns.
Similarly, research by Richards and Kritzer (2002; see also Kritzer
and Richards 2003)[12] examines how particular precedents establish
jurisprudential regimes that systematically affect judicial behavior in
subsequent cases. Lax (2007) examines a different aspect of the law
when he explains why collegial courts (rather than courts presided
over by a single judge) adopt specific legal rules for the disposition
of future cases. This research yields extremely important insights into
the effects of one aspect of the "legal model"—precedent.

In this book, our research focuses on another component of the
"legal model"—legislative statutes. In particular, we develop and test
an empirical measure of the plain meaning of legislative statutes. As
we note earlier, the concept of the plain meaning of the law "holds that

judges rest their decisions in significant part on the plain meaning of
the pertinent language" in statutes and other legal authorities (Segal
and Spaeth 2002, 53). However, previous research has been severely
hampered in testing this influence. Though we cite Segal and Spaeth
(2002, 59) in Chapter 1, it is important to reiterate their claim in relation to our present work:

> No proponent has even suggested a falsifiable test for this
> component of the legal model . . . [This] requires . . . that
> some method of determining plain meaning in some cases
> be established *a priori*; corroboration of the model might
> require . . . that *ceteris paribus*, justices must systematically
> react positively in some meaningful degree to such arguments.
> Of this, we have no evidence.

We take up this charge by providing a direct empirical test
that includes both a set of falsifiable hypotheses and a systematic
method for determining the plain meaning of the law. We then provide a series of empirical tests to fill the lacuna identified by Segal
and Spaeth. At this point, it is important to acknowledge a potential
objection to our operationalization of plain meaning. Obviously, we
recognize that in order to determine the substantive meaning of a
statute, one must identify specific words and discern their meaning.
Unfortunately, until more advances develop with computer assisted
content analysis software, such an enterprise is extremely difficult
for a large-N study. Yet, we can use the logic of plain meaning to
focus on a related aspect: the amount of discretion provided by a
statute. On average, if the language of a statute is clear (i.e., plain)
then judges will possess little discretion to deviate from the statute's
intended outcome. Conversely, if the language is ambiguous or vague
then judges will possess more discretion as they interpret the statute's
meaning. As we explain in greater detail below, examining the level of
discretion provided in statutes allows us to determine the conditions
under which judges are more likely (or less likely) to render decisions
according to their individual ideological preferences. We argue that a
more continuous measure, grounded within an applicable theoretical framework, is essential to understanding the potential legal constraints judges encounter when adjudicating disputes.

Placing Judicial Decision Making into a
Broader Theoretical Context

Before we develop and discuss our specific theoretical model, it is important to place our conceptualization of judicial decision making into a broader theoretical context. Why should legislative statutes influence judges? As explained earlier, the fundamental tenets of the attitudinal model argue that judges make decisions solely on the basis of their ideological preferences; any use of the law serves only as a means to justify these proclivities. Consequently, there should be little reason to suspect that the law operates as a significant influence on judicial behavior. Yet, from a normative perspective, one can argue that the law should guide judges. Without such fealty to the law the accountability and legitimacy of the entire constitutional system in the United States would suffer. Thus, any theoretical model should capture these characteristics in order to provide a rich explanation concerning judicial behavior.

Ironically, it is precisely because of the fundamental tenets of the attitudinal model that reasons exist helping to understand why the law should matter. If legislators want to ensure that judges do not make decisions solely based on their individual ideological preferences they have a strong incentive to write laws with clear and unambiguous language that prescribes specific outcomes and/or policies. By providing less discretion into the law itself, legislators limit the ability of judges to offer differing interpretations over the law's meaning. In turn, this limitation over statutory interpretation hinders the ability of judges to use the law only as a means to justify their ideological preferences. For example, if legislators wish to limit the ability of judges to provide lenient sentences to hardened criminals, they can enact laws that not only prescribe tougher sentences (such as California's "three strikes and you're out" laws) but also provide sufficient detail to limit judges' discretion; thereby ensuring fealty to the law. Yet, as Mayhew (1974) notes in *Congress: The Electoral Connection*, legislatures may not be able to draft clear statutes due to a variety of circumstances including political compromises and position taking by individual members. Thus, statutes may become vague or ambiguous, which in turn provides more discretion to judges when they interpret the law.

If one wishes to conceptualize the potential tension between the legislature and the courts in this manner, then Corwin's (1957, 171) "invitation to struggle" essentially becomes a battle between a legislative principal versus judicial agents over the meaning of the law. Though principal-agent theory most often is employed to examine tensions between the legislature and the bureaucracy, it also has applications to legislative-judicial interactions. The fundamental premise of this theory is that the principal seeks outcomes and/ or results which reflect his or her preferences. Yet, due to a lack of resources the principal cannot act alone (see Brehm and Gates 1997). Consequently, the principal "delegates some rights . . . to an agent who is bound . . . to represent the principal's interests" (Eggertson 1990, 40).

Inevitably, tension arises within this relationship because the agents seek outcomes reflective of their preferences which may diverge from those of the principal. Thus, the principal must establish effective control mechanisms or incentives to ensure that agents do not deviate from the principal's preferred positions (Shepsle and Bonccheck 1997). These mechanisms are essential because over time various disjunctures develop between the principal and the agents. These disjunctures (which include information asymmetries and knowledge expertise developed by the agents) provide agents with incentives to shirk the principal's wishes and act according to the agents' preferences. Consequently, the central empirical question for principal-agent models is the extent to which the principal makes its preferences known to the agents *a priori* and subsequently, the extent to which agents shirk from the principal's preferences.

Returning to the tension between the legislatures and the judiciary, it becomes a relatively straightforward exercise to frame these interactions according to principal-agent theory. As the principal, legislatures must either develop *ex ante* or *ex post* mechanisms to control the decisions made by agents. Because legislatures have few *ex post* monitoring mechanisms—there are no specific oversight committees for the judiciary, unlike for bureaucratic agencies—they must rely on *ex ante* mechanisms to control the behavior of agents. As Wood and Waterman (1993, 23) demonstrate "one tool for accomplishing this end" is for the principal to develop a "contract" that effectively binds the actions of the agent. We argue that legislative statutes serve as effective 'contracts' because they stipulate the preferences of the legislature *a priori* and if written properly (i.e., with enough specific detail) influence judges to vote according to the law. When legislatures choose to provide explicit direction to the courts, they write extremely detailed statutes that identify specific and well-defined outcomes, including copious citations of other laws, definitions of various concepts, and other detail that can instruct a judge on the intent of the law. Conversely, when legislatures cannot agree on more specific or detailed language their statutes become vague and ambiguous, thus giving judges more discretion to make decisions. Therefore, the empirical question involves properly measuring this "contract" and determining the extent to which it influences judicial behavior because judges are *agents* of the law. The next two sections discuss more specifically, both theoretically and operationally, how we make these determinations.

However, before we proceed to the next section we offer an important observation concerning previous research on principal-agent models. Historically, most studies assume that all agents have incentives to shirk from the preferences of the principal. Thus, the approach typically employed is to search for evidence of agent shirking. Yet, in reality shirking is but one possible option for agents. Since agents are not monolithic entities, each individual possesses different political inclinations and preferences over policy. Consequently, while some agents may be inclined to shirk, others share the principal's preferences and have incentives to utilize these preferences in order to more aggressively pursue particular ideological outcomes. The dynamic relationship that exists over time is therefore not merely one between the principal and agents, but also among the agents themselves.

Unfortunately, principal-agent studies tend to treat all agents as having the same incentives and motives. Stated another way, previous research tends to place all agents within a "black box" and treat them as a single, solitary actor. While this approach is understandable given the availability of data when examining the bureaucracy, treating agents as solitary actors severely limits our theoretical understanding in two fundamentally important ways. First, our knowledge of principal-agent relations is based on aggregate measures of bureaucratic preferences and behavior rather than on the characteristics of individual agents. Second, since bureaucratic agents possess limited authority our knowledge derives from limited agent options (i.e., either enforce the law or shirk) rather than exploring a wider range of potential responses (such as declaring laws unconstitutional, or using the law to enhance one's ideological proclivities). These limitations consequently prevent our ability to examine more dynamic principal-agent relationships.

Our book therefore contributes to the literature on principal-agent theory because we have the unique ability to unlock the "black box" of agents and examine the behavior of individual judges. By focusing on individual level data, we can identify important variations in agent responses to cues from the same principal. This allows us to examine situations in which the preferences of one agent converge with the principal while simultaneously analyzing when the preferences of another agent diverge. Furthermore, our individual level focus allows us to examine agent responses to principal cues under a variety of different institutional settings, including those in which the judges are appointed initially by the principal but cannot be removed to those where the judges are selected at regular intervals either through public elections or directly by the principal. Our individual level focus therefore provides a basis for a rigorous and theoretically rich analysis not only of why the law matters, but also how individual judges respond to the language of legislative statutes.

The Model of Contingent Discretion

A key step in developing and testing any theoretical model involves the identification of a suitable measure representing the plain meaning of legal or statutory influence. In a recent study of the bureaucracy, Huber and Shipan (2002, 31) argue, ". . . legislation is potentially the most definitive set of instructions that can be given to bureaucrats with respect to the actions they must take during policy implementation." In their examination of the implementation of Medicaid laws, they discover the impact of statutes on the discretion of bureaucrats. "Legislative statutes are blueprints for policymaking. In some cases, legislatures provide very detailed blueprints that allow little room for other actors . . . to create policy on their own. In other cases, legislatures take a different approach and write statutes that provide only the broad outlines of policy, which gives bureaucrats the opportunity to design and implement policy" (2002, 76). As we acknowledge in the previous chapter, judges are not the same as bureaucrats, whose role is to administer or implement the law. Bureaucrats do not have the authority to determine which laws are constitutional, nor can they strike down specific provisions within statutes. Yet, the key concept captured by Huber and Shipan is the *level of discretion* provided by legislation, and this concept is certainly relevant to the judicial setting.

Building upon the work of Huber and Shipan, we develop a theoretical explanation for judicial behavior—called the *model of contingent discretion*. In this model, we posit that judicial decision making is contingent on the level of discretion afforded by the law. Consequently, we expect to observe judges voting according to their ideological preferences when they interpret vague or ambiguous statutes that provide high levels of discretion. Conversely, when courts encounter statutes that prescribe more detailed outcomes, and therefore reduce the level of discretion, then we expect the ability of judges to decide cases attitudinally will be affected. Yet, it is important to note that not all judges will experience these potential effects at the same time in the same manner. Those judges whose ideological preferences differ with the principal will discover that the detailed law acts as a constraining influence. Other judges whose ideological preferences converge with the principal may rely on the language of the same detailed statute to facilitate or enhance their ability to vote ideologically. That is, the law can provide "legal cover" to these judges thereby allowing them to vote even more forcefully in accord with their ideological preferences. Thus, the contingent effect can operate in two ways—it can constrain judges from voting according to their ideological preferences or it can facilitate the influence of ideology.

While a facilitation effect may seem counterintuitive at first glance, upon further reflection it should seem extremely plausible. Why should the law only have a constraining effect? Should we not also expect the same laws to guide ideologically sympathetic judges? If a legislature passes a broad statute with ambiguous language to prescribe policy outcomes, then one would expect judges to interpret that statute based on their ideological preferences. Yet, if that legislature passes a detailed statute which prescribes a conservative outcome, one would expect liberal judges who subsequently interpret that statute to be constrained from voting in a liberal fashion, whereas conservative judges could rely on the same statutory language to facilitate their conservative votes (and vice versa). This *Model of*

Contingent Discretion is therefore dynamic in the sense that some judges may encounter statutory language that constrains their behavior while others concomitantly are facilitated to rule ideologically.

To measure this discretionary influence, and examine the effects of statutory constraint on the *Model of Contingent Discretion*, we borrow from the research of Huber, Shipan, and Pfahler (2001) and Huber and Shipan (2002). In their analyses of statutory constraint on bureaucratic behavior they employ a proxy measure based on the length of the statute. As they (2002, 73) indicate,

> Our qualitative and quantitative investigation of a huge number of statutes suggests that the more words a legislature puts into legislation on the same issue, the more it constrains other actors who will implement policy on that issue. Similarly, the fewer words it writes, the more discretion it gives to other actors.

After conducting a series of validity tests on this measure for Medicaid statutes, their analyses reveal that the length of statutes successfully accounts for variation caused by differences among (1) fairly meaningless generalizations, (2) situations where legislators deliberately pass vague consensus statutes, and (3) instances where legislators move beyond mere platitudes to enact statutes.

In a similar vein, we conducted a series of validity tests to determine whether longer statutes contained more detailed language that might limit the discretion of judges.[13] For each issue area we content analyzed a sample of statutes: some with shorter word lengths, some with lengths near the overall mean for that issue, and some with longer word lengths. From our analysis it is apparent that statutes with higher word counts contained more detailed language pertaining to its legal implications. For example, the federal criminal statute 18 USC 658 contains 128 words succinctly describing illegal activities related to a specific type of property fraud. In contrast, 18 USC 844 contains 1,801 words listing various penalties associated with illegal possession and/or transportation of explosives. This variation in overall length directly affects the degree of detail included in the statutes. Additionally, the criminal statutes 18 USC 2510 and 18 USC 921 provide definitions of illegal activities related to recording and/or intercepting communications and possession of firearms, respectively. The former contains 1,213 words describing various types of "communication" that are included in the statute, while the latter contains 2,922 words pertaining to possession of firearms. While both statutes provide descriptions of the various activities deemed criminal by Congress and definitions of various technical terms, the reader has a better understanding of the intent of Congress (including the desired outcomes of the legislators) in the latter statute than with the former.

Additionally, we conducted a series of validity tests for state statutes to determine if they followed patterns similar to their federal counterparts. To verify this, we examined a sample of state statutes (stratified by state and issue area). Specifically, we analyzed some statutes with longer word counts (greater than two standard deviations above the mean), with smaller word counts (less than two standard deviations below the mean), and with counts near the mean. Our examination is consistent with the conclusions of the previous validity tests—statute length is a valid indicator of the degree of legislative instruction regarding interpretation of the statute, rather than simply the result of multi-part statutes getting at multiple issues. That is, longer statutes contain a greater degree of detail with respect to the meaning and purpose of the law, as well as instructions on its implementation and application. Furthermore, longer statutes include more cross-references to additional relevant statutes and previous court decisions.[14] In contrast, shorter statutes tend to be more ambiguous. These statutes tend to use very broad language with few clearly defined terms, statements of purpose, directions on application, or cross-references.

An example of two Texas criminal statutes provides clarification of this distinction. Tex. Penal Code § 38.122, provides for the crime of Falsely Holding Oneself Out As a Lawyer. At only 1,967 words, the statute provides little detail as to what constitutes the elements of the crime and leaves a great deal of gap-filling for judges applying the statute to a given case. Additionally, it contains few references to prior judicial decisions or other statutes to assist judges applying the law to a specific situation. In contrast, the Aggravated Sexual Assault statute—Tex. Penal Code § 22.021—is not only substantially longer (166,493 words), but it also provides clearer instructions to judges applying the law in particular cases. In addition to clearly defining all of the key terms in the statute, it also references many prior judicial decisions and other statutes. Thus, the longer statute provides greater detail, leaving less discretion to judges when applying the law to specific cases.[15]

In making these observations, we recognize that judges may be called upon to examine only a specific section of the statute rather than the entire law. Whenever possible we recorded specific portions of statutes, as determined by the judicial case record. For example, in one case adjudicated by the Connecticut Supreme Court, the justices were asked to interpret Connecticut General Statute § 21a–278; and in a second case the same court was asked to interpret Connecticut General Statute § 21a–278a. In many instances, however, it is difficult to determine with certainty whether judges also reference the remaining portions of the bill in order to obtain contextual information on the intended effect or purpose of the legislation passed. The notable canon of statutory interpretation *noscitur a sociis* (it is known from its associates) "dictates that words be read in context with surrounding words in the same document (Breger 1987, 366). Thus, judges are encouraged to examine surrounding portions of the statute in order to more precisely determine the context under which a particular section is referenced. If the judges examine other portions, then relying on the overall word count of the statute as a measure of constraint does not systematically bias the analysis. Yet, if the judges only examine the specific section under dispute, then our inclusion of the overall word count poses a higher threshold for determining statistically significant relationships. For example, if a dispute occurs involving a large statute, our theory predicts that the behavior of judges will be constrained by the statute's language. However, if the judges only examine a specific section of that statute and ignore the remaining language, then their behavior will not be affected according to our prediction. Consequently, the empirical results will not display a statistically significant relationship for our measure of constraint.

Under this more stringent test, if judges are affected by the *model of contingent discretion*, we expect more ambiguous laws to provide more discretion to alter policy according to their individual ideological preferences, generally speaking. Conversely, statutes containing more detailed language will constrain judges from casting ideological votes. This leads to our initial hypothesis:

Statutory Constraint Hypothesis: *If the model of contingent discretion affects judicial behavior, as the level of statutory detail increases we expect judges to have less discretion to vote ideologically.*

Yet, as we stated earlier, the contingent effect can operate in two ways—it can constrain some judges from voting according to their ideological preferences and for others it can facilitate the influence of ideology. To support this contention we offer some anecdotal evidence from justices of the U.S. Supreme Court. Obviously, one should not expect to observe instances in which the majority opinion states "we rely on the language of the statute to make a more ideological ruling." Justices are savvier than that and will rely on appropriate language to help mask this phenomenon. For example, in *Allied-Bruce Terminix Cos. V. Dobson*, 513 U.S. 265 (1995), Justice Breyer writes the following in the majority opinion:

> After examining the statute's language, background, and structure, we conclude . . . [that] a broad interpretation of this language is consistent with the Act's basic purpose. Conversely, a narrower interpretation is not consistent with the Act's basic purpose.

While Breyer's explanation offers some insight into the Court's use of broad statutory interpretations to facilitate ideological outcomes, it is rare to encounter such language in a majority opinion, because the justices often deliberately obscure these occurrences. Yet, when this happens we can turn to the dissenting justices to highlight what is happening in the majority's decision. Consequently, the opinions of dissenting justices offer opportunities to identify situations in which relatively explicit statutes are given "broad interpretations" by the majority opinion. One such example comes from the obscenity decision in *United States v. Alpers* 338 U.S. 680 (1950). In this case, the dissenting opinion by Justice Black criticizes the majority for incorporating new media (based on recordings) into a congressional statute that explicitly prohibited indecent materials that people could read.

> In the provision relied on, as well as elsewhere in the Act, Congress used language carefully describing a number of 'indecent' articles and forbade their shipment in interstate commerce. This specific list applied censorship only to articles that people could read or see; the Court now adds to it articles capable of use to produce sounds that people can hear. The judicial addition here may itself be small. But it is accomplished by

a technique of broad interpretation which too often may be successfully invoked by the many people who want the law to proscribe what other people may say, write, hear, see, or read. I cannot agree to any departure from the sound practice of narrowly construing statutes which by censorship restrict liberty of communication.

A second example comes from the dissenting opinion of Justice Stevens in the case *United States v. James* 478 U.S. 597 (1986). Here, Justice Stevens criticizes the majority opinion for incorporating a broad interpretation to a statute that prescribes an explicit outcome. He states:

But when a critical term in the statute suggests a more limited construction, and when the congressional debates are not only consistent with this construction . . . a narrower interpretation is more faithful to the objective of Congress.

Justice White's dissent in *United States v. National Association of Securities Dealers, Inc.* 422 U.S. 694 (1975) provides a third example. In this case, the dissenting opinion focuses on the explicit language of the statute and he criticizes the majority for broad interpretations that are not supported by the text.

For several reasons, the majority's conclusions are infirm under the controlling authorities. It is plain that the Act itself contains no express exemptions . . . It is equally plain that the Act does not expressly permit the specific restrictions at issue here . . . It would be incredible even to suggest that Congress intended to give participants . . . carte blanche authority to impose whatever restrictions were thought desirable and without regard to the policies . . . Never before has the Court labored to find hidden immunities . . . and the necessity for the effort is itself at odds with our precedents.

As we stated earlier, these examples demonstrate situations in which the majority opinion relies on the language of the legislative statute, through the use of broad interpretations, to facilitate its ideological ruling. This qualitative evidence supports the conclusions offered by principal-agent theory and our own empirical findings concerning the facilitation effect on agents. We should not expect a conservative legislature to pass conservative laws that effectively constrain conservative justices. Instead, if an effect exists we should observe conservative legislation constraining liberal judges (and vice versa for liberal legislation constraining conservative justices). Therefore, if liberal judges experience constraining effects from detailed statutory language, then conservative judges should be able to rely on the legislative statute to facilitate their ideological voting. Doing so provides these judges with a greater opportunity to vote ideologically because the language of the statute offers "legal cover" for an expression of political ideology. That is, judges can cast more conservative votes or announce more conservative policy positions and rely on the statutory language to justify these outcomes from a legal perspective. This leads to our second hypothesis:

> **Statutory Facilitation Hypothesis:** *If the model of contingent discretion affects judicial behavior, for judges of the opposite ideology (i.e., opposite from those judges who are constrained), as the level of statutory detail increases we expect an increase in ideological voting.*

While precisely measuring the policy motivations of legislatures is beyond the scope of our analyses, we can deduce general expectations about statutory effects for specific issue areas, and based on conventional wisdom we offer three. First, criminal statutes tend to prescribe conservative outcomes by specifying the authority of the government over individuals and outlining the various options of punishment for transgressions. Consequently, if criminal statutes affect levels of judicial discretion, it is reasonable to expect that liberal judges (who tend to rule in favor of the individual and against governmental authority, and also impose more lenient punishments) would be most *constrained*. Conversely, since conservative judges generally desire a conservative outcome in criminal cases, more detailed statutes make it easier for them to reach decisions in line with their ideological preferences. Consequently, their ideological voting will be *facilitated* by more detailed criminal statutes.

A second area of law involves civil liberties. As with criminal law, most state statutes in this area negatively impact individual rights by asserting greater state authority at the cost of individual liberty. This general trend is exemplified by many of today's most salient political issues, from abortion rights to hate crimes speech; states frequently pass laws restricting individual civil liberties in the name of state authority. Thus, if these statutes have an impact on the level of discretion of judges, it should be liberal judges that are constrained. Conversely, the level of ideological voting of conservative judges should be facilitated by greater levels of specificity in the language of state civil liberty statutes. As most of these laws will prescribe outcomes in accordance with the ideological preferences of conservative judges, greater detail simply makes it easier for them to vote according to their attitudinal predispositions.

One notable exception involves civil rights statutes. In the civil rights arena legislative statutes tend to prescribe more liberal outcomes by specifying the rights of individuals that cannot be usurped by governmental authority. One needs to look no further than the Civil Rights Act of 1964 or the Voting Rights Act of 1965 for examples of these statutes. Consequently, if federal civil liberties statutes affect judicial discretion, it is plausible to argue that there would be greater constraint for conservative judges (who tend to rule in favor of state authority over individual rights). Conversely, liberal judges should be able to rely on the statutory language to facilitate their ideological voting.

Finally, with regard to economic legislation we do not expect a significant statutory effect to exist—primarily because of the influence exerted by the bureaucracy on areas of economic policy. When courts review economic disputes, not only must they consider the policy prescriptions implied by the federal statutes, they must also interpret subsequent rules and regulations drafted by bureaucratic agencies involved with the implementation of these statutes and any quasi-judicial rulings enacted by these agencies. Consequently, the regulatory imprint may be more pronounced during adjudication, which in turn mitigates the potential effects of any statutory language. Therefore, because bureaucratic agencies operate more visibly in the economic policy arena—instead of the criminal or civil liberties arena where the judiciary is more visible—we expect the effects of statutory language on judicial discretion to be less evident.

Operationalization of Statutory Discretion

Theoretically, our independent variable of primary interest is *Statutory Detail*. Following the Huber and Shipan methodology, we examine the length of legislative statutes. To measure length we first identify the statute in question based on information included in three judicial databases—the Supreme Court Database (compiled by Harold J. Spaeth), the U.S. Courts of Appeals Database (compiled by Donald R. Songer), and the State Supreme Court Database (compiled by Paul Brace and Melinda Gann Hall).[16] For each statute under consideration we subsequently employ LexisNexis and the "word count" feature in the Web browser Firefox. While this strategy provides a raw count of the number of words per statute, there are important reasons why the raw number is not useful in an empirical model. Theoretically, we expect the impact of statutory detail to possess diminishing marginal returns. For example, while increasing the length of a statute from 1,000 to 2,000 words dramatically reduces the ambiguity of that particular law (and doubles the length of the statute), a similar 1,000-word increase to a statute containing 100,000 words will have a more muted effect on the influence of judicial discretion. Furthermore, from a methodological standpoint, using the raw number of words is problematic both because of the inherent noise associated with a raw count and the considerable skewedness in the measure. Consequently, because we are interested in the effects brought by substantial differences among statutes, it is reasonable to take the natural log of each statute as our operationalization of the variable *Statutory Detail*. This approach allows us to capture empirically the theoretical notion of diminishing marginal returns while simultaneously allowing us to minimize the noise associated with raw counts; thereby addressing both a theoretical and methodological issue with the use of the raw word count.

Additionally, our hypotheses indicate a theoretical expectation that statutory detail operates differently between liberal and conservative judges (based on particular issue areas). This suggests that an interaction term is necessary to capture more specifically, the differential effects across these two groups. Therefore, we include a dummy variable *Liberal* to control for the presence of liberal judges on specific courts.[17] We then create the interaction term *Liberal Statutory Detail* to measure this potential dynamic and interdependent relationship. For those issue areas where the legislative statute prescribes a conservative outcome (such as criminal cases) this interaction term should reflect a constraining effect on judicial behavior.[18] Conversely, increases in statutory detail in these issue areas should facilitate (i.e., increase) the likelihood of ideological voting for conservative judges. Due to the presence of an interaction term, these effects will be observed in the original *Statutory Detail* variable.

Conclusions

In this chapter, we outline the theoretical foundations for our *model of contingent discretion*. Based on this theory, our expectation is that judicial decision making is contingent on the level of discretion afforded by the law. Consequently, we expect to observe judges voting according to their ideological preferences when they interpret vague or ambiguous statutes that provide high levels of discretion. Conversely, when courts encounter statutes which prescribe more detailed outcomes, and therefore reduce the level of discretion, then we expect the ability of judges to decide cases attitudinally will be constrained. Yet, as we stated earlier, it is important to note that not all judges will experience these potential constraining effects at the same time in the same manner—even when some judges are constrained from voting ideologically, the law can facilitate the expression of ideological voting among others. Thus, the contingent effect can operate in two ways—it can constrain judges from voting according to their ideological preferences or, among another set of judges, it can facilitate the influence of ideology.

In the remaining chapters, we subject the *model of contingent discretion* to several empirical tests across multiple judicial institutions. In Chapter 3we focus our attention on the U.S. Courts of Appeals—an institution that interprets Congressional statutes under mandatory jurisdiction (i.e., it cannot pick and choose which cases to adjudicate but must accept all appeals from lower courts). In Chapter 4 we examine the U.S. Supreme Court—an institution that also reviews Congressional statutes, but with discretionary control of its docket (i.e., it can selectively determine which cases to review). In Chapter 5 we turn our attention to state supreme courts (which operate under a variety of different institutional contexts) and an examination of state statutes. Finally, in Chapter 6 we return to the U.S. Supreme Court but focus our attention on a different aspect of statutory influence—whether the effects identified in Chapter 4 change over time.

3

U.S. Courts of Appeals

When the language is narrowly drawn, the constraints are fairly strict; when it is drawn loosely they're more generous, but in either case they do exist.

—Judge Alex Kozinski (2004, 79)

In the previous chapter we outline our theoretical argument for the *model of contingent discretion*. We posit that the statutory language interpreted by judges affects their ability to render decisions according to their ideological preferences. In this chapter, we present the first empirical test of our theory by systematically examining judicial behavior on the U.S. Courts of Appeals. In many ways, this judicial institution contains the ideal environment to test our theory. First, though the Courts of Appeals are divided into twelve different circuits, they essentially possess an identical institutional structure. The appellate judges all possess life tenure, according to Article III of the U.S. Constitution; the courts adjudicate appeals primarily through the use of three-judge panels (with judges assigned randomly); and they interpret statutes passed by a single legislative principal—the U.S. Congress. Second, the Courts of Appeals all possess mandatory jurisdiction. This means that they cannot pick and choose which cases to adjudicate, but rather, must review all appeals filed by litigants.[1] Consequently, if the *model of contingent discretion* systematically affects voting patterns as we expect, then this influence should be most prominent in the federal appellate courts.

In this chapter, we therefore examine the U.S. Courts of Appeals to determine whether the language included in Congressional statutes has a systematic impact on judicial behavior. We begin by first discussing the historical development of the Courts of Appeals. We then provide anecdotal evidence from judges' opinions about the importance of statutory language; followed by several empirical tests of the *model of contingent discretion.*

Historical Development of the Federal Appellate Courts

The establishment of the United States government, under the Articles of Confederation, did not coincide with the creation of an identifiable judicial branch. Virtually all governmental functions were handled by a single-chamber legislature. As the Founding Fathers gathered to replace the Articles of Confederation, the debate over the necessity of a separate judicial entity fostered disagreement. Two proposals were offered pertaining to a judicial branch. The first, commonly referred to as the Virginia Plan, called for the establishment of a single supreme court and a number of inferior federal courts. Opponents to this plan, concerned over a potentially powerful and centralized judiciary, presented the New Jersey Plan. This proposal would have created a single supreme court with the jurisdiction to hear appeals from state courts—where all trials would commence (Carp and Stidham 2001, 25). Similar to other aspects in the development of the U.S. Constitution, a compromise occurred among the delegates, which led to the drafting of Article III: "The Judicial Power of the United States, shall be vested in one supreme Court, and in such inferior Courts as the Congress may from time to time ordain and establish."

Upon ratification of the Constitution, Congress immediately worked to establish the initial judicial structure of the federal government. With the passage of the Judiciary Act in 1789, Congress created a three-tiered judicial structure. The Supreme Court consisted of a Chief Justice and five associate justices. Three circuit courts were established, each staffed by a district court judge and two Supreme Court justices. Finally, thirteen district courts were created, one for each ratifying state (plus a court each for Maine and Kentucky). In addition to creating a formal judicial structure, the Act established the jurisdictional relationships among the three tiers. The district courts served as minor trial courts and the circuit courts presided over more important civil and criminal trials, as well as handling diversity disputes (between citizens of two different states). The Supreme Court possessed original jurisdiction in a limited number of areas, and appellate jurisdiction from the circuit courts, district courts and state courts (Murphy, Pritchett, and Epstein 2002).

As the United States developed throughout the nineteenth century the inadequacy of this initial system became readily apparent. In 1891, Congress passed the Evarts Act, which created the circuit courts of appeals. These new courts were responsible for reviewing most of the appeals from the federal district courts. Ironically though, the Evarts Act did not abolish the old circuit courts. Consequently, for the next twenty years the federal judicial system included four tiers, two of which were trial tribunals: district courts and circuit courts; and two of which possessed appellate jurisdiction: circuit courts of appeals and the Supreme Court. In 1911, Congress passed additional legislation dissolving the old circuit courts and in 1948, the remaining intermediate appellate tribunals officially became known as the Courts of Appeals. The modern appeals courts are organized in eleven circuits, each possessing jurisdiction over a specific geographic region. A twelfth circuit reviews cases from Washington, DC (including many federal agencies) and a thirteenth circuit—the Federal Circuit created in 1982—possesses specific subject-matter jurisdiction.[2]

Since its inception in 1891, the U.S. Courts of Appeals has occupied a "pivotal position as the vital center of the federal judicial system" (Howard 1977). Songer (1991) states, "as the number of litigated cases grows both quantitatively and in complexity, while the number of cases reviewed by the Supreme Court remains static, the role of the courts of appeals as the final authoritative policymaker in the interpretation of many areas of federal law expands apace." According to the Administrative Office of the U.S. Courts, the annual caseload of the appeals courts has increased substantially each year with the total number of cases reviewed in 1990 reaching approximately 38,000 (Songer, Sheehan, and Haire 2000, 15–16). More recently, the Administrative Office reports a peak of cases commenced in the Appeals Courts at 70,375 in 2006. Therefore, for a large majority of cases, the U.S. Courts of Appeals serve as the court of last resort, since "fewer than one-half of 1% of appeals courts decisions are reviewed by the Supreme Court" (Songer 1991).[3] Consequently, this pivotal position provides the appeals courts with several opportunities to review questions pertaining to the structure, authority, and conduct of the federal government. For the majority of interpretations of federal law (i.e., Congressional statutes), the Courts of Appeals provide the final say. Thus, in testing the *model of contingent discretion*, it is extremely important to determine whether Congressional statutes influence federal appellate judges. To help answer this question, we first turn to actual court opinions—under the assumption that if judges are influenced by statutory language, one should expect to observe references of this influence in the official court opinions.

Anecdotal Evidence from Appeals Court Judges

In Chapter 1, we present several cases to illustrate the importance placed on statutory language by judges. In this section we elaborate on these general illustrations to provide examples taken specifically from the U.S. Courts of Appeals. As we indicate earlier, if appellate judges are influenced by statutory language, then we should expect to see references of this influence written directly into their statements—either in court opinions directly, or within certain academic writings. While this evidence does not demonstrate the systematic impact of statutory language—empirical tests discussed later in this chapter provide better evidence—anecdotal references illustrate how judges respond to statutory language.[4]

In this regard, Judge Alex Kozinski (2004, 79) of the Ninth Circuit offers an important discussion about language, generally speaking. He states:

> Let me give you an example of one principle that I think is extremely important: Language has meaning. This doesn't mean every word is as precisely defined as every other word, or that words always have a single, immutable meaning. What it does mean is that language used in statutes, regulations, contracts, and the Constitution place an objective constraint on our conduct. The precise line may be debatable at times, but at the very least the language used sets an outer boundary that those interpreting and applying the law must respect. When the language is narrowly drawn, the constraints are fairly strict; when it is drawn loosely they're more generous, but in either case they do exist.

In a similar fashion, Judge Frank H. Easterbrook of the Seventh Circuit offers insights into the debate between textualism and legislative intent. He states (2004, 258):

Doubts about the value of legislative history arise not because the context of a law is unimportant, but because snippets from the debates so often have been used in lieu of the text, or as an excuse to nudge the law closer to the view of the losers in the legislative battle (a class that may include the judge). The text of a statute—and not the intent of those who voted for or signed it—is the law.

In her article "Some Thoughts on Judging . . ." Chief Judge Patricia M. Wald (1987, 899) of the District of Columbia Circuit acknowledges the importance of legislative statutes and their influence on judicial behavior. She observes:

The legislature's role as the primary lawmaker has proved to be a major check on judicial discretion. The kind of reasoning a judge engages in when construing a statute differs from common law reasoning, in which the judge extracts principles from cases involving a variety of fact situations. In statutory construction, the principle is already laid down by the legislature; the judge's role is to locate it and apply (or not apply) it to varying fact situations. A judge construing a statute concentrates primarily on the meaning of the text, the purpose of the law, and the intent of the drafters, not the direction in which judge-made law should evolve . . . In statutory construction, the judge is performing a derivative function, searching for meaning in a static document.

These statements provide interesting insights into the general approaches taken by several federal appellate judges when interpreting legislative statutes. However, beyond examining the academic writings of specific individuals, it is also useful to examine select court opinions to determine if references to statutory influence become part of the "official record." To this end, we offer a few examples. The first involves the Fifth Circuit's interpretation of 18 U.S.C.A. § 1623(d); a recantation provision of 18 U.S.C.A. § 1623 which is a Congressional criminal statute dealing with knowingly making false material declarations. In the case *United States v. Scrimgeour* 636 F.2d 1019 (1981) Judge Frank M. Johnson, Jr. states (at 1022):

We must keep in mind several basic principles that relate to the construction of criminal statutes: A federal criminal statute should be construed narrowly in order to encompass only that conduct that Congress intended to criminalize . . . Although a criminal statute must be strictly construed, it must not be construed so strictly as to defeat the clear intention of the legislature . . . A basic canon of statutory construction is that words should be interpreted as taking their ordinary and plain meaning . . . Although in interpretation of statutory language reference should first be made to the plain and literal meaning of the words, the overriding duty of a court is to give effect to the intent of the legislature . . . A statute should be ordinarily interpreted according to its plain language, unless a clear contrary legislative intent is shown.

A second example comes from the case *Guidry v. Sheet Metal Workers National Pension Fund.*[5] In this case the court of appeals for the Tenth Circuit reviewed a trial court order that placed a constructive trust on an individual's pension benefits pursuant to a guilty plea involving the embezzlement of union funds. The dispute arose, in part, because of a conflict between provisions in the Labor-Management Reporting and Disclosure Act of 1959 and the Employee Retirement Income Security Act of 1974 (ERISA). In writing for the majority, Judge Moore indicates (1988, 1461) that:

Congress emphasized on several occasions the broad scope of remedies available under ERISA. In addition to the previously mentioned statutory language giving the courts authority to fashion remedies . . . the legislative history of the Act indicates Congressional intent to provide a broad variety of remedies for redressing the interests of participants and beneficiaries when they have been adversely affected. . . .

A somewhat contradictory example exists in the case *J. C. Penney Co. v. Commissioner of Internal Revenue* 312 F.2d 65 (1962). In writing for a unanimous majority, Judge Henry J. Friendly of the Second Circuit states in his first sentence (at 66), "This petition for review presents the rare case in which it is as clear as anything ever can be that Congress did not mean what in strict letter it said." Later in the opinion (at 68), Judge Friendly elaborates by stating that, "Congress is free, within constitutional limitations, to legislate eccentrically if it should wish, but courts should not lightly assume that it has done so. When the 'plain meaning' of statutory language has led to absurd or futile results [courts should look] beyond the words to the purpose of the Act" (1962, 68). Thus, though the Second Circuit in this instance ruled against the Congressional statute, Judge Friendly's opinion indicates that courts should begin their inquiry with an examination of the statutory language.

These examples, both the academic writings of federal appellate judges and the official opinions issued by the Courts of Appeals, reveal that judges examine the language of statutes carefully. Regardless of whether the individual judge is a strict textualist or is willing to discern legislative intent, it is obvious that the beginnings of all statutory inquiries focus on the language of the law. This anecdotal evidence therefore reinforces the importance of our initial question— to what extent does statutory language systematically influence the voting behavior of judges (in this case, judges on the U.S. Courts of Appeals)? In the next section we present empirical evidence to address this question.

Empirical Analysis of Statutory Influence

As we explain in Chapter 2, our basic argument is that judicial decision making is contingent on the level of discretion afforded by the law. Consequently, we expect to observe judges voting according to their ideological preferences when they interpret vague or ambiguous statutes that provide high levels of discretion. Conversely, when courts encounter statutes that prescribe more detailed outcomes, and therefore reduce the level of discretion, then we expect the ability of judges to decide cases attitudinally will be constrained. Yet, it is important to note that not all judges will experience these potential constraining effects at the same time—even when some judges are constrained from voting ideologically, the law can facilitate the expression of ideological voting among others. Thus, the contingent effect can operate in two ways—it can constrain judges from voting according to their ideological preferences or it can facilitate the influence of ideology.

In this section, we provide the initial empirical test of the *model of contingent discretion* and statistically evaluate both the statutory constraint hypothesis and the statutory facilitation hypothesis across several legal issue areas (including criminal law, civil liberties, and economic regulations). To examine the influence of statutory language we rely on data from the U.S. Courts of Appeals Database, compiled by Donald R. Songer; as updated by Susan Haire and Ashlyn Kuersten.[6] Though the full data contain a random sample[7] of cases from 1925–2002, we limit our analysis to those cases that include the interpretation of a congressional statute.[8] Since we are interested in the behavior of individual judges, we transpose the data to make our unit of analysis focus on individual judges.

The dependent variable for the analysis is whether the judge voted in an unconstrained or sincere manner.[9] We code the variable "1" if a liberal judge casts a liberal vote and '0' if that judge votes conservatively. Similarly, the variable is coded "1" if a conservative judge votes conservatively and "0" if that judge casts a liberal vote.[10]

As we indicate in Chapter 2, our independent variable of primary interest is *Statutory Detail.* Following the Huber and Shipan methodology, we examine the length of legislative statutes. To measure length we rely on information pertaining to the relevant statute in each case that is included in the Courts of Appeals Database.[11] Also, as we explain in the previous chapter, because we are interested in the effects brought by substantial differences among statutes, we take the natural log of each statute as our operationalization of the variable *Statutory Detail.*

Additionally, our hypotheses indicate a theoretical expectation that statutory detail operates differently between liberal and conservative judges (based on particular issue areas). This suggests that an interaction term is necessary to capture more specifically, the differential effects across these two groups.[12] Therefore, we include a dummy variable *Liberal* to control for the presence of liberal judges. We then create the interaction term *Liberal * Statutory Detail* to measure this potential dynamic and interdependent relationship. For those issue areas where the legislative statute prescribes a conservative outcome (such as criminal cases) this interaction term should reflect a constraining effect on judicial behavior. Conversely, increases in statutory detail in these issue areas should facilitate (i.e., increase) the likelihood of ideological voting for conservative judges. Due to the presence of an interaction term, these effects will be observed in the original *Statutory Detail* variable.

While the concept of statutory constraint/facilitation is related to the legal model, the attitudinal model indicates that judicial decision making is also the result of individual ideological preferences (Segal and Spaeth 2002). Since this theory was initially developed for the U.S. Supreme Court, and because of its unique institutional characteristics, several refined measures of ideology exist (Segal and Cover 1989; Martin and Quinn 2002). Unfortunately, comparable measures of ideology for appellate judges are not as refined. Yet, several scholars demonstrate the validity of the ideological preferences of an appellate judge's appointing president as a reliable surrogate for judicial ideology.[13] However, Giles, Hettinger and Peppers (2001) discover that the presence of senatorial courtesy can also affect the ideological tendencies of appellate judges. Thus, we rely on their empirical measure of ideological preferences in our variable *Ideological Intensity*. These scores represent a continuous measure of ideology and, as the authors demonstrate in their article, substituting the appropriate score—based on a judge's appointing president and confirming senator—offers a suitable surrogate for judicial ideology. Thus, judges appointed by more liberal presidents, from states with more liberal senators, will possess more liberal ideology scores and vice versa. Since our theory argues that statutory constraint will limit ideological influences over judicial behavior, we "fold" the Giles, Hettinger and Peppers measure into a continuum from the most moderate judges to the most extreme ideologues.[14] Consequently, we hypothesize that judges with strong ideological preferences will be more likely to render unconstrained or sincere decisions. A positive relationship should therefore exist between our variable *Ideological Intensity* and the dependent variable.

In addition to the two primary variables of interest and the interaction term, our model includes one other variable to control for relevant factors. It measures whether the Courts of Appeals are requested to review the constitutionality of the statute. If the appellate panels exercise their power of *Judicial Review*, we expect the judges to be more likely to cast sincere votes (i.e., we do not expect a substantial effect to exist when the constitutionality of the statute is questioned).

Before turning to the more sophisticated empirical models, it is useful to examine some descriptive statistics concerning Congressional statutes. Table 3.1 presents an overall description for all Congressional statutes interpreted by the U.S. Courts of Appeals in our sample. We can see that the average statute length (in raw number of words) is 2,074 words with a standard deviation of 3,687 words. The shortest statute contains only 22 words while the longest interpreted by the appellate courts contains 26,308 words. Since our empirical models measure statute length in terms of natural logs, we present these numbers as well. The average length (measured by its natural log) is 6.592 with a standard deviation of 1.505. The shortest statute contains a natural log of 3.091 while the longest has a natural log of 10.178.

Additionally, we observe a substantial amount of variation across specific issue areas in terms of statute length. As seen in Table 3.2, the average criminal statute passed by Congress contains 1,495 words (with an average natural log of 6.540) and a standard deviation of 2,042 words (with a natural log of 1.346). Additionally, the shortest criminal statute contains only 25 words (with a natural log of 3.219) while the longest criminal statute possesses 22,336 words (with a natural log of 10.014). Similarly, civil liberties statutes are slightly longer: containing an average number of 2,195 words (with a natural log of 6.347) and a standard deviation of 4,344 words (with a natural log of 1.630). The shortest civil liberties statute contains only 22 words

Table 3.1. The Nature of Congressional Statutes Under Review

Raw Number of Words	
Average Length	2074
Standard Deviation	3687
Minimum Length	22
Maximum Length	26308
Natural Log	
Average Length	6.592
Standard Deviation	1.505
Minimum Length	3.091
Maximum Length	10.178

Table 3.2. Congressional Statutes Under Review by Issue Area

Criminal Statutes

Raw Number of Words

Average Length	1495
Standard Deviation	2042
Minimum Length	25
Maximum Length	22336

Natural Log

Average Length	6.540
Standard Deviation	1.346
Minimum Length	3.219
Maximum Length	10.014

Civil Liberties Statutes

Raw Number of Words

Average Length	2195
Standard Deviation	4344
Minimum Length	22
Maximum Length	24420

Natural Log

Average Length	6.347
Standard Deviation	1.630
Minimum Length	3.091
Maximum Length	10.103

Economic Statutes

Raw Number of Words

Average Length	2304
Standard Deviation	3763
Minimum Length	22
Maximum Length	26308

Natural Log

Average Length	6.781
Standard Deviation	1.467
Minimum Length	3.091
Maximum Length	10.178

(with a natural log of 3.091) while the longest has 24,420 words (with a natural log of 10.103). Finally, economic statutes generally speaking are the longest laws passed by Congress with an average 2,304 words (translating into a natural log of 6.781) and a standard deviation of 3,763 words (with a natural log of 1.467). The shortest economic statute contains only 22 words (with a natural log of 3.091) while the longest possesses 26,308 words (and a natural log of 10.178).

Examining the information in the previous two tables immediately raises the question, What are examples of short Congressional statutes? One example is 18 U.S.C. § 1464—Broadcasting Obscene Language—that states, "Whoever utters any obscene, indecent, or profane language by means of radio communication shall be fined under this title or imprisoned not more than two years, or both." Note that this section does not contain definitions for the terms obscene, indecent, or profane language. This criminal statute has a length of 28 words. A second example is 28 U.S.C. § 1341—Taxes by States— that declares "The district courts shall not enjoin, suspend or restrain the assessment, levy or collection of any tax under State law where a plain, speedy, and efficient remedy may be had in the courts of such state." This statute has a length of 36 words. Again, note that none of the terms are defined. Consequently, while these statutes prescribe outcomes, they are extremely vague in nature, thus providing judges with greater discretion to define and apply the relevant terminology.

While the information in the previous two tables is interesting, it does not directly address the question whether statutory language systematically affects judicial behavior on the Courts of Appeals. To better understand these influences, we turn to Table 3.3 where the results of our empirical models are on display. Model 1 examines appellate decision making for criminal cases and the results provide empirical support for both the Statutory Constraint and Statutory Facilitation hypotheses. As we explain in Chapter 2, our expectation is that longer criminal statutes will exert a constraining effect on liberal judges while simultaneously providing a facilitation effect for conservative judges. Examining the interaction term *Statutory Detail * Liberal Judge Interaction* indicates that the coefficient is statistically significant and negative.[15] This means that as criminal statutes become more detailed (i.e., longer) they significantly constrain liberal appellate judges from casting sincere (i.e., liberal) votes. Conversely, the variable *Statutory Detail* is statistically significant and positive.

Table 3.3. Probit Analysis of Appellate Decisions

	Model 1 Criminal	Model 2 Civil Liberties	Model 3 Economic
Statutory Detail	.065*	.032	−.017
	(.034)	(.038)	(.025)
Liberal Judge	−.828**	−.022	−.331
	(.332)	(.347)	(.242)
Statutory Detail * Liberal Judge Interaction	−.099**	−.092*	.046
	(.050)	(.053)	(.034)
Ideological Intensity	−.726***	.503**	.224
	(.215)	(.247)	(.143)
Judicial Review	—	−.168	.310**
		(.324)	(.157)
Constant	.752 (.238)	.083 (.255)	.153 (.179)
N	1472	880	2396
Log Likelihood	−781.264	−574.404	−1648.196
LR/Wald Test	387.11	59.27	8.27
Probability > χ	.000	.000	.014
Pseudo R^2	.218	.050	.003
Null Model	58.5%	55.5%	53.7%
Correctly Predicted	76.2%	62.1%	54.3%
Reduction of Error	42.6%	15.0%	0.9%

Dependent Variable: unconstrained or sincere vote (1), constrained vote (0)
Values represent parameter estimates with robust standard errors in parentheses
* p < .10   ** p < .05   *** p < .01

Due to the inclusion of the interaction term, the variable *Statutory Detail* measures the effects of statute length on conservative judges. Its significant and positive coefficient indicates that as Congressional criminal statutes become more detailed, conservative judges are significantly more likely to cast sincere (i.e., conservative) votes.[16]

To determine the substantive impact of the significant coefficients for *Statutory Detail* and the *Statutory Detail * Liberal Judge Interaction*, we graphed in Figure 3.1 the probability of a sincere vote

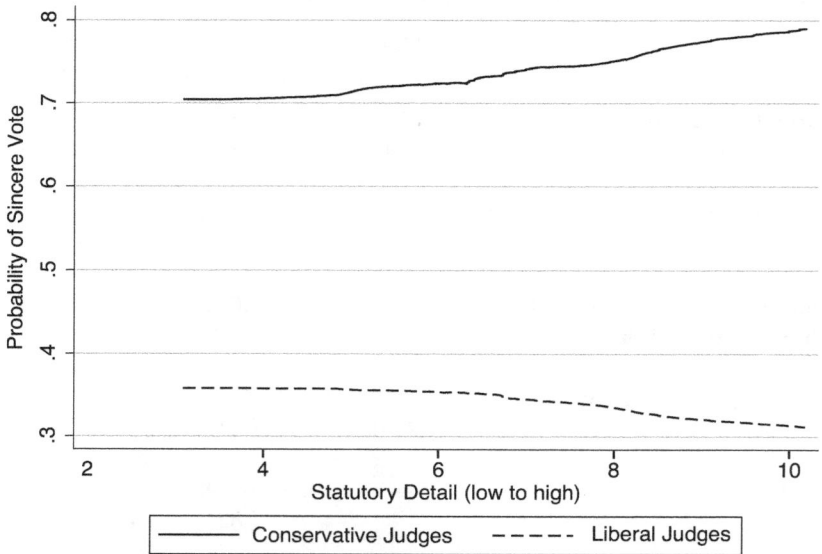

Figure 3.1. Impact of Statutory Detail on Sincere Voting in Criminal Cases.

against our measure of statute length. The solid line represents the likelihood of a sincere vote cast by conservative judges while the dotted line represents the probability of a sincere vote from liberal judges. Examining the pattern for conservative judges indicates that the probability of a conservative vote starts at approximately .700 and increases to approximately .790 as Congressional criminal statutes become more detailed. Thus, the statutory language facilitates almost a 10 percent increase in conservative voting by these conservative judges. In contrast, the probability of liberal judges casting sincere votes in criminal cases begins at approximately .350. As Congressional statutes become more detailed, however, the probability of a liberal vote decreases to approximately .310. Consequently, it is apparent that increases in statutory detail constrain liberal judges from casting liberal votes.

To determine if similar effects exist across other issue areas we examine both civil liberties cases (in Model 2) and economic cases (in Model 3). However, in neither model is *Statutory Detail* or the

*Statutory Detail * Liberal Judge Interaction* statistically significant.[17] However, the variable *Ideological Intensity* possesses a significant coefficient for civil liberties cases (in Model 2) indicating that judges with stronger ideological preferences are more likely to cast sincere votes.

At first glance, the results from Model 2 seem to provide little support for our expectation about the effects of statutory language on judicial behavior in civil liberties cases. However, it is important

Table 3.4. Probit Analysis of Appellate Decisions

	Model 4 Civil Rights	Model 5 Individual Liberties
Statutory Detail	.061 (.051)	.076 (.074)
Liberal Judge	.008 (.482)	.855 (.740)
Statutory Detail * Liberal Judge Interaction	−.088 (.072)	−.212** (.102)
Ideological Intensity	.304 (.332)	.746 (.540)
Judicial Review	−.077 (.362)	−.577 (.738)
Constant	−.101 (.358)	−.380 (.535)
N	471	225
Log Likelihood	−311.352	−145.252
LR/Wald Test	26.29	20.37
Probability > χ	.000	.001
Pseudo R^2	.041	.067
Null Model	54.3%	52.5%
Correctly Predicted	61.5%	63.0%
Reduction of Error	15.3%	22.5%

Dependent Variable: unconstrained or sincere vote (1), constrained vote (0)
Values represent parameter estimates with robust standard errors in parentheses
* $p < .10$ ** $p < .05$ *** $p < .01$

to note that this model examines *all civil liberties* cases and there are substantial differences between statutes designed to combat discrimination (such as the Civil Rights Act of 1964 or the Voting Rights Act of 1965) and laws designed to regulate aspects of free speech and expression, or place limits on abortion, or restrict privacy protections. These latter examples tend to involve legislation aimed at prescribing conservative outcomes whereas civil rights laws (such as the former examples) tend to prescribe liberal outcomes. If this reasoning is accurate, then one should expect conservative judges to experience constraining effects from more detailed civil rights legislation (with liberal judges experiencing facilitation effects) and liberal judges to experience constraining effects from more detailed statutes regulating other individual liberties (with conservatives experiencing facilitation effects).

To examine this possibility, in Table 3.4 we split the more general civil liberties cases into Civil Rights (Model 4) and Individual Liberties (Model 5). As one reviews the results of the Civil Rights analysis (Model 4) it is readily apparent that the level of statutory detail does not exert a significant influence on U.S. Courts of Appeals judges. Neither the variable *Statutory Detail* nor the *Statutory Detail * Liberal Judge Interaction* is statistically significant.

Though the influence of statute length is not apparent in Civil Rights cases, we observe a somewhat different situation when federal judges adjudicate disputes of Individual Liberties cases. Examining the results of Model 5 reveals that while the variable *Statutory Detail* is not statistically significant (indicating the conservative judges are not affected by statute length), the variable *Statutory Detail * Liberal Judge Interaction* is significant and negative. We notice also that the baseline variable *Liberal Justices* is significant and positive. Taken together, these two variables lead to the conclusion that liberal justices are generally more likely to cast sincere votes in individual liberties cases, *except* when the presence of detailed congressional statutes constrains their behavior; as the level of constraint increases liberal justices are less likely to cast sincere votes.

To better understand the substantive impact of this result, we graphed the probability of a sincere vote in individual liberties cases against our measure of statute length. Turning to Figure 3.2, we immediately observe substantially more variation across both liberal and conservative judges than was apparent in criminal cases (represented in Figure 3.1). As we examine the voting behavior of conser-

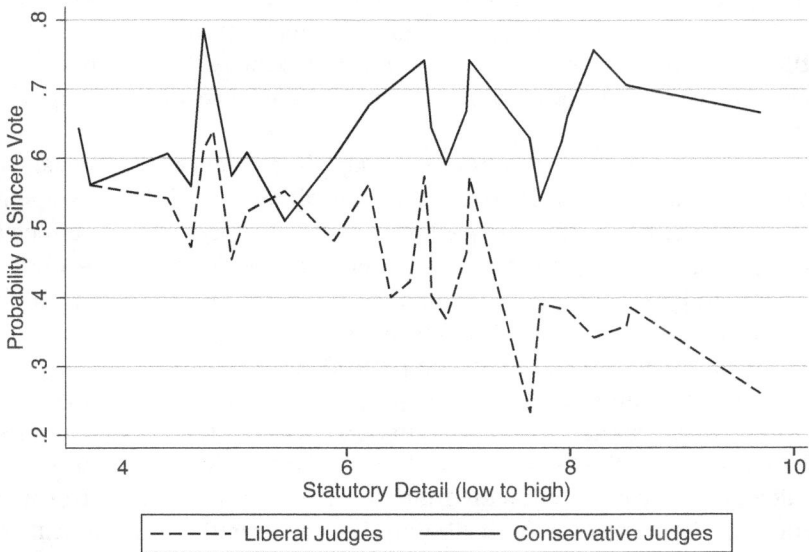

Figure 3.2. Impact of Statutes on Sincere Voting in Individual Liberties Cases.

vative judges (represented by the solid line) it is difficult to identify
an observable trend through the wild fluctuations. Perhaps there is
a slight increase in the probability of sincere voting (from an initial
probability of .65 to .68). However, as we examine the voting behavior
of liberal judges (represented by the dashed line) it is easier to dis-
tinguish the continuous decline in the probability of sincere voting.
Liberal judges begin with a probability of a sincere vote around .65
(similar to their conservative colleagues) when statutory detail is low.
As Congressional statutes become longer and more detailed, though,
the probability of a sincere vote from liberal judges decreases substantially to around .26. Consequently, it is apparent that increases
in statutory detail constrain liberal judges from casting liberal votes.

Circuit-Specific Analyses of Statutory Influence

The results reported in Figure 3.1 raise new questions concerning the
applicability of statutory influence across all circuits. Are all judges
influenced by Congressional statutes in a similar manner, or is there

one particular circuit (or maybe a limited number of circuits) whose judges are more susceptible to this influence than others? To address this question we examine the voting behavior of judges in specific circuits as they review criminal appeals. These results are reported in Figure 3.3.

Upon initial examination of the graphs in Figure 3.3, one can see that a similar general trend exists across all circuits. Generally speaking, conservative judges experience a positive, facilitation, effect as Congressional criminal statutes become more detailed. Conversely, liberal judges experience a negative, constraining, effect from the same statutory language. Therefore, generally speaking, the patterns revealed in Figure 3.3 reflect the pattern displayed in Figure 3.1.

Yet, as one delves a bit deeper and examines the graphs a bit more closely, some noticeable differences across the circuits emerge. First, judges in the District of Columbia Circuit display a more complicated pattern of behavior than the remaining circuits. The non-monotonic curves for both liberal and conservative judges indicate that statutory language only affects judicial behavior at the extremes— either when the statutes are significantly vague (i.e., short statute lengths) or when they contain substantial details (i.e., long statute lengths). Second, judges in the Third Circuit seemingly are immune to the influences of statutory language. Examining the voting patterns of liberal and conservative judges reveals relatively flat lines for both groups. To confirm this pattern, we ran a separate probit model (not reported) on just the Third Circuit; indicating that any influence of Congressional statutes is not persuasive among these judges, unlike their brethren in other circuits. This is the only circuit where statutory influences are not statistically significant. It is unclear why these judges are not affected in a similar fashion; a closer examination of the statutes litigated in the Third Circuit does not offer any insight into this anomaly.

An Alternative Specification

One final question may involve our use of the likelihood of a sincere vote as the dependent variable for these models. Admittedly, we had our initial qualms about this particular operationalization. Certainly, the accepted approach is to model the dependent variable in terms of

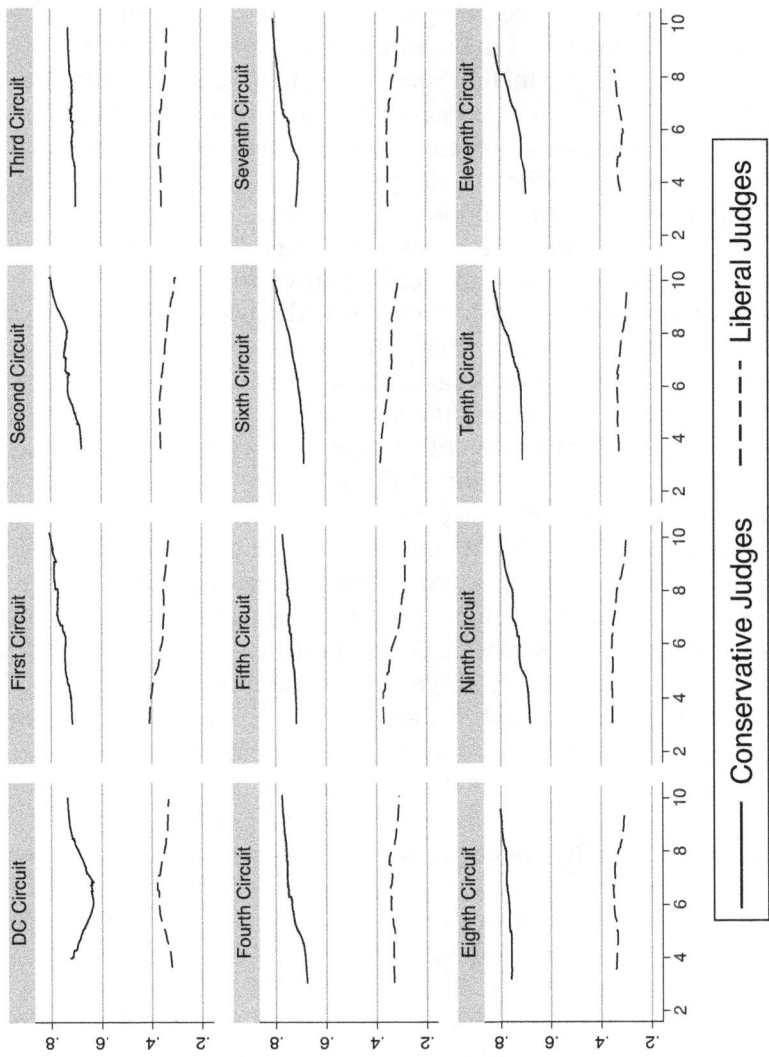

Figure 3.3. Impact of Statutory Detail Across Circuits.

a straight liberal or conservative vote; and, while this approach may be accepted more generally, we ultimately rejected it for theoretical reasons. As we explain in Chapter 2, the fundamental theoretical argument is whether statutory language can induce judges (both federal and state) from voting according to pure ideological predilections— not, whether statutes will make judges vote more conservatively or more liberally. This distinction may sound like we are splitting hairs or arguing semantics, but we believe it is an important distinction to make. By framing our argument (and by extension our dependent variable) in terms of whether judges vote sincerely, we allow for a more accurate conceptualization of the theory. As we argue in Chapter 2, if there is an influence of statutory language on judicial voting behavior, our expectation is that conservative and liberal judges will experience different effects—one set will discover their ideological voting supported (or facilitated) by the statute while the other set will find their ability to vote ideologically constrained by the law.

At the very least, framing the analyses in terms of sincere voting keeps us from having to constantly remind readers whether a positive relationship confirms (or refutes) the statutory constraint or statutory facilitation hypothesis—aspects which change depending on the specific issue area and whether one references liberal or conservative judges. That said we recognize that framing the argument in terms of the effects of statutory language on the likelihood of sincere votes has some disadvantages as well. One in particular involves the voting behavior of more moderate judges. For these individuals, it is more difficult to determine whether the vote cast is truly sincere or not than it is to identify whether the vote was liberal or conservative. In the eyes of some readers, this difficulty may be enough to cast doubt on the reliability of our results. Therefore, to test whether our use of sincere voting as a dependent variable is appropriate and not inherently biased, we reanalyzed Courts of Appeals adjudication of criminal disputes using the more conventional "ideological directionality of the case" as the dependent variable. The results of this alternative specification are reported in Table 3.5 under Model 6.

When examining the results from this table, it is important to note that the dependent variable is coded "1" for a conservative vote and "0" for a liberal vote. Therefore, the coefficients of this table should be interpreted with that frame in mind. As we see from Table 3.5 both the variables *Statutory Detail* and *Statutory Detail * Liberal*

Table 3.5. An Alternative Specification for Criminal Cases

	Model 6 Alternative Specification
Statutory Detail	.076* (.042)
Liberal Judge	–.271 (.395)
Statutory Detail * Liberal Judge **Interaction**	.104* (.059)
Ideology	–.127 (.223)
Judicial Review	—
Constant	.052 (.313)
N	1456
Log Likelihood	–665.129
LR/Wald Test	644.35
Probability > χ	.000
Pseudo R^2	.326
Null Model	58.6%
Correctly Predicted	81.1%
Reduction of Error	54.1%

Dependent Variable: conservative vote (1), liberal vote (0)
Values represent parameter estimates with robust standard errors in parentheses
* $p < .10$ ** $p < .05$ *** $p < .01$

Judge Interaction are significant and positive. This confirms the validity of the initial results in Model 1. Substantively, the results indicate that both conservative and liberal judges are more likely to cast conservative votes as criminal statutes become more detailed (i.e., longer). Since conservative judges prefer this outcome ideologically, the result supports our statutory facilitation hypothesis. Conversely, since liberal judges would prefer a liberal outcome, this result supports our statutory constraint hypothesis.

Conclusions

As we stated at the outset of this chapter, the Courts of Appeals contain the ideal environment in which to test our theory of contingent discretion because they possess mandatory jurisdiction and must review all appeals referred by lower courts. As such, they cannot pick and choose which cases to review. And it is interesting to note that we find support for the theory of contingent discretion in the analysis of criminal cases and a subset of civil liberties statutes. On the other hand, the evidence with regard to economic and civil rights cases does not support our main hypotheses.

What is also interesting about these results is the varying significance of ideology across these several models. When either the variable *Statutory Detail* or the *Statutory Detail * Liberal Judge Interaction* term is statistically significant there is no influence for the variable *Ideological Intensity*. This holds for criminal statutes (in Table 3.3), individual liberty (i.e., non-civil rights) statutes (Table 3.4) and the alternative specification (in Table 3.5). Conversely, when the ideological variable is statistically significant, neither of the statutory variables attain significance.

Taken together, these two results may lead initially to the general conclusion that law and ideology operate as "trade-offs" to each other. That is, either the law dominates or ideology possesses the primary influence. Yet, we also identify a facilitation effect among conservative judges in criminal cases; this is not consistent with a 'trade-off' perspective. Furthermore, as we demonstrate in later chapters of this book, the relationship between law and ideology is much more dynamic and complex and not simply a tradeoff between influences. This chapter provides a hint at the dynamic interchange between law and ideology when we observe some appellate judges experiencing constraining effects attributable to statutory language while others experience facilitating effects. The next chapter offers further evidence of the conditions under which law and ideology concomitantly affect judicial behavior in the U.S. Supreme Court.

4

The U.S. Supreme Court

By far the greatest part of what all federal judges do is to interpret the meaning of statutes . . . The text is the law, and it is the text that must be observed.

—Justice Antonin Scalia (1997, 13–30)

In Chapter 2, we explain the theoretical foundations for our *model of contingent discretion*—that the statutory language interpreted by judges affects their ability to vote according to their individual ideological preferences. Then, in Chapter 3 we provide the first empirical test of this model, using data on judicial behavior in the U.S. Courts of Appeals. As we discuss, the federal appellate courts possess the ideal environment to test our theory because of similar institutional contexts across the circuits, including mandatory jurisdiction.

In contrast, the Supreme Court represents the most difficult institution in which to test our model. This difficulty stems from two different characteristics affecting Supreme Court behavior. The first involves the possession of *discretionary jurisdiction* by the justices. Unlike judges on the federal appellate courts who must review every appeal, the justices of the Supreme Court can pick and choose which cases receive review. In order for any single case to receive attention, the justices must first grant *certiorari*.[1] During this process, the justices formally vote on whether to review an appeal, and four justices must agree in order for a petition to receive a writ of *certiorari* (see Perry 1991 for more details on the *certiorari* process).

Several scholars have examined the *certiorari* process to better understand what factors influence the justices to grant the writ (for example, see Brenner 1979; Songer 1979; Teger and Kosinski 1980; Brenner and Krol 1989; and Tanenhaus et al. 1989). These factors include organized interest groups who submit *amicus curiae* briefs requesting grants of *certiorari* (Caldeira and Wright 1988; 1990), attorney influences (McGuire and Caldeira 1993), signals from the lower courts (Cameron, Segal, and Songer 2000), the *en banc* process (George and Solimine 2001), and strategies of the federal government (Zorn 2002). Because of the nature of the *certiorari* process, several scholars conclude that these votes often reflect justices' preferences on the merits of a case (see Ulmer 1972; 1984; Boucher and Segal 1995; and Caldeira, Wright, and Zorn 1999). Furthermore, recent research indicates that the Supreme Court justices often signal to potential litigants which types of cases they wish to review in order to develop particular areas of legal policy (Baird 2004; 2007).

The second institutional feature of the Supreme Court that separates it from the Courts of Appeals involves the frequency of judicial review. Though both judicial institutions possess the authority to adjudicate the constitutionality of specific statutes, the Supreme Court exercises this authority in a larger percentage of cases than the appellate courts. This greater frequency is due, in large part, to the fact that the Supreme Court only decides approximately 80 cases per year compared to the thousands of cases decided by the Courts of Appeals. However, the greater frequency is also due to the fact that the Supreme Court often selectively reviews cases that present constitutional issues. Several scholars argue about the importance of judicial review and the potential effects this authority has on the Supreme Court (Franck 1996; Shipan 1997; and Howard and Segal 2004). Because of the frequency of judicial review exercised by the Supreme Court (as compared to other judicial institutions in the United States) we conduct a separate empirical test of the *model of contingent discretion* on these cases to determine if the patterns exhibited by Supreme Court justices during normal statutory interpretation cases holds when the constitutionality of those statutes is questioned.

In sum, because of these two institutional differences—the presence of discretionary jurisdiction through the *certiorari* process and the relatively high frequency of judicial review—the Supreme Court presents a more difficult environment in which to test empirically the validity and applicability of our *model of contingent discretion*. This is to say that our initial expectation points to a low probability of observing similar statutory constraining/facilitating effects that we find influencing the behavior of judges on the Courts of Appeals. The remaining sections of this chapter first examine the historical development of the Supreme Court. We then peruse anecdotal evidence concerning statutory influences from the writings of the justices; followed by several empirical tests of our theory.

Historical Development of the Supreme Court

In many ways, the history of the Supreme Court reflects Alexander Hamilton's contention, in *Federalist* No. 78, that the Court is the "least dangerous branch" of government. The inferiority of the institution is demonstrated in myriad ways. For example, it was not until 1935 that the Supreme Court moved into its own building. Prior to that year, the Court met in the basement of the Capitol Building in Washington, DC.[2] Additionally, early Supreme Court justices were required to "ride circuit" in order to hear cases across the judicial circuits. These examples (plus many others) prompted some justices to resign from the Court for what we today would consider less prestigious positions; including the first Chief Justice, John Jay, who resigned to become the Governor of New York.

Yet, in 1803, the Supreme Court rendered a decision that arguably transformed it into a more viable and politically relevant institution. Under the direction of Chief Justice John Marshall, the majority opinion in *Marbury v. Madison* (1 Cranch 137) declared, "it is emphatically the province and duty of the judicial department to say what the law is." The remainder of Marshall's opinion developed the foundation for the "vitally important legal principle" (Rehnquist 2001, 21) of judicial review—the ability of the judiciary to invalidate statutes based on provisions of the Constitution. Yet, though Marshall's opinion garnered this authority for the Supreme Court, he did not exercise it again to review a congressional statute (although it was applied to several state statutes). Rather, the next exercise of judicial review against a federal law came from the Taney Court, reviewing the Missouri Compromise, in the infamous *Dred Scott* case.[3]

With the establishment of judicial review as a legitimate and recognized authority possessed by the Supreme Court, it became a more viable institution in the checks and balances system of government. As the Court developed into a more vibrant institution, it became embroiled in more aspects of society; eventually leading Justice Oliver Wendell Holmes to observe that it is a "storm centre" of political controversy (quoted in O'Brien 2005, xiii). Yet, throughout its institutional evolution, the Court remained (and continues to remain) bound by congressional legislation for several aspects of its normal operations. First, though the Constitution specifically outlines its original jurisdiction, the Supreme Court relies on Congress to set the boundaries of its appellate jurisdiction. As Chief Justice Salmon P. Chase notes in the case *Ex parte McCardle*, "Without jurisdiction the court cannot proceed at all in any cause. Jurisdiction is the power to declare the law, and when it ceases to exist, the only function remaining to the court is that of announcing the fact and dismissing the cause."[4] Second, the Court relies on congressional statutes to determine the number of justices. The current number—nine—was set with the passage of the Judiciary Act of 1869, although prior to this year Congress changed the number of justices from five to ten.[5] This number has remained despite additional calls to change the number of justices, the most famous of which came from President Franklin Delano Roosevelt during the New Deal in which he proposed increasing to fifteen the number of justices, in order to "pack the Court" with his own appointees.[6]

These examples have led scholars to examine various aspects of congressional influence on the voting behavior of Supreme Court justices. One recent article concludes that Congress can introduce legislation aimed at curbing specific operations of the Court to induce the justices to adjust their voting behavior (Clark 2009). Our question is whether other congressional statutes—aimed at general policymaking rather than Court curbing—induce the justices to adjust their voting behavior. To address this question initially, we turn to the writings (both academic and from official opinions) of the justices themselves. As one can see, the justices claim to be highly sensitive to the preferences of Congress when they interpret legislation.

Anecdotal Evidence from Supreme Court Justices

In Chapter 3, we present anecdotal evidence from appellate judges demonstrating the influence that Congressional statutes have on their writings. In this section we elaborate on these general illustrations to provide examples taken specifically from the U.S. Supreme Court. As we indicate earlier, if the justices are influenced by statutory language, then we should expect to see references of this influence written directly into their statements—either in court opinions directly, or within certain academic writings. While this evidence does not demonstrate the systematic impact of statutory language—empirical tests discussed later in this chapter provide better evidence—anecdotal references help to illustrate how justices respond to statutory language.

To begin this discussion, we turn to Justice Felix Frankfurter (2004, 247) who highlights the difficulties involved with the interpretation of statutes. He notes:

> Anything that is written may present a problem of meaning, and that is the essence of the business of judges in construing legislation. The problem derives from the very nature of words. They are symbols of meaning. But unlike mathematical symbols, the phrasing of a document, especially a complicated enactment, seldom attains more than approximate precision. If individual words are inexact symbols, with shifting variables, their configuration can hardly achieve invariant meaning or assured definiteness. Apart from the ambiguity inherent in its symbols, a statute suffers from dubieties. It is not an equation or a formula representing a clearly marked process, nor is it an expression of individual thought to which is imparted the definiteness a single authorship can give. A statute is an instrument of government partaking of its practical purposes but also of its infirmities and limitations, of its awkward and groping efforts.

After expressing the difficulties associated with statutory interpretation, Justice Frankfurter continues (2004, 253–255) to explain the following:

> We must, no doubt, accord the words the sense in which Congress used them. That is only another way of stating the central problem of decoding the symbols. It will help to determine for whom they were meant. Statutes are not archaeological documents to be studied in a library. They are written to guide the actions of men. If a statute is written for ordinary folk, it would be arbitrary not to assume that Congress intended its words to be read with the minds of ordinary men. If they are

addressed to specialists, they must be read by judges with
the minds of specialists . . . Legislation has an aim; it seeks
to obviate some mischief, to supply an inadequacy, to effect
a change of policy, to formulate a plan of government. That
aim, that policy is not drawn, like nitrogen, out of the air; it
is evinced in the language of the statute, as read in the light
of other external manifestations of purpose. That is what the
judge must seek and effectuate, and he ought not be led off
the trail by tests that have overtones of subjective design. We
are not concerned with anything subjective. We do not delve
into the mind of legislators or their draftsmen, or committee
members . . . Violence must not be done to the words chosen
by the legislature . . . In the end, language and external aids,
each accorded the authority deserved in the circumstances,
must be weighed in the balance of judicial judgment. Only if its
premises are emptied of their human variables, can the process
of statutory construction have the precision of a syllogism.[7]

In addition to the insights articulated by Justice Frankfurter, Justice Antonin Scalia—perhaps the most vocal advocate of the strict
textualist approach—offers glimpses into the importance of statutory
language. In his book, *A Matter of Interpretation*, he writes the following (1997, 13-30):

Every issue of law resolved by a federal judge involves interpretation of text—the text of a regulation, or of a statute, or
of the Constitution . . . By far the greatest part of what I and
all federal judges do is to interpret the meaning of federal
statutes and federal agency regulations . . . The text is the
law, and it is the text that must be observed . . . Words do
have a limited range of meaning, and no interpretation that
goes beyond that range is permissible . . . My view that the
objective indication of words, rather than the intent of the
legislature, is what constitutes the law leads me, of course, to
the conclusion that legislative history should not be used as
an authoritative indication of a statute's meaning.

While these academic writings provide a useful understanding
of the theoretical issues surrounding statutory interpretation, it is also

important to determine what the justices say in their official written opinions. To this end, we offer a few examples. The first pertains to the case *FDA v. Brown & Williamson Tobacco Co.*,[8] in which the Supreme Court determines whether Congress explicitly granted the Food and Drug Administration (FDA) jurisdiction to regulate tobacco products. In writing for the majority to declare that Congress did not expressly grant such authority, Justice Sandra Day O'Connor elaborates on several canons of statutory interpretation used by the Court. She states (at 132–133):

> In determining whether Congress has specifically addressed the question at issue, a reviewing court should not confine itself to examining a particular statutory provision in isolation. The meaning—or ambiguity—of certain words or phrases may only become evident when placed in context . . . It is a 'fundamental canon of statutory construction that the words of a statute must be read in their context and with a view to their place in the overall statutory scheme' . . . A court must therefore interpret the statute 'as a symmetrical and coherent regulatory scheme' . . . and fit, if possible, all parts into an harmonious whole . . . Similarly, the meaning of one statute may be affected by other Acts, particularly where Congress has spoken subsequently and more specifically to the topic at hand.

A second example is seen in the majority opinion written by Justice Anthony Kennedy in the case *Amoco Products Co. v. Southern Ute Indian Tribe*.[9] Here, the Court was asked to resolve a dispute concerning land patents issued pursuant to the Coal Land Acts passed by Congress in 1909 and 1910. The question involved whether Congressional regulations pertaining to coal explicitly also covered coalbed methane (CBM) gas. In writing for the Court, Justice Kennedy states (at 877–878) the following:

> There is some evidence of limited and sporadic exploitation of CBM gas as a fuel prior to the passage of the 1909 and 1910 Acts . . . It seems unlikely, though, that Congress considered this limited drilling for CBM gas. To the extent Congress had an awareness of it, there is every reason to think it viewed the extraction of CBM gas as drilling for natural gas, not mining

coal. That distinction is significant because the question before us is not whether Congress would have thought that CBM gas had some fuel value, but whether Congress considered it part of the coal fuel. When it enacted the 1909 and 1910 Acts, Congress did not reserve all minerals or energy resources in the lands. It reserved only coal, and then only in lands that were specifically identified as valuable for coal. It chose not to reserve oil, natural gas, or any other known or potential energy resources. The limited nature of the 1909 and 1910 Act reservations is confirmed by subsequent congressional enactments. When Congress wanted to reserve gas rights that might yield valuable fuel, *it did so in explicit terms* (emphasis added).

Finally, the case *Chevron v. Natural Resources Defense Council*[10] offers additional insights into the importance of Congressional statutes. The *Chevron* case is most notable for the ruling that courts should give deference to administrative agencies when Congressional legislation is ambiguous. In writing for the majority, Justice John Paul Stevens provides an excellent summary as to how judges should approach matters of statutory interpretation (at 842–843):

When a court reviews an agency's construction of the statute which it administers, it is confronted with two questions. First, always, is the question whether Congress has directly spoken to the precise question at issue. If the intent of Congress is clear, that is the end of the matter; for the court, as well as the agency, must give effect to the unambiguously expressed intent of Congress. If, however, the court determines Congress has not directly addressed the precise question at issue, the court does not simply impose its own construction on the statute, as would be necessary in the absence of an administrative interpretation. Rather, if the statute is silent or ambiguous with respect to the specific issue, the question for the court is whether the agency's answer is based on a permissible construction of the statute.

These examples, both the academic writings of individual justices and the official opinions issued by the Supreme Court, reveal that the justices examine the language of statutes carefully. Regardless of whether the individual is a strict textualist or is willing to discern legislative intent, it is obvious that the beginnings of all statutory inquiries focus on the language of the law. This anecdotal evidence therefore gives greater force to our initial question—to what extent does statutory language systematically influence the voting behavior of the Supreme Court? In the next section we present a variety of empirical evidence to address this question.

Empirical Evidence of Statutory Influence

In Chapter 3, we offer an initial empirical test of our theory of contingent discretion and its relationship to the voting behavior of judges on the U.S. Courts of Appeals. These results provide some support for our theoretical expectations concerning the *model of contingent discretion*, particularly in the areas of criminal law and individual liberty cases. Yet, as we also explain, the appellate courts contain what we consider to be the best environment in which to test this theory, in part because of the lack of discretionary control over their dockets and because of the possibility of review by the Supreme Court. Additionally, since we find no evidence of the effects of contingent discretion at the appellate level in civil rights and economic cases, our test in the Supreme Court takes on even greater significance. Are these effects limited to certain areas of law and only in the Courts of Appeals? This is a key question because identifying empirical evidence for the model in only one judicial institution or a few types of cases does not provide broad support for our theory.

Because the U.S. Supreme Court presents an entirely different venue for examining the influence of the law, it represents not merely an opportunity to replicate our analyses from Chapter 3, but also provides a stricter test of the contingent discretion thesis. The threshold for finding a relationship between the law and judicial behavior should be higher with Supreme Court justices, for all the reasons just described. Consequently, an examination of the nation's highest court represents a critical test of our model's generalizability.

Importantly, the Supreme Court is not encumbered by a lack of discretionary control over its docket, or by the possibility of review by a higher court. Although Court decisions may be "reversed" through subsequent Congressional legislation, the justices possess the ability to review the new statutes. Congress may also choose to adopt an amendment to the Constitution, but such a process is exceedingly difficult and therefore does not represent a credible threat to the justices. Thus, in terms of principal-agent theory, the Supreme Court operates much less as an agent of Congress than the Courts of Appeals. Consequently, the justices of the Supreme Court possess substantially more leeway than appellate court judges to decide cases according to their ideological preferences.

Therefore, in this section we conduct empirical tests under the more difficult institutional context of the U.S. Supreme Court. Data for this analysis come from the three justice-centered Supreme Court databases compiled by Harold J. Spaeth.[11] Though the original datasets contain the universe of formally decided cases,[12] we limit our analysis to those cases in which the Supreme Court interprets a congressional statute. Consequently, we analyze approximately 28,000 justice-votes from 1953 to 1998.[13]

Similar to the previous chapter, the dependent variable for the analysis is whether a justice voted in an unconstrained or sincere manner.[14] We should also note that in the construction of the dataset we follow standard practice and eliminate those cases where a clear ideological decision does not exist. Thus, the 28,000 justice-vote observations all include an identifiable ideological directionality.

As we indicate in Chapter 2, our independent variable of primary interest is *Statutory Detail*. To measure length we rely on information in the Spaeth database to identify the statute in question.[15] Also, as we explain in the previous chapter, because we are interested in the effects brought by substantial differences among statutes, we take the natural log of each statute as our operationalization of the variable *Statutory Detail*. We also include a dummy variable *Liberal Justices* to control for the presence of liberal justices on specific courts. We then create the interaction term *Liberal Justices * Statutory Detail* to measure this potential dynamic and interdependent relationship. For those issue areas where the legislative statute prescribes a conservative outcome (such as criminal cases) this interaction term should reflect a constraining effect on judicial behavior. Conversely, increases in statutory detail in these issue areas should facilitate (i.e., increase) the likelihood of ideological voting for conservative justices. Due to the presence of an interaction term, these effects will be observed in the original *Statutory Detail* variable.

While the concept of statutory constraint is related to the legal model, the attitudinal model indicates that judicial decision making is also the result of individual ideological preferences (Segal and Spaeth 2002). To measure the individual ideological preferences of Supreme Court justices, we rely on the ideology scores developed by Martin and Quinn (2002). We employ these measures (rather than the scores generated by Segal and Cover 1989) because they are a more dynamic measure. Using a Bayesian analysis, Martin and Quinn develop annual ideology scores for each individual justice. Rather than a static measure of general ideology, we use a measure that changes over time and better captures the potential dynamics of ideological influences. Thus, we rely on their empirical measure of ideological preferences in our variable *Ideological Intensity*. Because our theory posits that statutory constraint will limit ideological influences over judicial behavior, we "fold" the Martin and Quinn measure into a continuum from the most moderate justices to the most extreme ideologues.[16] Consequently, we hypothesize that justices with stronger ideological preferences will be more likely to render unconstrained or sincere decisions. A positive relationship should therefore exist between our variable *Ideological Intensity* and the dependent variable.

In addition to the two primary variables of interest and the interaction term, our model includes three other variables to control for various relevant factors. The first measures whether the Supreme Court is requested to review the constitutionality of the statute. If the Court exercises its power of *Judicial Review*, we expect the justices to be more likely to cast sincere votes (i.e., we do not expect substantial constraint to exist when the constitutionality of the statute is questioned). Therefore, a positive relationship should exist between this variable and the dependent variable. The second control variable *Lower Court Congruence* measures the case disposition by the lower court (most often a Court of Appeals). The variable is coded "1" if the lower court rendered a decision in opposition to the justice's ideological preferences, "2" if the lower court rendered a mixed decision, and "3" if the directionality of the lower court decision is congruent with the justice's ideological preferences. Because the Supreme Court has a tendency to reverse decisions of the lower courts (see Epstein et al. 1996) we expect this variable to be negatively related to the likelihood of casting a sincere vote. Finally, we control for the presence of a *Minimum Winning Coalition*, positing that in these situations the justices are more likely to vote according to their individual ideological preferences because of the contentious nature of the case; therefore generating a positive expected relationship between this variable and the dependent variable.

Before turning to the more sophisticated empirical models, we examine some descriptive statistics concerning Congressional statutes. Table 4.1 presents an overall description for all Congressional statutes interpreted by the Supreme Court in our sample. We can see that the average statute length (in raw number of words) is 1,449 words with a standard deviation of 2,784 words. The shortest statute contains only 21 words while the longest interpreted by the appellate courts contains 26,308 words. Since our empirical models measure statute length in terms of natural logs, we present these numbers as well. The average length (measured by its natural log) is 6.315 with a standard deviation of 1.381. The shortest statute contains a natural log of 3.044 while the longest has a natural log of 10.178.

Additionally, we observe a substantial amount of variation across specific issue areas in terms of statute length. As seen in Table 4.2, the average criminal statute passed by Congress contains 1,171 words (with an average natural log of 6.339) and a standard deviation of 1,643 words (with a natural log of 1.240). Additionally, the shortest criminal statute contains only 34 words (with a natural log of 3.526) while the longest criminal statute possesses 10,981 words

Table 4.1. The Nature of Congressional Statutes Under Review

Raw Number of Words	
Average Length	1449
Standard Deviation	2784
Minimum Length	21
Maximum Length	26308
Natural Log	
Average Length	6.315
Standard Deviation	1.381
Minimum Length	3.044
Maximum Length	10.178

Table 4.2. Congressional Statutes Under Review by Issue Area

Criminal Statutes

Raw Number of Words

Average Length	1171
Standard Deviation	1643
Minimum Length	34
Maximum Length	10981

Natural Log

Average Length	6.339
Standard Deviation	1.240
Minimum Length	3.526
Maximum Length	9.304

Civil Liberties Statutes

Raw Number of Words

Average Length	2087
Standard Deviation	4228
Minimum Length	22
Maximum Length	24420

Natural Log

Average Length	6.362
Standard Deviation	1.563
Minimum Length	3.091
Maximum Length	10.103

Economic Statutes

Raw Number of Words

Average Length	1452
Standard Deviation	2457
Minimum Length	21
Maximum Length	26308

Natural Log

Average Length	6.459
Standard Deviation	1.316
Minimum Length	3.044
Maximum Length	10.178

(with a natural log of 9.304). Similarly, civil liberties statutes are longer; containing an average number of 2,087 words (with a natural log of 6.362) and a standard deviation of 4,228 words (with a natural log of 1.563). The shortest civil liberties statute contains only 22 words (with a natural log of 3.091) while the longest has 24,420 words (with a natural log of 10.103). Finally, economic statutes generally speaking are slightly longer than criminal statutes, but shorter than the civil liberties laws with an average 1,452 words (translating into a natural log of 6.459) and a standard deviation of 2,457 words (with a natural log of 1.316). The shortest economic statute contains only 21 words (with a natural log of 3.044) while the longest possesses 26,308 words (and a natural log of 10.178).

Finally, we thought it would be useful to briefly compare the statute length of laws reviewed by the Courts of Appeals to those reviewed by the Supreme Court. As we indicate at the beginning of this chapter, since the Supreme Court possesses discretionary control of its docket, the justices are able to pick and choose which cases they review. Consequently, it is possible that they deliberately avoid granting *certiorari* to cases containing Congressional statutes that provide little discretion; preferring, instead to review cases where the legislation provides greater discretion. If this is true, then we should expect to see longer statutes litigated in the Appeals Courts and shorter ones reviewed by the Supreme Court. Examining the comparison listed in Table 4.3 provides initial evidence supporting this assertion. As one can see by looking at the average length of statutes across all three issue areas, the Courts of Appeals adjudicate longer statutes than the Supreme Court—criminal statutes are 324 words longer (on average), civil liberties statutes 108 words longer, and economic statutes 852 words longer. What is also striking is that the minimum and maximum length of statutes for civil liberties and economic cases is virtually identical between appellate panels and the Supreme Court. However, the longest criminal statute reviewed by the Courts of Appeals is 11,355 words longer than the longest statute reviewed by the Supreme Court. This is a tremendous difference; the appellate statute is over twice as long as the longest law reviewed by the Supreme Court. One can only speculate as to the cause of this difference. Perhaps the justices strategically avoid criminal cases where the Congressional statutes provide little discretion. Conversely, it is plausible that the longer criminal statutes adjudicated in the

Table 4.3. Appeals Courts—Supreme Court Comparison

	Appeals Courts	Supreme Court	Difference
Criminal Statutes			
Average Length	1495	1171	324
Minimum Length	25	34	–9
Maximum Length	22336	10981	11355
Civil Liberties Statutes			
Average Length	2195	2087	108
Minimum Length	22	22	0
Maximum Length	24420	24420	0
Economic Statutes			
Average Length	2304	1452	852
Minimum Length	22	21	1
Maximum Length	26308	26308	0

appellate courts do not raise issues that are important, substantial, or salient enough for the Supreme Court to review. Since many criminal appeals are considered frivolous, it is quite reasonable to observe the justices denying *certiorari* to those petitions. Future research into this question would help us better understand the motivations behind, and statutory influences upon, the *certiorari* process.

While the information in the previous tables is of interest, it does not directly address the question whether statutory language systematically affects judicial behavior on the Supreme Court. To better understand these influences, we turn to Table 4.4 and the results of our empirical models. Because our dependent variable is dichotomous, we employ a series of probit models—across specific issue areas—to evaluate the empirical relationships. The first table examines the effects of statutory constraint across three general issue categories: Model 1 examines criminal appeals,[17] Model 2 focuses on civil liberties cases,[18] and Model 3 analyzes economic disputes.[19] Each of these models offers well-identified analyses as seen by an examination of the reduction of error coefficients (8.4 percent for criminal appeals, 9.9 percent for civil liberties cases, and 23.4 percent for economic disputes).

Table 4.4. Probit Analysis of Supreme Court Decisions

	Model 1 Criminal	Model 2 Civil Liberties	Model 3 Economic
Statutory Detail	.009	.067***	–.071***
	(.028)	(.019)	(.014)
Liberal Justices	–.718***	1.392***	.012
	(.271)	(.197)	(.144)
Statutory Detail * Liberal Justices Interaction	.065	–.175***	.087***
	(.042)	(.030)	(.022)
Ideological Intensity	.148***	.169***	.062***
	(.020)	(.018)	(.011)
Judicial Review	.098*	.104**	.067
	(.055)	(.051)	(.073)
Lower Court Congruence	–.461***	–.431***	–.535***
	(.053)	(.046)	(.028)
Minimum Winning Coalition	.568***	.673***	.428***
	(.071)	(.060)	(.045)
Constant	.352 (.184)	–.358 (.128)	.448 (.097)
N	2619	3569	8303
Log Likelihood	–1584.549	–2098.744	–5202.253
LR/Wald Test	202.43	363.26	876.30
Probability > χ	.000	.000	.000
Pseudo R^2	.068	.086	.088
Null Model	64.8%	65.7%	55.5%
Correctly Predicted	67.8%	69.0%	66.0%
Reduction of Error	8.4%	9.9%	23.4%

Dependent Variable: unconstrained or sincere vote (1), constrained vote (0)
Values represent parameter estimates with robust standard errors in parentheses (clustered by individual justice)
* p < .10   ** p < .05   *** p < .01

Despite the higher threshold provided by an analysis of the Supreme Court, the empirical evidence provide some support for our hypotheses, though admittedly this support is more mixed than what we observed for the Courts of Appeals. As we explained in Chapter 2, our expectation is that longer criminal statutes will exert a constraining effect on liberal justices while simultaneously providing a facilitation effect for conservative justices. The variable *Statutory Detail* is not statistically significant indicating that conservative justices are not influenced by the presence of more detailed criminal statutes.[20] However, the variable *Statutory Detail * Liberal Justices Interaction* has a conditional negative effect on liberal justices.[21] This indicates that liberal justices are increasingly constrained from casting sincere votes as congressional statutes become more detailed.

That we discover patterns of behavior among Supreme Court justices similar to those observed among appellate judges is quite remarkable. However, an important distinction remains between these two levels and that involves the effect of ideology among the justices. The statistical significance and positive coefficient for the variable *Ideological Intensity* reveals that both liberal and conservative justices are more likely to cast sincere votes as their ideological preferences become stronger. This influence was not present in the Courts of Appeals, and it serves to reinforce the central tenet of the Attitudinal Model. Consequently, our results demonstrate the separate effect of ideology as well as the dynamic interdependence between ideology and the law.

As for the remaining variables in the model, the measure of *Judicial Review* is statistically significant and indicates that questions of constitutionality increase the likelihood of sincere voting. The variable *Lower Court Congruence* is significant and negative indicating that justices are likely to cast sincere votes in order to reverse lower court decisions which diverge from the justices' ideological preferences. Finally, the variable *Minimum Winning Coalition* is significant and positive. This finding supports the general expectation that the justices are more likely to cast sincere votes when the majority coalition is small (i.e., minimum winning).

Model 2 focuses on the voting behavior of justices during the resolution of civil liberties cases. The data indicate that the variable *Statutory Detail* is significant and positive, revealing that conservative justices are more likely to cast sincere votes as congressional statutes become more detailed. Yet, the interaction term *Statutory Detail * Liberal Justices Interaction* is statistically significant and negative.[22] The results reported in Model 2 also reveal that Supreme Court justices are significantly influenced by their ideological preferences; the coefficient for the variable *Ideological Intensity* is significant and positive. As the ideological preferences of liberals and conservatives increase (i.e., become stronger) these justices are more likely to cast sincere votes. The variable *Judicial Review* is significant and positive indicating that questions of constitutionality increase the likelihood of sincere voting. Additionally, the variable *Lower Court Congruence* is significant and negative, indicating that the justices are more likely to cast sincere votes in order to reverse lower court decisions. Finally, the variable *Minimum Winning Coalition* is significant and positive, supporting our expectation that justices cast sincere votes when the majority coalition is narrow.

The final column of Table 4.4 examines patterns of voting behavior when Supreme Court justices adjudicate economic disputes. We notice that the variable *Statutory Detail* is significant and negative, indicating that conservative justices are constrained in their ideological voting when the plain meaning of congressional statutes becomes clearer and more detailed. Yet, the conditional effect of the *Statutory Detail * Liberal Justices Interaction* is not statistically significant,[23] indicating that liberal justices are not affected by the language of congressional economic statutes. Additionally, the variable *Ideological Intensity* is significant and positive revealing that as the ideological preferences of liberals and conservatives increase (i.e., become stronger) these justices are more likely to cast sincere votes. Model 3 also reveals that the presence of *Judicial Review* does not affect voting behavior. Furthermore, the variable *Lower Court Congruence* is significant and negative, indicating that the justices are more likely to cast sincere votes in order to reverse lower court decisions. Finally, the variable *Minimum Winning Coalition* is significant and positive, supporting our expectation that justices cast sincere votes when the majority coalition is narrow.

Initially, the results from Table 4.4 partially support our hypotheses concerning the effects of the *model of contingent discretion* on Supreme Court behavior. However, closer inspection of both civil liberties cases and economic disputes reveals that the inclusion of these two general-issue categories does not completely capture patterns of voting behavior. Therefore, we re-estimate the analyses by focusing on subsets of these general issues. These results are reported in Table 4.5: Model 4 examines only civil rights cases,[24] Model 5 examines non-civil rights cases,[25] and Model 6 focuses on a subset of economic disputes—federalism cases.[26] Overall, these three additional models perform remarkably well—each produces a sizeable reduction of error (9.9 percent for civil rights cases, 15.6 percent for non-civil rights cases, and 32.4 percent for federalism cases). Since the analysis is most concerned about the effects of statutory constraint versus individual ideology, the remaining discussion will focus only on the primary independent variables of interest.

Examining the results in Model 4 (civil rights) reveals that conservative justices are not affected by the language of congressional statutes; the variable *Statutory Detail* is not statistically significant. Consequently, there is neither a constraining nor facilitating effect on conservative judges. However, the conditional effect of the interaction term *Statutory Detail * Liberal Justices Interaction* is significant and positive,[27] indicating that liberal justices are more likely to cast sincere votes—a facilitation effect—as congressional civil rights statutes become more detailed. Finally, the variable *Ideological Intensity* is significant and positive. This result indicates that justices possessing stronger ideological preferences are more likely to cast sincere votes.

Since we examined the discrimination cases separately, we also analyze the remaining civil liberties cases (First Amendment, due process, and privacy cases).[28] These results are reported in Model 5 (non-civil rights). We hypothesized that conservative justices would encounter significant statutory constraints in civil liberties cases. Yet, in these cases conservative justices are significantly more likely to cast sincere votes as statutory language becomes more detailed (i.e., the variable *Statutory Detail* is significant and positive). Conversely, liberal justices are significantly constrained by the presence of detailed congressional statutes—the variable *Statutory Detail * Liberal Justices Interaction* is significant and negative. We notice also that the baseline variable *Liberal Justices* is significant and positive. Taken together, these two variables lead to the conclusion that liberal justices are generally more likely to cast sincere votes in non-civil rights cases, *except* when the presence of detailed congressional statutes constrains their behavior; as the level of constraint increases

Table 4.5. Probit Analysis of More Specific Categories

	Model 4 Civil Rights	Model 5 Non-Civil Rights	Model 6 Federalism
Statutory Detail	.024	.131***	.097**
	(.023)	(.033)	(.039)
Liberal Justices	.634***	2.665***	.759*
	(.242)	(.372)	(.386)
Statutory Detail * Liberal Justices Interaction	.031	-.409***	-.107*
	(.038)	(.054)	(.059)
Ideological Intensity	.184***	.151***	.108***
	(.022)	(.031)	(.032)
Judicial Review	.189**	.078	.969***
	(.080)	(.080)	(.201)
Lower Court Congruence	-.499***	-.325***	-.853***
	(.057)	(.082)	(.085)
Minimum Winning Coalition	.743***	.547***	.063
	(.078)	(.099)	(.127)
Constant	-.138 (.158)	-.689 (.243)	-.336 (.266)
N	2387	1176	1099
Log Likelihood	-1381.847	-681.652	-664.004
LR/Wald Test	288.13	124.93	160.64
Probability > χ	.000	.000	.000
Pseudo R^2	.102	.098	.124
Null Model	65.4%	65.7%	54.0%
Correctly Predicted	69.0%	71.1%	69.0%
Reduction of Error	9.9%	15.6%	32.4%

Dependent Variable: unconstrained or sincere vote (1), constrained vote (0)
Values represent parameter estimates with robust standard errors in parentheses
* $p < .10$ ** $p < .05$ *** $p < .01$

liberal justices are less likely to cast sincere votes.[29] Therefore, the empirical evidence indicates that longer congressional statutes in these areas of the law significantly *constrain the ideological voting of liberal justices*, while simultaneously *facilitating the ideological voting of conservative justices*. This empirical finding makes sense due to the fact that many congressional statutes pertaining to First Amendment, due process or privacy rights prescribe conservative outcomes (for example, the Defense of Marriage Act banning homosexual marriage; the "Hyde Amendment" to the Medicaid statute limiting federal funding for abortions; or the Bipartisan Campaign Finance Reform Act (McCain-Feingold Act) placing new limits on campaign contributions). Therefore, it is plausible to expect liberal justices to experience constraining effects from these statutes and conservative justices to rely on the detailed language to support or facilitate voting according to their ideological preferences.

The final model (Model 6) examines the effects of statutory language during the resolution of federalism disputes. In this issue area, we observe effects similar to those identified in Model 5 (non-civil rights cases). The variable *Statutory Detail* is significant and positive, indicating that conservative justices are more likely to cast sincere votes as congressional statutes become more detailed. However, liberal justices encounter opposite effects from these statutes. As shown by a significant and negative coefficient on *Statutory Detail * Liberal Justices Interaction*, these justices are less likely to cast sincere votes when congressional statutes become more detailed. At first this appears to be a somewhat counterintuitive result since one might initially believe congressional statutes would proscribe liberal outcomes by detailing the power of the federal government in relation to the states. However, further inspection of the federalism statutes reveals that many spell out areas of state authority in detail, thereby dictating conservative outcomes (i.e., in favor of states). Consequently, it is plausible that liberal justices would experience the constraining effects of these statutes while conservatives view the statutory language as supporting their ideological preferences.

In sum the results we provide from the various models offer compelling empirical evidence that the *model of contingent discretion* provides both constraining and facilitating influences on Supreme Court behavior, though the facilitating effect is more broadly identified. Even when justices are influenced by their ideological pref-

erences, this influence is contingent on the level of discretion afforded
by the law; it can facilitate the expression of ideological voting among
some justices while also constraining ideological voting among others. This is an important discovery because our results demonstrate
that law and ideology do not merely compete for dominance in the
judicial decision calculus. Rather, they interact in a substantially more
dynamic manner, contingent on the discretion afforded by the law.

To examine the substantive implications of these results, we
graphed the relationships among statutory detail, individual ideological preferences, and the probability of casting a sincere vote.[30]
Figure 4.1 presents these influences on the probability of a sincere
vote for justices adjudicating *non-civil rights* cases.[31] Initially, we
hypothesized that any effects of statutory constraint would be experienced by conservative justices, and that these justices would be less
likely to cast sincere votes as levels of constraint increase. Examining
Figure 4.1 reveals that individual ideology exerts a substantial influ-

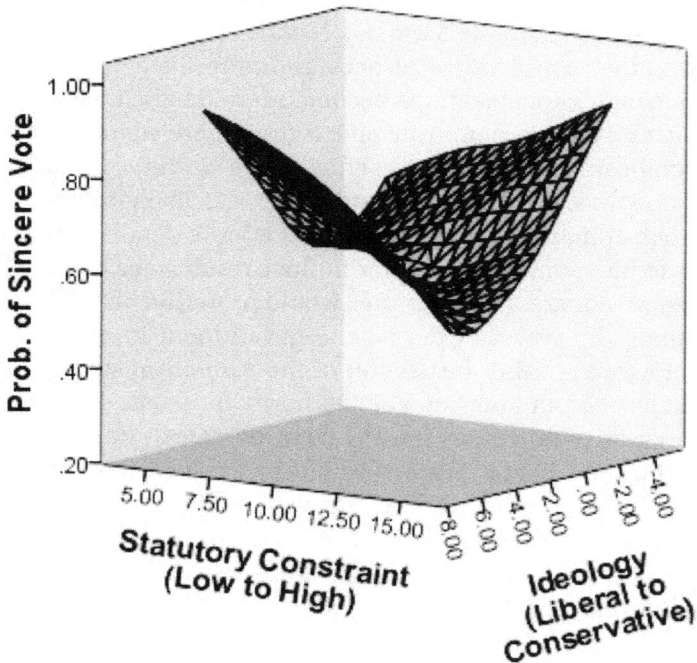

Figure 4.1. Impact of Constraint and Ideology in *Non-Civil Rights* Cases.

ence on judicial behavior.[32] As the preferences of justices become stronger (in either direction), the probability of casting sincere votes increases by approximately 30 to 40 percent regardless of whether the justices are liberal or conservative.[33]

Yet, when one accounts for the *model of contingent discretion*, and factors in the effects of the statutory language, new voting patterns emerge; patterns that depend on whether justices are liberal or conservative. If we focus on the behavior of liberal justices (illustrated by the "leading edge" of the graph) we see that they possess a high probability of casting sincere votes when statutory constraint is low. However, as constraint increases, the probability of casting sincere votes decreases dramatically—by approximately 35 percent. Conversely, Figure 4.1 displays a different result for conservative justices (illustrated by the "trailing edge" of the graph). When statutory constraint is low, these justices possess a relatively high probability of casting sincere votes (though not as high as that experienced by liberal justices). As the language of statutes becomes more clear and detailed, Figure 4.1 reveals that the probability of conservative justices casting sincere votes increases by approximately 15 percent.

Justice-Specific Analyses of Statutory Influence

While the results in Figure 4.1 are based on a statistical analysis that focuses on the votes of individual justices, they do not offer glimpses into potential variation across the justices. This is important to better understand the "black box" of principal-agent theory. As we indicate in Chapter 2, one of the limitations of traditional principal-agent models is the lack of ability to examine the behavior of individual agents. Our analysis of the Supreme Court provides an ideal opportunity to delve into the "black box" and examine each justice specifically to understand how he/she responds to legislative statutes. We do so in Figure 4.2 where we graph the probability of a sincere vote for each specific justice[34] based on the level of detail (i.e., length) included in the Congressional statute for cases involving non-civil rights issues.

Immediately, one can see the tremendous variation among individual justices in terms of the constraining and facilitating effects of statutory language. For example, for the more liberal justices (such as Marshall, Brennan, Stevens, Souter, Ginsburg, Breyer, Warren, and

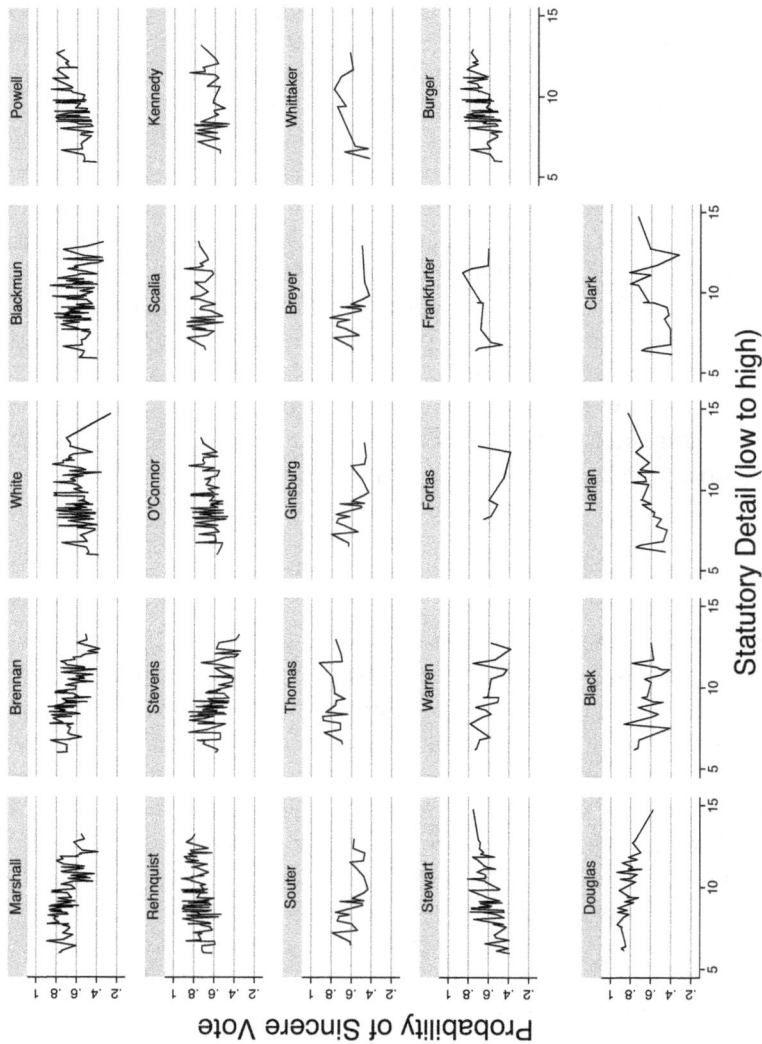

Figure 4.2. Impact of Statutory Detail Across Individual Justices.

Douglas), while they all exhibit declines in the probability of casting sincere votes as statute length increases (as expected), the rates at which these occur vary substantially. Conversely, the more conservative justices (such as Powell, Rehnquist, Scalia, Thomas, Stewart, and Burger) exhibit increases in the probability of casting sincere votes as statute lengths increase, and their rates vary considerably as well. Perhaps most notable among the conservative justices is the pattern displayed by Scalia—arguably the most vocal advocate of strict textualism. While his graph indicates a slight increase in sincere voting, it is apparent that the language of Congressional statutes (in non-civil rights cases) affects him differently than other justices. Perhaps this trend reflects Scalia's professed desire to interpret the law as dictated by Congress. Regardless, what is evident is that these individual graphs support our contention that more detailed Congressional statutes will exert constraining effects on some justices (i.e., liberal justices in these cases) while simultaneously facilitating the ideological voting of other justices. Additionally these results demonstrate the importance of delving into the "black box" of agent behavior because the magnitude of these effects varies dramatically with each individual.

An Alternative Specification

In Chapter 3, we raise one final question about the use of the likelihood of a sincere vote as the dependent variable for these models. Our answer, as we explain in Chapter 2, is that the fundamental theoretical argument is whether statutory language can induce judges (both federal and state) from voting according to pure ideological predilections—not, whether statutes will make judges vote more conservatively or more liberally. That said, we also recognize that framing the dependent variable in terms of sincere voting has some disadvantages as well—in particular for observations concerning moderate justices.

To address this potential concern, we reanalyze Supreme Court voting behavior in criminal cases using the more conventional "ideological directionality of the case" as the dependent variable. The results of this alternative specification are reported in Table 4.6 under Model 7. When examining the results from this table, it is important to note that the dependent variable is coded "0" for a conserva-

Table 4.6. An Alternative Specification for Criminal Cases

	Model 7 Alternative Specification
Statutory Detail	–.045*** (.017)
Liberal Judge	–.189 (.217)
Statutory Detail * Liberal Justice **Interaction**	–.074** (.032)
Ideology	.148*** (.020)
Judicial Review	–.152*** (.056)
Lower Court Congruence	.162*** (.051)
Minimum Winning Coalition	.151** (.061)
Constant	.161 (.202)
N	2618
Log Likelihood	–1644.344
LR/Wald Test	277.92
Probability > χ	.000
Pseudo R^2	.083
Null Model	56.5%
Correctly Predicted	64.7%
Reduction of Error	18.9%

Dependent Variable: conservative vote (0), liberal vote (1)
Values represent parameter estimates with robust standard errors in parentheses
* p < .10   ** p < .05   *** p < .01

tive vote and "1" for a liberal vote. Therefore, the coefficients of this table should be interpreted with that frame in mind. As we see from Table 4.6 both the variables *Statutory Detail* and the *Statutory Detail * Liberal Justice Interaction* are statistically significant. The negative coefficient on the variable *Statutory Detail* reflects that conservative justices are less likely to cast liberal votes as criminal statutes become longer. This supports our expectation concerning the Statutory Facilitation Hypothesis. Conversely, the negative coefficient on the *Statutory Detail * Liberal Justice Interaction* indicates that liberal justices are also less likely to cast liberal votes as the length of criminal statutes increases. This result supports our expectation concerning the Statutory Constraint Hypothesis. Substantively, the results indicate that both conservative and liberal judges are more likely to cast conservative votes as criminal statutes become more detailed.

Examination of Statutes Under Judicial Review

As we mention at the beginning of this chapter, the Supreme Court presents a more difficult empirical test of our theory because of the frequency with which the justices examine questions of constitutionality—the exercise of judicial review. Several scholars argue about the importance of judicial review and the potential effects this authority has on the Supreme Court (Franck 1996; Shipan 1997; and Howard and Segal 2004). In particular for our theory, confirmed by the empirical analyses above, is that the exercise of judicial review is likely to affect how justices approach statutory interpretation. Our expectation is that justices will be less likely to experience either the constraining or the facilitating effects of Congressional statutes when the constitutionality of those laws is called into question. To test this expectation, we select only those cases involving either criminal or non-civil rights statutes. This selection is made because of the hypothesized directionality of influence discovered in the previous empirical analyses (see Models 1 and 5). In both issue areas, liberal justices experience constraining effects as Congressional statutes increase in length, while conservative justices experience facilitating effects.

Before turning to the empirical test of this assertion, we first examine some basic descriptive statistics for those statutes examined by the Court under judicial review. Table 4.7 presents these numbers in comparison to the overall descriptive statistics from Table 4.1. As can be seen, when the Supreme Court grants *certiorari* to cases calling for an exercise of judicial review, the statutes in question are substantially more ambiguous than the ones examined overall. This should not be much of a surprise, since more detailed statutes are likely to raise fewer questions concerning unsettled areas of the law that would require intervention by the Supreme Court; whereas less detailed statutes are likely to receive more constitutional challenges in order to resolve legal disputes. What is more important for our theoretical expectation is that less detailed statutes (i.e., shorter statutes) allows for more discretion by the Court. This confirms our expectation that the effects of statutory language should be less pronounced (or even non-existent) when the justices exercise their power of judicial review.

However, the results displayed in Table 4.8 follow the same patterns exhibited in earlier models. Though the justices examine the constitutionality of criminal and non-civil rights laws (which on average provide more judicial discretion), they are still significantly influenced by the length of Congressional statutes. The variable *Statutory Detail* possesses a positive coefficient indicating that conservative justices are likely to increase the probability of casting a sincere vote as statute length increases—confirming the Statutory Facilitation

Table 4.7. Questioning the Constitutionality of Congressional Statutes

	Overall	Under Judicial Review
Raw Number of Words		
Average Length	1449	1221
Standard Deviation	2784	1871
Minimum Length	21	28
Maximum Length	26308	12862
Natural Log		
Average Length	6.315	6.216
Standard Deviation	1.381	1.377
Minimum Length	3.044	3.332
Maximum Length	10.178	9.462

Table 4.8. Probit Analysis of Statutes Under Judicial Review

	Model 8 Judicial Review
Statutory Detail	0.86***
	(.024)
Liberal Judge	1.180***
	(.359)
Statutory Detail * Liberal Justice **Liberal Justice Interaction**	–.142*** (.035)
Ideology	.161***
	(.023)
Lower Court Congruence	–.340***
	(.065)
Minimum Winning Coalition	.712***
	(.079)
Constant	–.558 (.244)
N	1791
Log Likelihood	–1037.968
LR/Wald Test	170.53
Probability > χ	.000
Pseudo R^2	.083
Null Model	67.6%
Correctly Predicted	69.5%
Reduction of Error	5.9%

Dependent Variable: sincere vote (1), non–sincere vote (0)
Cases represent criminal and non–civil rights statutes
Values represent parameter estimates with robust standard errors in parentheses
* $p < .10$ ** $p < .05$ *** $p < .01$

Hypothesis. Conversely, the *Statutory Detail * Liberal Justice Interaction* has a negative coefficient revealing that these justices are less likely to cast sincere votes as statutes become longer—confirming the Statutory Constraint Hypothesis.

These results raise some interesting questions concerning the conventional wisdom about judicial review and its effects on the behavior of the Supreme Court. Most scholars (ourselves included) would readily agree that the Court treats judicial review cases differently. At the very least, these cases present the justices with arguably the greatest opportunity to influence policy because constitutional decisions cannot be overturned by future Congressional statutes. The only way for a constitutional decision from the Supreme Court to be overturned is for the adoption of a new amendment to the Constitution—something that has happened only five times in the history of the United States. The Eleventh Amendment (adopted in 1795) overturned the Court's decision in *Chisholm v. Georgia* (1793); the Thirteenth Amendment (adopted in 1865) overturned part of the *Dred Scott* cases—*Scott v. Sandford* (1857); the Fourteenth Amendment (adopted in 1868) overturned another part of the *Dred Scott* case; the Sixteenth Amendment (adopted in 1913) overturned *Pollock v. Farmer's Loan and Trust Co.* (1895); and the Twenty-Sixth Amendment (adopted in 1971) overturned the Court's decision in *Oregon v. Mitchell* (1970).

Given the difficulty of overturning a constitutional (i.e., exercise of judicial review) decision by the Supreme Court, we therefore expected that the justices would not experience similar facilitating or constraining effects of statutory language. This is especially true for the constraining effects and thus the results in Table 4.8 are very interesting and somewhat counterintuitive. Certainly, they raise additional questions about the nature of the Court's decision-making process under judicial review. Hopefully, future research can explore this relationship in more detail.

Corollary Analysis of Statutes and Unanimous Decisions

In addition to the analyses described above there is one last question pertaining to the influence of legislation—whether statute length is related to the likelihood of unanimous decisions. These decisions historically have posed problems for advocates of the attitudinal model because a strict adherence to its tenets leads to the prediction of no unanimous decisions on the Supreme Court. Yet, the empirical evidence reveals that the Court reaches unanimous consensus in approximately one-third of its decisions. Consequently, the attitudinal model in its purest form either excludes unanimous decisions completely or substantially downplays their importance—claiming that these cases represent non-salient often mundane areas of the law.

One of the implications from our *model of contingent discretion* is that longer statutes should increase the likelihood of unanimous decisions. Since the empirical evidence demonstrates that some justices are constrained from voting sincerely while others have their sincere voting facilitated by the statute, the implication is that all justices will vote for the same outcome. Consequently, this movement in a similar direction translates into an increased likelihood of unanimous decisions.

To test this implication we ran a simple bivariate regression model with the proportion of unanimous decisions per Court term as the dependent variable and our measure of statute length (i.e., the natural log of a statute's word count) as the independent variable.[35] The substantive results of this regression are presented in Figure 4.3, where we graph the proportion of unanimous decisions (in the Y-axis) against the average statute length (in the X-axis). Examining the graph

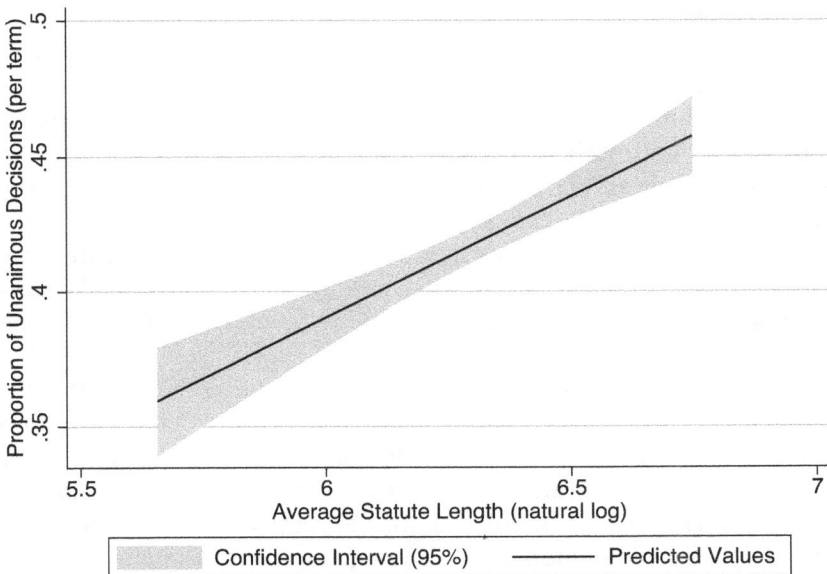

Figure 4.3. Influence of Statute Length on Unanimous Decisions.

reveals that the proportion of unanimous decisions per term moves from a low of .360 when statutes are vague to approximately .460 when statutes are detailed.[36] Thus, as the law becomes more precise the judges adjudicating that law increasingly reach consensus about its meaning.

Conclusions

The empirical results presented in this chapter provide additional evidence concerning constraining and facilitation effects of the model of contingent discretion and its applicability to both the Courts of Appeals and the Supreme Court. At each level of the federal judiciary the evidence demonstrates that detailed congressional statutes affect judicial voting. Some individuals are constrained from voting ideologically while others are facilitated to vote according to their preferences. These effects are often concomitant—some statutes lead to constraining effects for liberal justices while their conservative colleagues are facilitated; and some statutes facilitate the ideological voting of liberal justices while simultaneously constraining their conservative brethren. *Consequently, these dynamic patterns provide the most convincing evidence yet that the language of congressional statutes matters.*

Our analyses also offer some interesting insights into the variation across both judicial institutions, for while we find evidence of contingent discretion in both courts, the effect is not identical. At the appellate court level when the effects of contingent discretion exist, the influence of ideology vanishes. Perhaps this is due to the possible review of panel decisions by the Supreme Court. Appellate judges may attempt to minimize this probability by eschewing ideology in favor of the law.

Conversely, for Supreme Court justices the ideological influence remains significant even when the effects of contingent discretion operate. It is quite plausible that this difference is the result of the non-discretionary nature of appellate court dockets versus the discretionary docket control afforded to the Supreme Court; statutes reaching the justices may simply contain more ambiguous language. From a principal-agent perspective, it is also possible that judges on the Courts of Appeals must be more concerned with multiple principals (both Congress and the Supreme Court) when they interpret statutes; hence they demonstrate a greater propensity to sacrifice ideological preferences for the law. Regardless, the results suggest that the nature of judicial institutions matters. While the *model of contingent discretion* applies to both federal courts, the dynamic is far different.

Furthermore, the analyses in this chapter demonstrate how Supreme Court justices respond to the language written in congressional statutes. Contrary to arguments raised by advocates of the attitudinal model, liberal and conservative justices do not search the statutes merely to procure legal authority consistent with their preordained ideological disposition. If this proposition was accurate we would only find evidence of a facilitation effect. Rather, our empirical evidence indicates that when the justices find legal authority consistent with their attitudes they use it. But, when the law is inconsistent or contradicts these ideological views it serves as a significant constraint on judicial behavior.

In sum, the results in this chapter provide strong evidence that the *model of contingent discretion* is not limited to one type of judicial institution or to a few specific policy areas. Yet, the question remains whether its tenets are generalizable to judicial institutions that reach beyond the federal courts. Specifically, does this model also apply to the decision making of state supreme courts? We turn to this question in the next chapter.

5

State Supreme Courts

Kirk A. Randazzo, Richard W. Waterman, and Michael P. Fix[1]

> When reviewing issues of statutory interpretation, we are mind-
> ful that the first rule in considering the meaning and effect of
> a statute is to construe it just as it reads, giving the words their
> ordinary and usually accepted meaning in common language.
> When the statute is plain and unambiguous, there is no need to
> resort to rules of statutory interpretation.
>
> —Justice Robert L. Brown of the Supreme Court of Arkansas[2]

In the previous two chapters we examine how Congressional statutes
affect the voting behavior of judges on the U.S. Courts of Appeals and
justices of the U.S. Supreme Court. Consistent with our theoretical
expectations, the language of statutes systematically affects judicial
behavior. At times, for some judges, they are constrained from voting
sincerely and at other times, for other judges, the legislation facilitates their ideological voting. These insights are extremely important
because they help provide a better understanding of the conditions
under which judicial ideology interacts with statutory influences to
determine voting behavior.

Yet, the generalizability of these insights may be limited because
the statutes in question all come from a single legislative source—
the United States Congress. Additionally, the previous two chapters
examined voting behavior of federal judges and justices; all of whom
possess similar institutional characteristics (for example, they all possess life tenure). Therefore, to broaden the impact of this research,
we need to conduct examinations across multiple contextual and

institutional environments. If the results of these new examinations confirm the analyses of the federal judiciary then the conclusions become much more robust and generalizable.

To do so, we examine the voting behavior of state supreme courts and their interpretations of state statutes. Recognizing that courts as institutions are not merely a "collection of individuals . . . pursuing their individual policy preferences" (Gillman and Clayton 1999, 1), a more searching examination of the impact of legislative statutes must focus on judicial decision making under a variety of institutional contexts. As previous research demonstrates (see Brace and Hall 1995), state courts provide the ideal "natural experiment" for examining judicial behavior under a range of institutional variation. This allows researchers to fine-tune theoretical predictions through several contextual environments; thus reducing the likelihood of spurious findings due to institutional homogeneity. The central question of this analysis therefore examines whether state supreme court judges render decisions according to their ideological preferences (similar to federal judges) in lieu of the potentially constraining language of state statutes and other institutional influences (such as method of selection).

Influence of Law and Ideology on State Supreme Courts

In contrast to "the preoccupation . . . with attitudes and policy preferences of individual justices" (Gillman and Clayton 1999, 1) that dominates much of the research on the U.S. Supreme Court, state court scholars combine a "constellation of contextual, institutional, and attitudinal factors" into a single approach (Langer 2002, 26). Known as neo-institutionalism, this approach creates integrated models that incorporate these various factors (Brace and Hall 1990, 1997; Hall and Brace 1989).

In part, this line of research focuses on the institutional differences between state and federal courts. As with federal judges it is generally assumed that judges on state supreme courts are interested in furthering their personal policy preferences (Brace and Hall 1997; Langer 2002). Yet, lacking insulation from potential retaliation by other institutions (and in some cases by voters), these judges must consider possible sanctions when making decisions (Brace and Hall

1990, 1997; Langer 2002). For example, Douglas and Hartley (2003) demonstrate that, in some states, courts must be concerned with potential sanctions from other institutions in the form of attacks on their budgets and other financial resources.

Certain institutional factors have long been recognized as influencing the decision making of state court judges. In states with elected judges, scholars recognize that electoral considerations affect judicial behavior (Jaros and Canon 1971). In these states, supreme court judges face additional constraints on voting—for example, Hall (1992) demonstrates how judges facing reelection vote strategically in death penalty cases to minimize their chances of electoral defeat. Moreover, other research concludes that state court judges encounter a variety of significant influences beyond ideology and electoral pressures, such as the length of service (Brace and Hall 1997), specific case facts (Brace and Hall 1990), the complexity of a state's political environment (Brace and Hall 1990), state ideology (Brace and Hall 1997), and the presence of an intermediate appellate court (Hall and Brace 1989).

While there is a renewed focus on institutional approaches to decision making for the U.S. Supreme Court (see e.g., Clayton and Gillman 1999), the dominant theoretical approach continues to reside with the attitudinal model. This argument by Segal and Spaeth (1993, 2002) provides evidence that judges (in particular Supreme Court justices) render decisions according to their individual ideological preferences, *ceteris paribus*. Yet, even in the context of the U.S. Supreme Court, we are less certain about the impact of these ideological influences when other factors are not equal. Various legal considerations such as precedent, case facts, the plain meaning of the law (as we demonstrate in the previous chapters), and legislative intent may affect the ability of judges to rule ideologically. Stated another way, the impact of ideology on judicial behavior may be *contingent* on the degree of legal discretion afforded to judges.

At the state court level, there are few—if any—scholars who assert that a pure attitudinal model operates in this context. Moreover, there is a myriad of extant evidence that *both* law and ideology exert a significant influence on judicial decision making (Brace and Hall 1995, 1997). Yet, our understanding of how these potentially opposing influences operate is less clear. Are they truly independent, or is there a more dynamic interdependence between law and ideology?

If the former, then we should observe an opposing tension between these forces—as the effects of the law increase, the influence of ideology should decrease (and vice versa). Conversely, if a more dynamic interdependence exists then we should observe a more complex interaction in which some situations present the opposing tension between law and ideology, while others provide for a convergence of these influences

What is apparent from these various analyses is that state supreme courts possess a myriad of contextual and institutional characteristics and environments. Some state judges face electoral pressures—either from the public directly or through various appointment mechanisms within the legislature or governor's office. Others face more professionalized legislatures (as opposed to part-time legislatures) with larger staffs and more resources that can be invested in drafting legislation. Given this wide variation of institutional contexts it seems unlikely that our operationalization of statutory influence will exert an effect on the voting behavior of state court judges. Yet, if the empirical evidence supports our theoretical contentions about the *model of contingent discretion*, even in the highly diverse environment of state courts, then our conclusions gain additional validity. To examine whether state court judges are affected by statutory language similar to their federal brethren, we begin by examining their official writings.

Anecdotal Evidence from State Court Judges

In Chapters 3 and 4 we present anecdotal evidence from Courts of Appeals judges and Supreme Court justices demonstrating the influence that Congressional statutes have on their writings and opinions. In this section we explore this relationship in the context of state supreme court judges and state statutes. As we argue throughout this book, if judges are influenced by statutory language, then we should expect to see references of this influence written directly into their opinions. While this evidence does not demonstrate the systematic impact of statutory language, anecdotal references help to illustrate how state judges respond to statutory language.

To begin this discussion, we turn to a case from the Supreme Court of California, *Curle v. Superior Court of Shasta County*,[3] in which Chief Judge George dismisses a petition from a disqualified trial judge for a writ of mandate challenging the disqualification order. In interpreting the appropriate state statute, Chief Judge George states (at 1063):

> Our role in construing a statute is to ascertain the Legislature's intent so as to effectuate the purpose of the law. In determining intent, we look first to the words of the statute, giving the language its usual, ordinary meaning. If there is no ambiguity in the language, we presume the Legislature meant what it said, and the plain meaning of the statute governs. If the Legislature provided an express definition of a term, that definition is binding on the courts. Furthermore, we consider portions of a statute in the context of the entire statute and the statutory scheme of which it is a part, giving significance to every word, phrase, sentence, and part of an act in pursuance of the legislative purpose.

Similarly, the case *Kahlo Jeep Chrysler Dodge of Knightstown, Inc. v. DamilerChrysler Motors Company*[4] from the state of Indiana provides additional insight into the importance of proper statutory interpretation and the central focus on statutory language. In this case, involving franchise disputes between local car dealers and their parent company, Judge Barnes writes (at 527):

> If a statute is unambiguous, we may not interpret it but must give the statute its clear and plain meaning. If a statute is ambiguous, we must ascertain the legislature's intent and interpret the statute to effectuate that intent. A statute may be ambiguous if it is susceptible to more than one reasonable and intelligible interpretation. If interpretation is necessary, the express language of the statute controls and we apply the rules of statutory construction.

A third example is found in the case *Arkansas Department of Human Services v. Collier*,[5] where the Supreme Court of Arkansas resolves a dispute involving a county judge's order placing an unborn fetus in the custody of the state Department of Human Services. In his opinion, Justice Robert L. Brown states (at 778):

When reviewing issues of statutory interpretation, we are
mindful that the first rule in considering the meaning and
effect of a statute is to construe it just as it reads, giving the
words their ordinary and usually accepted meaning in common language. When the language of a statute is plain and
unambiguous, there is no need to resort to rules of statutory
construction. A statute is ambiguous only where it is open to
two or more constructions, or where it is of such obscure or
doubtful meaning that reasonable minds might disagree or be
uncertain as to its meaning. When a statute is clear, however,
it is given its plain meaning, and this court will not search for
legislative intent; rather, that intent must be gathered from
the plain meaning of the language used. This court is very
hesitant to interpret a legislative act in a manner contrary to
its express language, unless it is clear that a drafting error or
omission has circumvented legislative intent.

Numerous other examples could be cited that would echo the
statements given above. Therefore, rather than simply repeat the logic
of these statements, let us offer one more opinion that better highlights the difficulties judges encounter when interpreting legislative
statutes. This example comes from the Wisconsin Supreme Court
in the case *In re Byers*,[6] and involves the dissenting opinion written
by Chief Justice Shirley S. Abrahamson. In her dissent, Chief Justice
Abrahamson comments specifically on the problems of language and
statutory construction. She states (at 740–741):

A court begins with the language of the statute and then
considers all relevant evidence of legislative intent including
its 'scope, history, context, subject matter, and purpose.' All of
these factors bear on the interpretation of the language, and
no single one is exclusive or controlling. The language of a
given statute is without a doubt the most important indication of legislative 'intent.' After all, the words are the objective manifestation of the legislative intent we seek to discern.
More importantly, citizens obligated to follow the law, public
officials elected to carry out the law, and attorneys employed
to advise clients on the meaning of the law should be able to
rely upon the words written in the Wisconsin Statutes when

fulfilling these duties. Nevertheless, language, especially statutory language, is often ambiguous. "Anything that is written
may present a problem of meaning . . . The problem derives
from the very nature of words. They are symbols of meaning.
But unlike mathematical symbols, the phrasing of a document,
especially a complicated enactment, seldom attains more than
approximate precision." Language is further a product of its
time and context. A word is not a crystal, transparent and
unchanged, it is the skin of a living thought and may vary
greatly in color and content according to the circumstances
and the time in which it is used.

The last two sentences suggest that laws are not precise, and
consequently statutory interpretation is a vital aspect of judicial decision making. These examples help to reveal the importance state
court judges place on legislative statutes, and highlight the difficulties with which they must interpret those laws. Consequently, these
opinions reinforce the necessity of empirically examining our basic
research question—to what extent does statutory language systematically influence the voting behavior of state court judges? In the next
section we present empirical evidence to address this question.

Empirical Evidence of Statutory Influence

Again, our basic argument is that judicial decision making is contingent on the level of discretion afforded by the law. Recall from
Chapter 2, that we conduct a series of validity tests for state statutes
to determine if they followed patterns similar to their federal counterparts. To verify this, we examined a sample of state statutes (stratified
by state and issue area). Specifically, we analyzed some statutes with
longer word counts (greater than two standard deviations above the
mean), with smaller word counts (less than two standard deviations
below the mean), and with counts near the mean.

Our examination supports the conclusions of the previous validity tests—statute length is a valid indicator of the degree of legislative
instruction regarding interpretation of the statute, rather than simply the result of multi-part statutes getting at multiple issues. That is,
longer statutes contain a greater degree of detail with respect to the

meaning and purpose of the law, as well as instructions on its implementation and application. Furthermore, longer statutes include
more cross-references to additional relevant statutes and previous
court decisions.[7] In contrast, shorter statutes tend to be more ambiguous. These statutes tend to use very broad language with few clearly
defined terms, statements of purpose, directions on application, or
cross-references.

An example of two Texas criminal statutes provides clarification
of this distinction. Tex. Penal Code § 38.122, provides for the crime
of Falsely Holding Oneself Out As a Lawyer. At only 1,967 words, the
statute provides little detail as to what constitutes the elements of
the crime and leaves a great deal of gap-filling for judges applying
the statute to a given case. Additionally, it contains few references to
prior judicial decisions or other statutes to assist judges applying the
law to a specific situation. In contrast, the Aggravated Sexual Assault
statute—Tex. Penal Code § 22.021—is not only substantially longer
(166,493 words), but it also provides clearer instructions to judges
applying the law in particular cases. In addition to clearly defining
all of the key terms in the statute, it also references many prior judicial decisions and other statutes. Thus, the longer statute provides
greater detail, leaving less discretion to judges when applying the law
to specific cases.

As we state in Chapter 2, we recognize that judges may be called
upon to examine only a specific section of the statute rather than
the entire law. Whenever possible we recorded specific portions of
statutes, as determined by the judicial case record. For example, in
one case adjudicated by the Connecticut Supreme Court, the justices
were asked to interpret Connecticut General Statute § 21a–278; and
in a second case the same court was asked to interpret Connecticut
General Statute § 21a–278a. In many instances, however, it is difficult
to determine with certainty whether judges also reference the remaining portions of the bill in order to obtain contextual information on
the intended effect or purpose of the legislation passed.

To examine whether statutory language exerts a systematic influence on the voting patterns of state court judges, we rely on data from
the Judge-Level State Supreme Court Database, compiled by Chris W.
Bonneau, Paul Brace, and Kevin Arceneaux and archived at Rice University. The data contain cases from all fifty states from 1995 through
1998.[8] We examine each case in the dataset to determine whether the

state courts interpret a state statute, and subsequently confine our analysis to those cases. This yields approximately 41,233 individual state judge votes.[9]

The dependent variable for the analysis is whether a state judge votes in an unconstrained or sincere manner. Consistent with the previous chapters our independent variables of primary interest are *Statutory Detail*, and the interaction term *Liberal * Statutory Detail* to measure this potential dynamic and interdependent relationship. Again, because we expect criminal and civil liberties statutes to prescribe more conservative outcomes, we expect longer statutes to decrease the likelihood of sincere voting by liberal judges. Therefore, the interaction term *Liberal * Statutory Detail* should possess a negative relationship with the probability of a sincere vote. Conversely, increases in statutory detail in these issue areas should facilitate (i.e., increase) the likelihood of ideological voting for conservative judges.

Additionally, we recognize that our theoretical expectations concerning the impact of statutory language may be muted by the ideological extremity of a particular judge. That is, extreme ideologues may be more likely to vote in a sincere fashion than their moderate colleagues holding the level of statutory constraint constant. To measure this effect, we rely on the PAJID scores developed by Brace, Hall, and Langer (2000). These scores place state court judges on an ideological continuum from most conservative (with a score of 0) to most liberal (with a score of 100). Because our theoretical interest focuses on the intensity of a judge's ideology, regardless of his/her ideological directionality, we "fold" the PAJID scores into a continuum from the most moderate judges to the most extreme ideologues.[10] Consequently, we hypothesize that judges with stronger ideological preferences will be more likely to render unconstrained or sincere decisions. A positive relationship should therefore exist between our variable *Ideological Intensity* and the dependent variable.

In addition to these variables, our model includes six other control variables—one measured at the individual case level and the remaining five measured at the state level. The first measures whether the state court is requested to review the constitutionality of a statute. If the court is asked to exercise the power of *Judicial Review*, we expect the judges will be more likely to cast sincere votes (i.e., we do not expect substantial constraint to exist when the constitutionality of the statute is questioned). Therefore, a positive relationship should exist between this variable and the dependent variable. The second individual-level control variable measures the length of time that has elapsed from the passage of the original legislation to the state court's review. Thus, the variable *Age of Statute* measures the number of years between a statute's enactment and the actual court case reviewing the law.[11] We expect that more recent statutes will possess more influence over judicial behavior than older legislation. Consequently, this variable should have a negative relationship with the dependent variable.

Additionally, at the state level we include a control variable to measure the *Partisan Balance of the State Legislature.* This measure comes from Klarner (2003) and is a ratio of the proportion of seats held by Democrats versus the proportion held by Republicans.[12] We also include a dummy variable to control for the presence of an *Intermediate Appellate Court.* Previous research indicates that the presence of an IAC—combined with the corresponding increase in docket control for the state court of last resort—allows the state judges to review more salient and/or important cases; thereby increasing the likelihood of sincere votes (Arceneaux, Bonneau, and Brace 2008; Bonneau and Rice 2007). The third state level control variable measures the degree of *Judicial Professionalism* possessed by state court judges. We rely on Squire's (2008) professionalism measure, which assess the informational capacity of each state high court based on its degree of docket control, level of judicial salaries, and number of law clerks. Finally, we include two separate dummy variables to control for those states in which judges are subject to *Retention Elections* and those states in which judges experience *Partisan/Non-Partisan Elections.* Several previous studies of state court behavior demonstrate the different behavioral patterns exhibited by judges who are directly elected to the bench versus their appointed colleagues (see Hall 1992; Brace, Hall, and Langer 2001). Consequently, we control for these institutional differences across states.

Because our data represent individual choices nested within state-level influences, we employ a series of multilevel models to examine the effects of the *Model of Contingent Discretion* on state court judges. In so doing, we rely on a Bernoulli sampling specification with an accompanying logit link to examine the binary dependent variable. We initially define the logit link, $\Pr(Y_{ij} = 1) = \rho_{ij}$, which is the probability of a sincere vote for judge i in state j. We then define π_{ij} as the log-odds of ρ_{ij} (i.e., $\pi_{ij} = \log[\rho_{ij} / 1-\rho_{ij}]$), which allows us to specify the log-odds as a linear function of the level 1 independent variables. This equation is then conditioned on the Level 2 macro (i.e., state-level) effects. Therefore, the overall model estimates a two-level random coefficient model with the following specification:

(Level 1): $\pi_{ij} = \beta_{0ij} + \beta_{1ij}$ Statutory Constraint + β_{2ij} Liberal + β_{3ij} Liberal $*$ Statutory Constraint + β_{4ij} Ideological Intensity + β_{5ij} Judicial Review + β_{6ij} Age of Statute

(Level 2): $\beta_{0j} = \gamma_{0j} + \gamma_{1j}$ State Ideology + γ_{2j} Intermediate Appellate Court + γ_{3j} Judicial Professionalism + γ_{4j} Retention Election + γ_{5j} Partisan/Non-Partisan Election

In the Level 1 equation, the likelihood of a sincere vote (π_{ij}) for any individual judge is associated with the degree of statutory constraint (as interacted with whether the judge is liberal or conservative), the strength of the judge's ideological preferences, and whether the case involves an aspect of judicial review. β_{0ij} is a random intercept that varies across individual judges and states, and it can be conceptualized as the general propensity of a sincere vote. Furthermore, the Level 1 equation is also affected by differences among states (j). The term γ_{0j} is a random intercept that represents the general propensity for state j to experience sincere votes among its judges. Additionally, the Level 2 effects are also conditioned by state ideology, specific institutional features (such as an intermediate appellate court and professionalism), and the selection mechanism used to determine its judges.

Table 5.1 presents separate models for criminal law cases[13] and civil liberties cases.[14] Examining these results reveals that the *Model of Contingent Discretion* significantly influences state supreme court judges in the expected directions. For both criminal cases (Model 1) and civil liberties cases (Model 2) the coefficient for the variable *Statutory Detail* is statistically significant and positive. Recall that because of the inclusion of the interaction term, this variable now measures the effect of statutory language on conservative judges. Consequently, these results provide empirical support for our hypothesis—as statutes become more detailed, conservative judges are able to use the statutory language to reinforce and facilitate their ideological voting.

Table 5.1. Multilevel Model of Statutory Influence

	Model 1 Criminal Cases	Model 2 Civil Liberties Cases
Individual Level Effects (Level 1)		
Statutory Detail	.068***	.130*
	(.013)	(.062)
Liberal	.112	1.353
	(.168)	(.817)
Liberal * Statutory Detail	−.136***	−.253**
	(.018)	(.097)
Ideological Intensity	.001	−.009
	(.001)	(.006)
Judicial Review	.015	.019
	(.053)	(.198)
Age of Statute	.000	−.001
	(.000)	(.002)
State Level Effects (Level 2)		
Partisan Balance of the **State Legislature**	−.077	.599
	(.432)	(.531)
Intermediate Appellate Court	−.134	.207
	(.165)	(.213)
Judicial Professionalism	−.364	.540
	(.456)	(.718)
Retention Election	.198	.211
	(.186)	(.253)
Partisan/Non−Partisan Election	.050	−.006
	(.168)	(.211)
Constant	.311	−.703
	(.385)	(.799)
N	29429	910
Log−Likelihood	−19767.91	−1310.33
Wald χ^2	680.061	42.241
Probability $> \chi^2$	.000	.031

* p < .05   ** p < .01   *** p < .001

Dependent Variable: unconstrained or sincere vote (1), constrained vote (0)

Note: Estimates calculated with HLM 6.07 (Raudenbush, Bryk, and Congdon 2005).

In contrast, the interaction term *Liberal * Statutory Detail* is statistically significant but possesses a negative coefficient. This indicates that for both criminal and civil liberties cases, liberal state court judges are constrained from voting ideologically as state statutes become more detailed. The result for the interaction term provides empirical support for our hypothesis. Examining the remaining individual-level variables reveals that none of the coefficients attain statistical significance in either model. Additionally, turning our attention to the state-level effects reveals that none of the variables exert a statistically significant influence on individual behavior (although collectively it is still important to control for state-level effects).

While these empirical results confirm our hypothesis related to the *Model of Contingent Discretion*, they do not offer insights into the substantive effects of statutory language on judicial behavior. To provide a better understanding of the dynamic relationship between statutes and ideological preferences, we offer Figure 5.1. This graph presents the impact of increases to statutory detail on the probability of individual

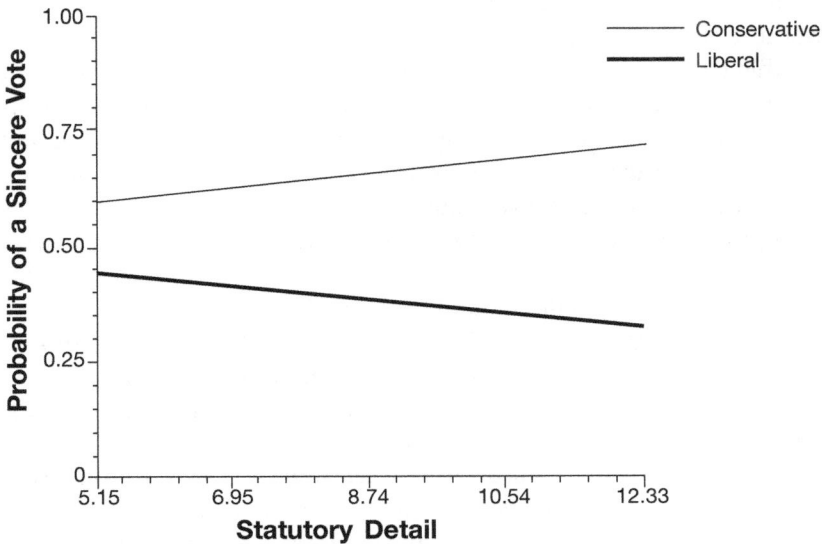

Figure 5.1. Impact of Constraint on Sincere Voting in Criminal Cases.

state judges casting sincere votes in criminal cases. Examining the dashed line (which represents conservative judges) reveals that as the length of legislation increases from its minimum to maximum value, the probability of conservative judges casting sincere votes increases by approximately .100 (from a probability of .600 to a probability of .700). Therefore, holding all other influences constant (including the degree of ideological extremism), for every ten criminal cases the average conservative state court judge reviews, we should expect to see one additional conservative vote when the statute involved contains more detailed language. Conversely, the solid line indicates that increases in the length of legislation from minimum to maximum decrease the probability of liberal judges casting sincere votes by approximately .100 (from a probability of .450 to a probability of .350). Thus, holding all other influences constant, the average liberal judge is expected to cast one less liberal vote in a set of ten criminal cases.

While these results further support our theoretical contention regarding the influence of statutory language, we acknowledge that many of these state court cases involve several different types of cases, including some that are either frivolous or not salient to the judges. It is quite possible that the effects of statutory language diminish as state judges engage in more important or more salient cases. To examine this possibility, we reanalyze the sample of criminal cases, but this time narrow the range to include only those cases involving the death penalty. These results are reported in Table 5.2. Immediately, one can observe that the results for death penalty cases are very similar to those for criminal cases generally speaking. The one noticeable difference involves the variable *Statutory Detail*—it is now not significant in death penalty cases, whereas it was significant and positive in general criminal cases. This indicates that increases in statutory detail do not facilitate ideological voting of conservative judges in death penalty cases. Yet, the interaction term *Liberal * Statutory Detail* remains significant and negative. This supports our hypothesis that liberal judges are constrained from casting sincere votes as death penalty statutes become more detailed.

Finally, one may question why we only examine statutes that prescribe relatively conservative outcomes; when in the two previous chapters we also examine statutes that prescribe relatively liberal outcomes and discover a similar effect (but one where liberal judges are facilitated in their ideological voting and conservatives are con-

Table 5.2. Multilevel Model of Statutory Constraint in Death
Penalty Cases

	Model 3 Death Penalty Cases
Individual Level Effects (Level 1)	
Statutory Constraint	.044 (.026)
Liberal	−1.235** (.440)
Liberal * Statutory Constraint	−.101* (.043)
Ideological Intensity	.018** (.003)
Judicial Review	−.077 (.089)
State Level Effects (Level 2)	
Partisan Balance of the State Legislature	.003 (.002)
Intermediate Appellate Court	.422 (.298)
Judicial Professionalism	.243 (.330)
Retention Election	−.135 (.149)
Partisan/Non-Partisan Election	−.049 (.160)
Constant	.067 (.419)
N	6324
Log–Likelihood	−3290.117
Wald χ^2	1757.55
Probability > χ^2	.000

* p < .05   ** p < .01   *** p < .001
Dependent Variable: unconstrained or sincere vote (1), constrained vote (0)
Note: Estimates calculated with HLM 6.02 (Raudenbush, Bryk, and Congdon 2005).

strained). The answer to this question involves the data available in the Judge-Level State Supreme Court Database. Quite simply, there are not enough cases containing liberally oriented statutes to conduct an appropriate empirical analysis. However, to test whether our *Model of Contingent Discretion* works similarly when state court judges adjudicate more liberal statutes, we conduct an analysis of discrimination cases. These results are reported in Table 5.3.

Table 5.3. Fixed Effects Model of Statutory Constraint in Discrimination Cases

	Model 4 Discrimination Cases
Statutory Detail	−.369* (.153)
Liberal	−3.340** (1.830)
Liberal * Statutory Detail	.468* (.204)
Ideological Intensity	−.001 (.012)
Judicial Review	−.162 (.585)
Retention Election	.125 (.405)
Partisan/Non-Partisan Election	−.535 (.405)
Constant	3.277 (1.541)
N	246
Log-Likelihood	−158.810
Wald χ^2	20.66
Probability > χ^2	.000

* p < .05   ** p < .01   *** p < .001
Dependent Variable: unconstrained or sincere vote (1), constrained vote (0)
Cell values calculated using fixed effects logit model with standard errors in parentheses

At the outset we caution against reading too deeply into any conclusions generated by these results. The relatively small number of observations substantially limits the robustness of this analysis. Consequently, our discussion of this evidence will be limited as well. As we explain in Chapter 2, if judges are influenced by statutory language, then our expectation is that more detailed statutes will facilitate the ideological voting of liberal judges when those statutes prescribe liberal outcomes. Conversely, these same statutes should constrain the ideological voting of conservative judges. If these expectations are valid, then the empirical evidence should display a negative and statistically significant coefficient on the variable *Statutory Detail* (which measures the influence of statutory language for conservative judges) and a statistically significant and positive coefficient for the interaction term *Liberal * Statutory Detail* (which measures the influence of statutory language for liberal judges). Examining the results in Table 5.3 supports these expectations. The interaction term is significant and positive indicating that liberal judges rely on longer discrimination cases to facilitate their ideological voting. In contrast, conservative judges experience a constraining effect on their ideological voting when discrimination statutes become longer.

The combined findings for *Statutory Detail* and the *Liberal * Statutory Detail* interaction term suggest a theoretically important way of thinking about judicial behavior. Rather than conceptualizing the legal model and the attitudinal model as competitors (i.e., that there is a tradeoff between law and ideology), the empirical evidence suggests that legal influences and ideological influences also work in tandem among state supreme courts. These judges are influenced by the *Model of Contingent Discretion* and, occasionally, the traditional tension exists and statutory language constrains the judges from voting ideologically. However, in other instances these two influences operate in a more dynamic and interdependent manner and we observe statutory language facilitating the expression of ideological voting among the judges.

Corollary Analysis of Statutes and Judicial Elections/Appointments

While the previous analyses are useful in helping us understand the dynamic relationship between statutory language and ideological voting among state court judges, they also raise an additional question. Why are the state-level effects not more prominent in the model; in particular the method of judicial selection? In Model 1 and Model 2 neither the variable *Retention Election* nor *Partisan/Non-Partisan Election* is statistically significant. This indicates that elected judges and merit selected judges behave similarly to judges that are appointed to state supreme courts. This conclusion contradicts the general consensus among state court scholars: that elected judges encounter additional constraints as the result of electoral pressures from the public (see Bonneau and Hall 2003; Brace and Hall 1993, 1997; Hall 1992; Hall and Brace 1992; and Langer 2002).[15] As these studies demonstrate, electoral pressures often serve to constrain the ideological voting of individual judges.

To address this apparent contradiction, we conduct a corollary analysis on the determinants of statutory detail. In particular, we focus on whether some states are more likely to pass detailed statutes than others. For this analysis we utilize the *Statutory Detail* variable as the dependent variable, and we regress it on three independent variables: *Retention Election, Partisan/Non-Partisan Election*, and *State Ideology*.[16] The results reported in Table 5.4 for all cases (Model 5) and for criminal cases only (Model 6) provide extremely interesting information. In each model the coefficients for *Retention Election* and *Partisan/Non-Partisan Election* are significant and positive (even when controlling for *State Ideology*)—states that do not possess complete and direct control (i.e., states that do not appoint judges) over the makeup of their courts of last resort are significantly more likely to pass detailed statutes. Additionally, we ran an alternative specification (Model 7) for criminal cases in which we changed the baseline category from judicial appointments to retention elections. The results in Model 7 indicate that states with *Partisan/Non-Partisan Elections* are significantly more likely to pass more detailed statutes than states with retention elections.

The results of this corollary analysis help paint an extremely interesting portrait of legislative-judicial interactions at the state level. It is apparent from the empirical evidence in Table 5.4 that states with direct and complete control over the composition of their supreme courts (i.e., through judicial appointments) are significantly more likely to pass vague and ambiguous statutes. However, as state legislatures lose control over the makeup of their courts—as they move

Table 5.4. Determinants of the Level of Detail in State Statutes

	Model 5 All Cases	Model 6 Criminal Cases Only	Model 7 Alternative Specification
Retention Election	.252***	.556***	—
	(.013)	(.022)	
Partisan/Non—Partisan	.366***	.483***	.030*
Election	(.013)	(.024)	(.017)
State Ideology	.269***	.264***	.214***
	(.005)	(.009)	(.008)
Judicial Appointment	—	—	−.177***
			(.008)
N	101338	37783	37783
F	933.850	419.930	419.930
Probability > F	.000	.000	.000
R^2	.027	.032	.032
Adjusted R^2	.027	.032	.032

* $p < .10$ ** $p < .05$ *** $p < .01$

Dependent variable is *Statutory Constraint*. Estimates are OLS coefficients, standard errors are in parentheses.

Note: Models 5 and 6 use *Judicial Appointment* as the baseline category (for comparisons) and Model 7 uses *Retention Election* as the baseline (for comparisons).

to retention elections and then to partisan/non-partisan direct elections—they respond by passing more detailed legislation; legislation that according to our empirical evidence in Table 5.1 significantly influences judicial behavior. Stated another way, if the principal (i.e., the state legislature) possesses the ability to select the agents (state supreme court justices) directly, then they are significantly more likely to provide those agents with discretion. However, in states where the principal does not possess this authority, then additional control mechanisms (in the form of longer legislative statutes) become necessary to ensure agent compliance.

This finding highlights an important intervening variable that has heretofore been excluded in existing research. The scholarly con-

sensus agrees that state court judges facing electoral pressures are
more likely to deviate from voting according to their ideological preferences. For example, Hall (1992) demonstrates that liberal judges
seeking reelection in four relatively conservative states are significantly more likely to vote conservatively (and join conservative majority coalitions) in death penalty cases. Our corollary analysis suggests
that future research should explore the potentially mediating effects
of legislation on the impact of electoral pressures. It is possible that
judges in states with judicial elections are not simply encountering
direct electoral pressure as the previous research indicates. Rather,
these judges may face competing pressures—from both the electorate and from the state legislature that is attempting to make elected
supreme court judges more accountable to the legislative branch. Our
results suggest that scholars need to explore the potentially complex
intricacies of this dynamic relationship.

Conclusions

Are state supreme court judges influenced by the *Model of Contingent Discretion*, similar to their federal colleagues? Stated another
way, do these judges render decisions according to their ideological
preferences, or are they constrained by the language of state statutes?
Our examination into this question provides empirical evidence to
support the latter contention. The measure of statutory detail reveals
that more detailed language (resulting in statutes with higher word
counts) significantly limits the discretion afforded to liberal judges
while simultaneously facilitating the ideological voting of their conservative colleagues in both criminal and civil liberties cases.

      While these results suggest an important new theoretical direc-
tion for judicial behavior, the research also raises additional questions for future studies to address. First, though we provide evidence
concerning the passage of detailed legislative statutes in those states
with direct or retention elections of judges, more research is needed
to determine the precise nature of this relationship.[17] Second, since
our analysis is limited to only four years, future research is needed to
determine if these results are confined to the period under study or
whether they can be generalized to a broader context. In addition to
these temporal aspects it is important to see if these results hold in

other issue areas, specifically to areas where one would expect legislation to prescribe more liberal outcomes (e.g., civil rights statutes). If the *Model of Contingent Discretion* operates in these areas as well, we would expect to see patterns of constraint and facilitation reversed with more detailed legislation, making liberal judges more likely to vote in a sincere manner and conservative judges facing constraint. Empirically examining these questions in future research is important to determine additional aspects of the dynamic and interdependent relationship between statutory influences and ideological preferences.

6

Temporal Analysis of
Supreme Court Behavior[1]

In the previous chapters, we present several analyses examining the effects of statutory detail on judicial behavior. Throughout each model our argument is that the language of statutes—specifically the degree to which they limit or expand judicial discretion—systematically affects voting behavior. At times, for some judges, they are constrained from voting sincerely and at other times, for other judges, the legislation facilitates their ideological voting. These patterns exist regardless of whether one examines judges on the U.S. Courts of Appeals, justices of the U.S. Supreme Court or state supreme court judges. Fundamentally, the insights we generate are extremely important because they help provide a better understanding of the conditions under which judicial ideology interacts with statutory influences to determine voting behavior.

Yet, there remains one area that has not been explored and that involves the temporal nature of statutory interpretation. Our previous analyses operate on a purely cross-sectional level; ignoring the sequential nature of the struggle between Congress and the judiciary (in particular, the U.S. Supreme Court) over the establishment of law. For example, in response to the Supreme Court's decision in *Employment Division of Oregon v. Smith*,[2] Congress passed the Religious Freedoms Restoration Act (RFRA) in 1993. The primary purpose of the RFRA was to effectively nullify the *Smith* precedent and provide more effective freedoms related to the exercise of religion. However, the Supreme Court declared the RFRA unconstitutional in the case *City of Boerne v. Flores* in 1997.[3] In response to this decision, Congress passed the Religious Land Use and Institutionalized Persons Act (RLUIPA), which was designed in part, to protect individuals confined to governmental institutions from having their religious exercise freedoms substantially burdened. Currently, lower courts are still interpreting portions of the RLUIPA—a continuation of the dynamic process of interpretation and application of law in the United States.

Unfortunately, many theoretical models of judicial behavior operate from a more static conceptualization of reality. They typically focus on one or two primary determinants of judicial outcomes, such as ideological attitudes or legal factors (or perhaps a combination). Often, when legal factors are involved scholars treat these factors as discreet events that occur at a single point in time, such as the impact of a landmark precedent. Yet, as the example above demonstrates, there is an important *temporal* aspect to judicial interpretation. This chapter focuses explicitly on the temporal aspect as it integrates both ideological and legal factors into a single model of judicial behavior. Because we specifically examine the temporal nature in which the law is interpreted, revised, and reinterpreted over time, our model offers a more dynamic measure of the influences on judicial behavior.

To accomplish this goal we incorporate the effects of two distinct, but related, legal factors. The first is our measure of *Statutory Detail*, but rather than use it as a static measure, we focus more on the evolution of statutory language over time. The second legal factor examines *previous judicial interpretations* of a statute's language. This factor focuses the temporal and contextual dynamics of statutory interpretation. Specifically, it captures the additional judicial history that becomes part of the official U.S. Code (listed as judicial annotations) and offer subsequent clarity after passage of the original statute. Consequently, these additional annotations provide information related to prior judicial interpretations of a congressional statute. Our argument is that these additional annotations also affect the level of discretion afforded to judges by the law, but are not part of the original statute. Thus, the annotations offer further clarity over the plain meaning of the statute—clarity that comes from a judicial, not legislative, source.

The Temporal Nature of the Law

As we explain in Chapters 1 and 2, one of the primary limitations in the literature involves the inchoate development of theory combined with suitable empirical measures to assess the influence of legal factors on judges. Scholars recognize the importance of ideological preferences and numerous studies exist demonstrating their effect on the voting calculus of the justices. However, there is little empirical confirmation that the law possesses a similar systematic influence. Connected to this puzzle is the lack of clarity concerning the role of temporal factors—namely legal context—as an influence and/or potential constraint, on individual ideological preferences.

When Congress passes a statute it is essentially sending a set of codified instructions to other governmental institutions for handling various public issues. The exactness or specificity of these instructions varies from statute to statute. If a particular law is vague and does not clearly prescribe a particular method of application or clear interpretation, government agents (whether bureaucrats, judges, law enforcement officials, etc.) must use their own discretion when real-life circumstances so dictate. Naturally, the opportunity to use discretion invites one to inject his or her personal values or ideological preferences into the decision-making process. Conversely, the law can act as a clamp on such activities when Congress is clear and specific about how the law is to be applied or interpreted.

Additionally, one must remain cognizant of the fact that statutory meanings and definitions are not static phenomena. Although many statutes exist for long periods of time without formal amendments by Congress,[4] they often encounter adjudication in the courts—sometimes on multiple occasions. Each decision adds a new contextual layer to the congressional statute that may drastically alter the law. As statutes encounter multiple interpretations and reinterpretations the additional contextual information is recorded for use by future lawyers and judges.[5]

To enhance our understanding of the dynamic relationship between Congress and the courts (in particular, the Supreme Court) over the substantive meaning and interpretation of the law, we must account for the temporal struggle between these two institutions. Specifically, our models must recognize statutory interpretation as an ever-growing set of policy instructions, which may (a) serve to reaffirm the substantive intent of Congress; (b) conflict with the legislative intent of Congress; or (c) send multiple mixed messages. Additionally, as new challenges and controversies arise over a particular statute, the pertinent amalgamating case law either constrains judges from voting according to their ideological preferences or facilitates behavior consistent with their individual ideology. Our theoretical model (and subsequent empirical examinations) seeks to provide a more nuanced account of judicial behavior by incorporating these aspects directly.

Thus, as we have argued so far in this chapter, while laws are enacted discretely at one point in time, their effects are interpreted sequentially over time by a variety of different policy actors. In particular, judges at different levels of the adjudicatory process play a role in statutory interpretation. While researchers often tend to focus on the Supreme Court, the adjudication of statutes begins with lower courts, which must try to make sense of the meaning of the law. This often results in a series of cases at the federal level, with several district courts and sometimes multiple appellate courts interpreting the law, occasionally in contradictory ways. By the time the Supreme Court agrees to review a case, it therefore has been adjudicated, often at length, by a number of federal courts. In many cases, the decisions rendered by the lower courts are contradictory or at least have considerable variation in the decisions rendered by individual judges. The presence of such conflict among the circuits has been noted as one of the primary reasons for the grant of *certiorari* by the Supreme Court (see Perry 1991).

Unlike our measure of statutory language, which involves the express will of Congress on a particular subject, the *temporal context* of a statute often contains a cacophony of disparate and confusing judicial opinions regarding its interpretation. These judicial annotations therefore provide an evolving historical commentary of the opinions and decisions of the lower courts; factors that the Supreme Court may consider when it decides to hear an appeal. As noted, these decisions likely contain a variety of contradictory decisions and dissenting opinions.[6] Thus, unlike the plain meaning of a statute, the *temporal context* received by the Supreme Court is not always consistent. Consequently, whereas we expect longer statutes to provide more detailed information for judges, increases in judicial annotations may reflect greater levels of disagreement or confusion about interpretations of the law.

To better illustrate this point, we need to examine particular statutes and the annotations surrounding their interpretations. One congressional statute that exemplifies the dynamic nature of law is the Voting Rights Act (hereafter, VRA) of 1965 (42 U.S.C.S. § 1973). In a forthcoming book, Rivers (N.D.) discusses the myriad of competing influences—such as the Congressional Black Caucus and the Supreme Court—surrounding this statute. As a result, she demonstrates the "conflicting interpretations of the laws" pertaining to minority voting rights (p. 38). An examination of the judicial annotations related to the VRA reveals a plethora of additional interpretations rendered by judges, often to resolve unforeseen circumstances. For example, in the case *Solomon v. Liberty County* (1988)[7] the Eleventh Circuit Court of Appeals states that the "Goal of 42 U.S.C.S. § 1973 was not to maximize political clout, but rather to insure minority representation in government." Yet, the District Court for the Northern District of Illinois indicates that "nothing in the Voting Rights Act requires that there be proportional representation nor that any minority be guaranteed certain percentage of voters in ward" (*Ketchum v. City Council of Chicago* 1985).[8] Finally, in 1983 the District Court for the Eastern District of Louisiana provides further clarification by stating that "Congress has the authority to regulate state and local voting practices through provisions of the Voting Rights Act . . . and does not work unconstitutional abrogation of powers allocated to states by the Tenth Amendment . . ." (*Major v. Treen* 1983, 574 F. Supp 326).

From a principal-agent perspective these examples illustrate the difficulties encountered by the principal (in this case, Congress) when it wishes to enact a contract with its agents. Though the language of the contract (i.e., the Voting Rights Act) may contain explicit detail regarding the precise outcomes preferred by the principal, no one can anticipate all of the situations in which the statute may be applied. Consequently, the judicial annotations (which represent attempts by agents to interpret the law) preserve these additional interpretations in the law for future agents to review when they are called upon to provide subsequent interpretations of the statute. Therefore, while the principal-agent model generally assumes that the principal acts and agents respond (or shirk), these judicial annotations represent a measure of the extent to which agents try to make sense of the principal's cues.

Given this dynamic relationship between the principal and agents and also among the agents themselves, what then does the temporal dimension actually entail? It is a measure of judicial opinion pertaining to a specific congressional statute (i.e., statutory interpretation), often recorded by lower court judges (not necessarily by the

Supreme Court). Since we expect the judicial annotations to include a variety of opinions over a myriad of different situations, expressing both liberal and conservative views, we expect that the justices will have greater flexibility to base decisions on their individual ideological preferences as the number of annotations increases. Stated another way, if a liberal justice is constrained by the plain meaning of the law (i.e., the Congressional statute), increases in the judicial annotations over time should provide that justice with additional flexibility and legal rationale to vote according to the tenets of the attitudinal model. This leads to an additional hypothesis not stated in Chapter 2:

> **Judicial Annotation Hypothesis:** *The greater the attention paid to a statute by courts—represented by an increase in the number of words contained in the judicial annotations—the more likely it is that Supreme Court justices will vote according to their ideological preferences.*

Evolution of Congressional Statutory Language

Before we examine the results of specific empirical tests, it is important to better understand the evolution of statutes passed by Congress. Using our measure of *Statutory Detail,* which calculates the number of words in a statute, we track the year in which Congress passes a particular law. We then compute the average statute length for all laws passed in a specific year and graph the results in a variety of different ways.

Figure 6.1 represents the average statute length per year for all statutes passed by Congress over an approximately one-hundred-year time span.[9] Examining the results of this graph reveals some interesting patterns concerning the level of detail included in federal laws. First, it is apparent that in the early 1900s, Congress passed relatively vague statutes. However, with the advent of President Franklin Roosevelt's New Deal legislation in the 1930s, there is a tremendous spike in the average number of words—Congressional statutes in this era virtually double in length (from approximately 750 to 1,500 words). Then following World War II, though there is a slight decline, the average statute length never dips below 1,250 words. Overall, this graph indicates that federal statutes (on average) evolve into considerably

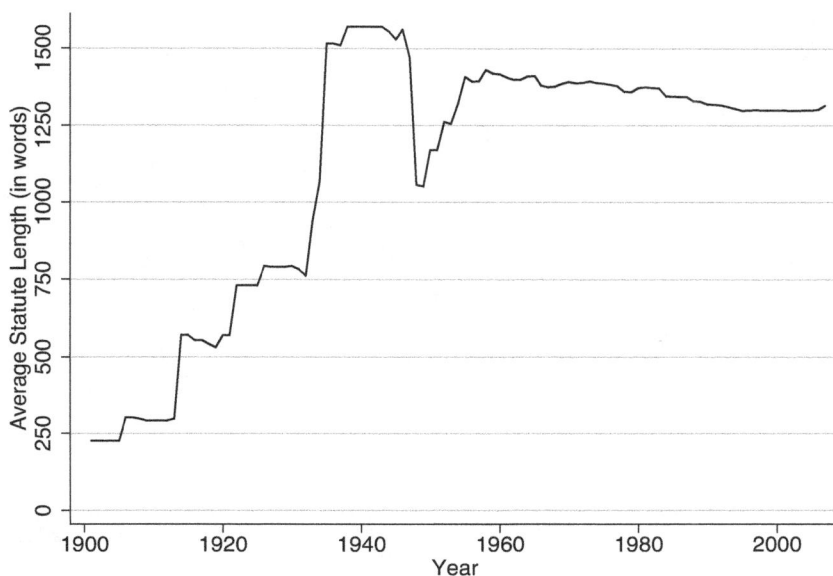

Figure 6.1. Changes in Statute Length over Time.

more detailed laws in the "modern era" (i.e., after the New Deal) and remain at a high level of detail into the new millennium.

To gain a slightly different perspective, we break the data from the previous figure into separate issue areas—criminal, civil liberties, and economic—and examine only those statutes specifically interpreted by the Supreme Court in our analysis of voting behavior. The graph displayed in Figure 6.2 contains the average statute length for criminal laws. While there is considerable fluctuation across the time-series, one can identify a slight increase starting in 1970 (possibly to counter the effects of pro-defendant decisions (such as *Miranda v. Arizona*) handed down by the Warren Court).

Figure 6.3 presents information pertaining to the average length of civil liberties statutes. Immediately, one can see how the landmark Civil Rights Act (1964) and Voting Rights Act (1965) compare to other civil liberties statutes. Congress was extremely deliberate in its choice of words and methodically developed detailed legislation specifically dictating particular objectives and outcomes. As we see in Chapter 4,

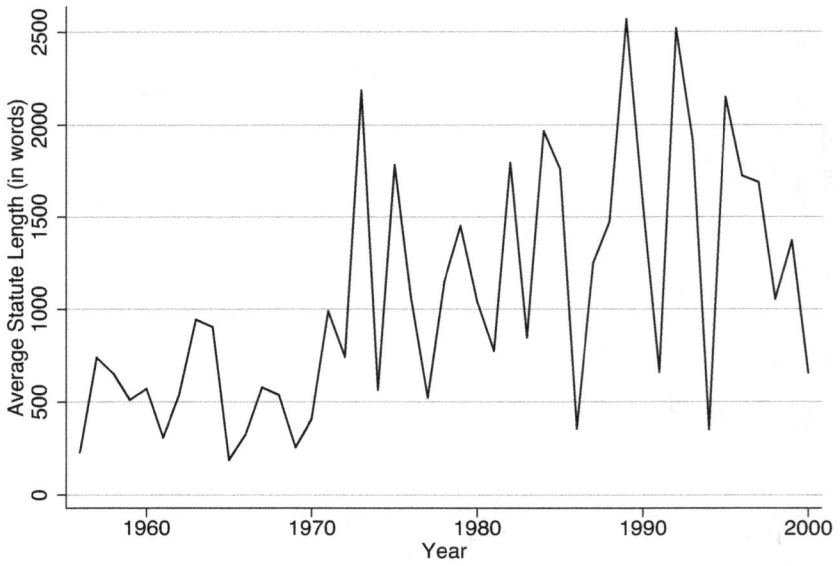

Figure 6.2. Changes in Criminal Statutes over Time.

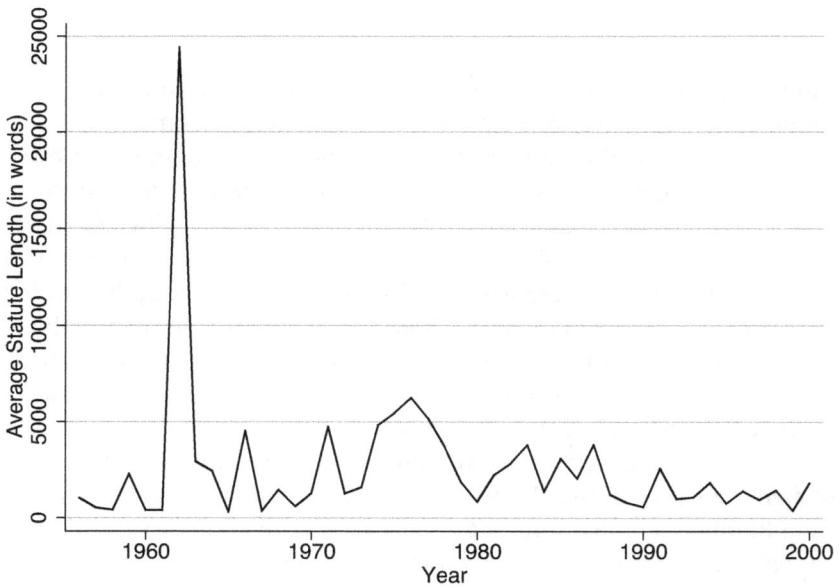

Figure 6.3. Changes in Civil Liberties Statutes over Time.

these statutes significantly affected the voting behavior of justices on the Supreme Court; in particular, the liberal justices relied on these details to facilitate their ideological voting.

Finally, in Figure 6.4 we examine the evolution of economic statutes over time. Looking at this graph does not reveal any easily identifiable patterns, unlike what we observe for criminal and civil liberties statutes. There is a general positive trend, though it is so slight that no significant differences occur. We speculate that the lack of any noticeable trend in statute length is a result of administrative agencies and their regulations. Because of the substantial expansion of the federal bureaucracy, it is plausible that Congress has not experienced any pressure to provide more detailed legislation; content to let administrative agencies develop more specific regulations. If this is correct, then one should expect to observe significant increases in agency pronouncements over the same time frame. Unfortunately, further investigation into this matter is beyond the scope of our analysis, though future research will hopefully explore this in more detail.

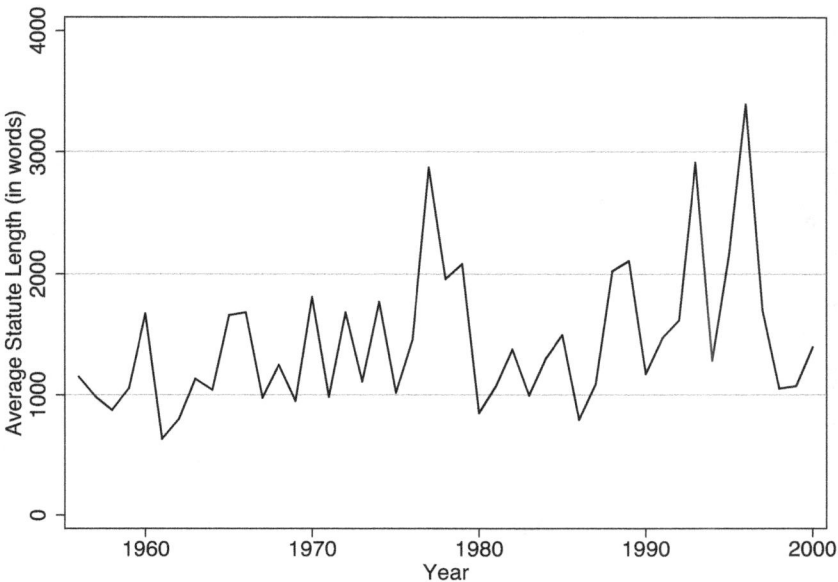

Figure 6.4. Changes in Economic Statutes over Time.

In order to understand the dynamic interplay between Congress and the federal courts over the interpretation of law, one must also examine how judicial annotations evolve over time. Recall that these annotations provide a running commentary of the opinions and decisions of the lower courts: factors that the Supreme Court may consider when it decides to hear an appeal. Consequently, the judicial annotations likely contain a variety of contradictory decisions and dissenting opinions. Examining the graph in Figure 6.5 illustrates the growing number of annotations over time. In the early 1900s relatively few annotations exist. However, as lower federal courts become more active, starting in the 1950s, the average number of judicial annotations increases exponentially. Whether this explosion in the number of annotations is a result of Congress passing more detailed statutes (as seen in Figure 6.1) following the New Deal era, or the result of federal courts becoming more politically active, is unclear from the graph.[10] What is apparent from Figure 6.5 is that by the time a case

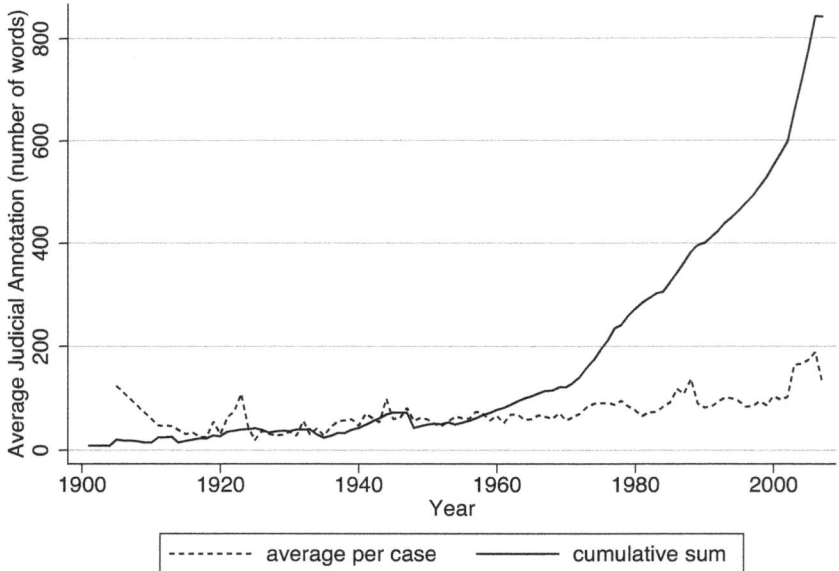

Figure 6.5. Changes in Judicial Annotations over Time.

reaches the Supreme Court, the justices have a plethora of judicial annotations that they can utilize to interpret congressional statutes.

Consequently, the focus of the question raised by the previous figures is, What effect does the increasing number of judicial annotations have on the influence of statutory language? As we state earlier in the "Judicial Annotation Hypothesis," our expectation is that this "increased noise" serves to ameliorate and dampen the influence of statutory language. And, without the presence of statutory influence affecting judicial behavior, we expect the justices will be more likely to vote according to their ideological preferences.

Empirical Analysis of Statutory Influence versus Judicial Annotations

To examine empirically the dynamics between statutory language and judicial annotations we reexamine the data on Supreme Court voting presented in Chapter 4. Recall that the data come from the three justice-centered Supreme Court databases compiled by Harold J. Spaeth.[11] Though the original datasets contain the universe of formally decided cases,[12] we limit our analysis to those cases in which the Supreme Court interprets a congressional statute. Consequently, we analyze approximately 28,000 justice-votes from 1953 to 1998.[13]

To keep this analysis comparable to the examination in Chapter 4 we retain the same dependent variable—whether a justice voted in an unconstrained or sincere manner.[14] We code the variable "1" if a liberal justice casts a liberal vote and "0" if that justice votes conservatively.[15] Similarly, the variable is coded "1" if a conservative justice votes conservatively and "0" if that judge casts a liberal vote.

We also retain the same set of independent variables from Chapter 4. These include our measure of *Statutory Detail* (coded as the natural log of each statute); a dummy variable, *Liberal Justices* to measure differences between liberal and conservative justices; the interaction term *Liberal Justices * Statutory Detail* to measure the potential dynamic of statutory influence across different sets of justices; and the measure of *Ideological Intensity* (calculated based on "folding" the Martin and Quinn (2002) ideology scores). Additionally we retain the same control variables from Chapter 4—*Judicial Review* (dummy variable coded "1" when the constitutionality of a statute is questioned); *Lower Court Congruence* (coded "1" if the lower court rendered a decision in opposition to the justice's ideological preferences, "2" if the lower court rendered a mixed decision, and "3" if the directionality of the lower court decision is congruent with the justice's ideological preferences); and *Minimum Winning Coalition* (dummy variable coded "1" when the decision is 5–4 or 4–3).

In addition to these independent variables, we include two others that better capture the temporal context described earlier. The first variable *Judicial Annotations* measures the number of words included in a statute's annotations. To code this variable we examine each congressional statute through LexisNexis to record the number of words in every annotation plus the year in which the annotation was added to the statute's official record. Then we calculated the cumulative sum of these several annotations for every subsequent year in which a statute is interpreted by the courts.[16] Consequently, this variable begins at zero (0) for each statute (i.e., when the statute is initially passed by Congress there are no annotations) and increases with every subsequent interpretation, provided that interpretation adds a new annotation to the statute's official record in Lexis. The second variable is an interaction term *Liberal Justices * Judicial Annotations Interaction* to measure any disparate effects between liberal and conservative justices.[17] If our hypotheses related to temporal context are correct then both of these variables should possess a positive influence on the likelihood of a sincere vote.

Table 6.1 presents the results of several empirical models involving criminal statutes before the Supreme Court. The first model (Model 1) restates the original analysis from Chapter 4.[18] We include this original specification for comparison purposes in order to better identify the impact of temporal context as measured by judicial annotations. Consequently, further discussion of the original model is not necessary. Rather, we draw attention to the remaining columns. In Model 2 we reexamine the original specification and add our two new variables measuring the influence of temporal context. Immediately noticeable from Model 2 (the pooled data) is that the variables *Judicial Annotations* and the *Liberal Justices * Judicial Annotations* are not statistically significant. However, the remaining aspects of the model are comparable to the original specification in terms of statistical significance and directionality. Consequently, the initial conclusion we

Table 6.1. The Interplay of Statutes and Annotations in Criminal Cases

	Model 1 Original	Model 2 Pooled Data	Model 3 Frequent Statutes
Judicial Annotations	—	−.002 (.034)	−.164** (.080)
Liberal Justices * Judicial Annotations Interaction	— (.051)	−.045 (.106)	.319***
Statutory Detail	.009 (.028)	.105*** (.029)	.218** (.085)
Liberal Justices	−.718*** (.271)	.808* (.473)	−1.253 (1.346)
Statutory Detail * Liberal Justices Interaction	.065 (.042)	−.086** (.041)	−.068 (.108)
Ideological Intensity	.148*** (.020)	.148*** (.021)	.171*** (.043)
Judicial Review	.098* (.055)	.164*** (.62)	.092 (.155)
Lower Court Congruence	−.461*** (.053)	−.481*** (.057)	−.864*** (.117)
Minimum Winning Coalition	.568*** (.071)	.528*** (.074)	.517*** (.160)
Constant	.352 (.184)	−.734 (.327)	−1.118 (1.022)
N	2619	2325	607
Log Likelihood	−1584.549	−1398.634	−331.747
LR/Wald Test	202.43	220.90	115.54
Probability > χ	.000	.000	.000
Pseudo R^2	.068	.073	.148
Null Model	64.8%	64.8%	66.0%
Correctly Predicted	67.8%	67.5%	70.8%
Reduction of Error	8.4%	7.8%	14.4%

Dependent Variable: unconstrained or sincere vote (1), constrained vote (0)
Values represent parameter estimates with robust standard errors in parentheses (clustered by individual justice)
* p < .10   ** p < .05   *** p < .01

draw from this analysis is that the addition of variables measuring the temporal context does not affect judicial behavior.

Yet, it is important to note that most statutes seldom appear before the Supreme Court. In fact, an examination of the frequency in which statutes appear before the Court reveals that the modal category is 1—the vast majority of statutes have only a single interpretation by the Supreme Court. Further examination reveals that the mean number of instances is 8.4 (with a standard deviation of 16.7). The statute most frequently litigated before the Supreme Court is the National Labor Relations Act (NLRA); specifically 29 U.S.C.S. 158(a)(3) which deals with unfair labor practices. This specific provision of the NLRA appears before the Supreme Court approximately 75 times during the time period under analysis.

Since the majority of statutes come before the Supreme Court only once, they have few or no annotations connected to them. Thus, it is somewhat unreasonable to include them in the analysis because there is very little temporal context available. Consequently, we construct a separate model (Model 3) that examines statutes frequently interpreted by the Supreme Court. In order for an observation to appear in this sample, the number of interpretations must be greater than the mean (8.4). Examining the results for this model (frequent statutes) reveals a very different pattern of behavior than Model 2 which includes all observations. The first noticeable difference involves the temporal context variables, which are both statistically significant. The variable *Judicial Annotations* has a negative coefficient, which indicates that as the length of annotations increases (measured as the natural log of its cumulative sum) conservative justices are significantly less likely to vote sincerely. In contrast, the *Liberal Justices * Judicial Annotations Interaction* possesses a positive coefficient indicating the liberal justices are more likely to cast sincere votes as annotations increase.

These results only partially support our hypothesis that the annotations would lead to higher probabilities of sincere voting, regardless of whether justices are liberal or conservative. We find support in the former case, but not the latter. Yet, what is most remarkable about the empirical evidence is that in some cases annotations counteract the effects of statutory language. Examining Model 3 reveals that the variable *Statutory Detail* remains significant and positive—this continues to support the statutory facilitation hypothesis we outline in Chapter 2. As congressional criminal statutes become longer, conservative justices are significantly more likely to vote sincerely. These results remain consistent from the original specification (Model 1) through the pooled data in Model 2 to the smaller sample of frequently litigated statutes in Model 3.

Based on the results for criminal statutes we also re-estimate one additional analysis from Chapter 4: non-civil rights statutes. These results are included in Table 6.2. The first column of this table (under Model 4) contains the results from the original specification outlined in Chapter 4 (for comparison purposes). Model 5 (listed in the second column) contains results for the entire set of non-civil rights statutes. Immediately noticeable is that our two new variables measuring temporal context are not statistically significant. Also, the remaining portions of Model 5 match (in terms of directionality of coefficients and their statistical significance) the original specification. Had we limited the analysis to the pooled set of non-civil rights statutes our conclusion would be that temporal context does not influence the voting behavior of Supreme Court justices.

However, similar to criminal statutes, non-civil rights statutes most often appear before the Supreme Court only once (i.e., the modal category is 1). Consequently, we estimate Model 6 for those statutes that appear frequently before the justices. Turning to these results we notice a completely different pattern. The variable *Judicial Annotations* is significant and negative; indicating the longer judicial annotations decrease the likelihood that conservative justices will vote sincerely. In contrast, the *Liberal Justices * Judicial Annotations Interaction* is significant and positive; indicating that longer judicial annotations increase the likelihood of liberal justices casting sincere votes. What is also remarkable about Model 6 (similar to what we observe in Model 3 for criminal statutes) is that the effects of annotations seem to countermand the influence of congressional statutes. The latter variables remain statistically significant and retain the same directionality of influence as the original specification. Thus, the variable *Statutory Detail* is positive; indicating that longer congressional statutes facilitate the sincere voting of conservative justices. But, the *Statutory Detail * Liberal Justices Interaction* remains negative; indicating the longer statutes constrain liberal justices from casting sincere votes.

To better understand the substantive impact of judicial annotations, in Figure 6.6 we graph their effects for both conservative (represented by the solid line) and liberal (represented by the dotted

Table 6.2. The Interplay of Statutes and Annotations in Non–Civil Rights Cases

	Model 4 Original	Model 5 Pooled Data	Model 6 Frequent Statutes
Judicial Annotations	—	-.016 (.053)	-.669** (.201)
Liberal Justices * Judicial Annotations Interaction	—	.104 (.082)	.526* (.269)
Statutory Detail	.131*** (.033)	.147*** (.037)	1.317*** (.307)
Liberal Justices	2.665*** (.372)	2.954*** (.543)	15.942*** (4.034)
Statutory Detail * Judicial Justices Interaction	-.409*** (.054)	-.347*** (.055)	-1.614*** (.419)
Ideological Intensity	.151*** (.031)	.164*** (.034)	.140** (.064)
Judicial Review	.078 (.080)	.070 (.098)	.211 (.397)
Lower Court Congruence	-.325*** (.082)	-.339*** (.092)	.039*** (.227)
Minimum Winning Coalition	.547*** (.099)	.455*** (.105)	.368 (.248)
Constant	-.689 (.243)	-1.286 (.396)	-11.814 (2.798)
N	1176	944	267
Log Likelihood	-681.652	-560.183	-144.244
LR/Wald Test	124.93	106.41	65.67
Probability > χ	.000	.000	.000
Pseudo R^2	.098	.087	.185
Null Model	65.7%	64.5%	62.1%
Correctly Predicted	71.1%	70.2%	75.6%
Reduction of Error	15.6%	15.9%	35.7%

Dependent Variable: unconstrained or sincere vote (1), constrained vote (0)
Values represent parameter estimates with robust standard errors in parentheses (clustered by individual justice)
* p < .10   ** p < .05   *** p < .01

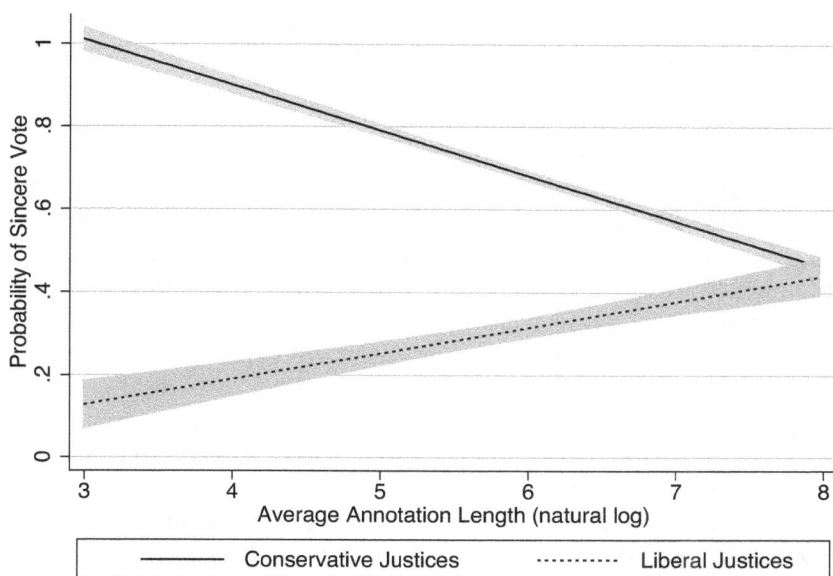

Figure 6.6. Impact of Judical Annotations on Sincere Voting.

line) justices. It is important to understand that these effects are calculated while holding the influence of congressional statutes and
ideology constant. What is immediately apparent from this figure—
beyond the contrasting slopes of the lines—is the differential impact
of judicial annotations on the justices. Conservative justices seem
substantially more prone to the influence of annotations than liberals. Across the range of the X-axis, the probability of conservative
justices voting sincerely decreases by approximately 55 percentage
points. In contrast the probability of liberal justices casting sincere
votes increases by approximately 30 percentage points. Consequently,
conservative justices are affected by judicial annotations significantly
more than their liberal colleagues, by an almost two-to-one margin.

Corollary Analysis of Statutes and Unanimous Decisions

In Chapter 4 we conduct a corollary analysis focused on the relation between congressional statutes and the proportion of unanimous

decisions rendered by the Supreme Court. Figure 6.7 reproduces the graph from Chapter 4 highlighting this relationship. You will recall we conclude that longer congressional statutes (as measured by the natural log of their word count) substantially increase the proportion of unanimous decisions (by almost 10 percent).

In this section we examine the impact of judicial annotations on the likelihood of unanimous decisions. Figure 6.8 displays this relationship based on non-civil rights cases (similar effects exist for other issue areas). Examining this graph reveals that more judicial annotations attached to statutes (as represented by the natural log of their cumulative sum) substantially decreases the likelihood of a unanimous decision by the Supreme Court (holding both statute length and ideology constant). Across the range of the X-axis, as annotations become longer the likelihood of a unanimous decision decreases by approximately 65 percent.

If one considers the effects of congressional statutes on unanimous decisions (displayed in Figure 6.7) in tandem with the results

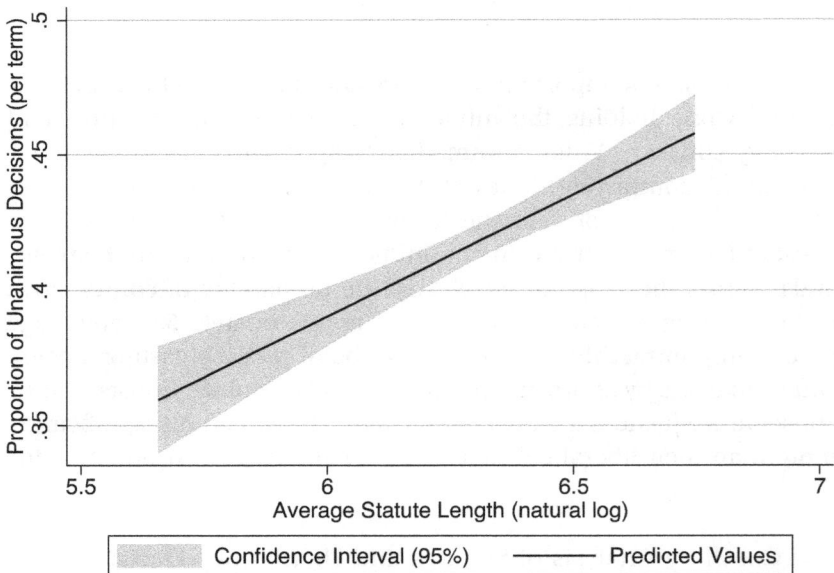

Figure 6.7. Influence of Statute Length on Unanimous Decisions.

of annotations (from Figure 6.8) a remarkable pattern emerges. Recall that the majority of congressional statutes come before the Supreme Court only once. Thus, for the bulk of the Court's statutory interpretation, the length of the law affects the likelihood of unanimous decisions by the justices. That is, more detailed statutes passed by Congress lead directly to more unanimous decisions by the Supreme Court. However, as statutes receive additional interpretations by judges, these interpretations (officially recorded as judicial annotations) substantially decrease the number of unanimous decisions. Stated another way increased judicial annotations lead to a growing lack of consensus among the justices.

Conclusions

In this chapter we depart slightly from previous chapters and examine a complementary influence to legislative statutes—the judicial anno-

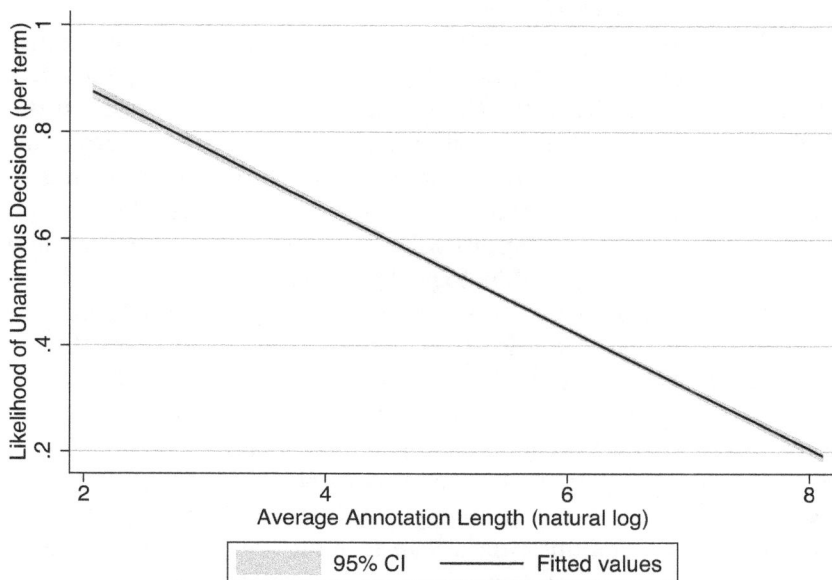

Figure 6.8. Influence of Judicial Annotations on Unanimous Decisions.

tations that become part of the official record. As we indicate earlier, our previous analyses operate on a purely cross-sectional level; ignoring the sequential nature of the struggle between Congress and the judiciary (in particular, the U.S. Supreme Court) over the establishment of law. In other words, we measure how disagreements among agents impact subsequent voting decisions. This chapter therefore focuses explicitly on the temporal aspect as it integrates both ideological and legal factors into a single model of judicial behavior. Because we specifically examine the temporal nature in which the law is interpreted, revised, and reinterpreted over time, the analyses presented here offer a more dynamic measure of the influences on judicial behavior.

To explore this more dynamic relationship, we examine the judicial annotations attached to congressional statutes after judges interpret those laws. As we explain, these annotations serve as a measure of judicial opinion pertaining to a specific congressional statute (i.e., statutory interpretation), often recorded by lower court judges (not necessarily by the Supreme Court). Since we expect the judicial annotations to include a variety of opinions, expressing both liberal and conservative views, we expect that the justices will have greater flexibility to base decisions on their individual ideological preferences. Stated another way, if a liberal justice is constrained by the plain meaning of the law (i.e., the Congressional statute), increases in the judicial annotations over time should provide that justice with additional flexibility and legal rationale to vote according to the tenets of the attitudinal model. Based on this argument, we hypothesize that increases in judicial annotations will allow the justices more flexibility to vote according to their ideological preferences.

The empirical results presented in this chapter partially support this contention, but only for frequently interpreted statutes. If one examines all statutes, there is no apparent effect for judicial annotations. However, most statutes appear before the Supreme Court only once, and consequently have few or no annotations attached. When one examines statutes that frequently appear before the Supreme Court, a different picture emerges. While we hypothesized that increases in annotations would lead to more sincere voting regardless of the ideological preferences of justices, what we observe is that annotations operate in a countervailing way. Thus, if justices are constrained by the language of the congressional statute, the annotations facilitate sincere voting. Conversely, if the sincere voting of justices is facilitated by congressional statutes, then the annotations serve to constrain this behavior.

Moreover, increases in judicial annotations lead to a substantial decrease in consensus among the justices—as observed by a decline in the likelihood of unanimous decisions. Again, this effect countermands congressional statutes, which increase the probability of unanimous decisions. Therefore it is apparent, in numerous ways, that judicial annotations serve to temper or contradict statutory influences among the justices.

Toward a New Paradigm

We began this book by asking a relatively simple question: From where does the law emerge? This question may be relatively simple, yet the answer is extremely complex and quite interesting. Thanks to the overlapping provisions provided by the U.S. Constitution, both the legislative and judicial branches of government can legitimately claim authority over the law. According to Article I, Congress has the authority to write statutes and Article III provides the courts with the authority to interpret those statutes.

Consequently, defining the lawmaking responsibilities of the legislative and judicial branches involves "a highly dynamic process sometimes overlooked" by many scholars of these institutions (Campbell and Stack 2001, xiii). Fisher (2001, 21) notes that "although it is conventional to view the judiciary—and especially the Supreme Court—as the ultimate and final arbiter of constitutional law, numerous examples over two centuries suggest a more dynamic and less hierarchical model." This dynamic process is also observed by Paschal (1992) when he notes that there is a "continuing colloquy" between the legislative and judicial branches over the meaning of the law. This ongoing dialogue raises important questions for scholars of the judiciary. To what extent do legal factors (such as legislative statutes) influence the behavior of judges and justices?

On one side of this debate are advocates of the "attitudinal model" who argue that judges are motivated primarily by their personal ideological policy preferences (Segal and Spaeth 1993, 2002). On the other side are legal advocates, who contend that the law is of paramount importance (Posner 2001). While numerous analyses exist which empirically demonstrate the influence of ideology, a similar pattern has not emerged for the quantitative analysis of legal influences. Though qualitative research reinforces the conventional wisdom about the influence of law, "the real question is not whether such behavior exists at all, but whether it exists at systematic and substantively meaningful levels" (Spaeth and Segal 1999, 7). Unfortunately, previous quantitative research of legal influences is plagued by inadequate measures. Our book addresses this inadequacy by developing an empirical measure of statutory influence, and testing the measure across decisions in state and federal courts.

To date, the empirical literature on congressional influence over the courts has focused primarily on the nomination process or congressional overrides of judicial decisions. However, these two aspects involve only a small fraction of the interactions between the two branches. Most exchanges between Congress and the judiciary occur after confirmation of judges and before attempts at overrides; namely, over the interpretation of statutes by courts. Yet, statutes have received relatively little attention in the empirical judicial literature, mostly because only rough measures (such as dummy variables) have been available to test their impact. This is unfortunate since, theoretically, statutes are extremely important because *they represent the primary opportunity legislatures have to ensure that those individuals who interpret or implement the law (e.g., judges and bureaucrats) will follow their preferences.* Hence, in those cases where lawmakers have clear policy preferences they can write legislation that encourages judges to strictly interpret the plain meaning of the law, a goal consistent with the legal model of judicial decision making. If legislatures do not write clear legislation, then it leaves open the possibility that judges will make decisions based on their own policy preferences in accord with the tenets of the attitudinal model. Consequently, an important empirical question remains unresolved—*To what extent do legislative statutes exert an influence on judicial behavior?*

To address this question we offer a new theoretical explanation for judicial behavior—called the *model of contingent discretion.* In this model, we posit that judicial decision making is contingent on the level of discretion afforded by the law. Consequently, we expect to observe judges voting according to their ideological preferences when they interpret vague or ambiguous statutes that provide high levels of discretion. Conversely, when courts encounter statutes that prescribe more detailed outcomes, and therefore reduce the level of discretion, then we expect the ability of judges to decide cases attitudinally will be constrained. Yet, it is important to note that not all judges will experience these potential constraining effects at the same time—even when some judges are constrained from voting ideologically, the law can facilitate the expression of ideological voting among others. Thus, the contingent effect can operate in two ways—it can constrain judges from voting according to their ideological preferences or it can facilitate the influence of ideology.

Summary of Empirical Evidence

Throughout the previous four chapters we present several parts of a puzzle and both qualitative and empirical evidence supporting the theoretical claims by our *model of contingent discretion*. Allow us to briefly summarize the findings. Consistent with the tenets of principal-agent theory and the notion of the law as a "contract" between principals and agents, our first and most fundamental finding is that legislative statutes systematically influence judicial behavior. Examining statute length is a legitimate strategy for developing an empirical measure of this influence. In repeated analyses our measure of statutory influence, and the hypothesized interaction terms with specific ideological groups, significantly predicts the likelihood of sincere voting. Whether one examines judges on the Courts of Appeals, state supreme courts, or justices of the U.S. Supreme Court the same conclusion appears—longer legislative statutes constrain some judges from voting sincerely, while simultaneously facilitating the ideological voting of other judges. Moreover, this result remains theoretically explicable, predictable, and occurs systematically, regardless of whether one examines statutes passed by the U.S. Congress or laws passed by individual state legislatures. Thus, these combined findings provide strong support for the external validity of our measure of statutory language.

Yet, the story does not end there because the presence of additional judicial annotations can also serve to countermand the effects of legislative statutes. For those statutes receiving frequent adjudication (especially by the U.S. Supreme Court) the presence of judicial annotations serves as a countervailing influence. Thus, if justices are constrained by the language of the congressional statute, the annotations facilitate sincere voting. Conversely, if the sincere voting of justices is facilitated by congressional statutes, then the annotations serve to constrain this behavior.

Consequently, we demonstrate repeatedly that two important legal factors (statutory detail and judicial annotations) systematically impact judicial behavior. The implications of these results reveal that empirical models that do not incorporate legal measures are likely underspecified and biased. Furthermore, theoretical arguments that depend solely on ideological or attitudinal influences, or that posit legal factors operate in only one direction, are simply not sufficiently robust. Our model of contingent discretion demonstrates a vibrant and dynamic interaction between ideology and law, and provides clarity for how judges balance their ideological proclivities with their duty to interpret the plain meaning of the law.

In addition to these primary results, there are several secondary results that help illustrate the complex and dynamic relationship between statutory influence and judicial behavior. For example, we note that adjudication of detailed statutes leads to a significant increase in the likelihood of unanimous decisions by the Supreme Court. This is an important discovery because it helps to explain *why* the Supreme Court renders unanimous decisions—a phenomenon not accounted for by the attitudinal model. The typical attitudinal analysis either completely excludes unanimous decisions, or substantially downplays their importance—claiming that cases resulting in unanimity represent non-salient often mundane areas of the law. Our results indicate that unanimous decisions are significantly influenced by the presence of detailed legislative statutes. Thus, as the law becomes more precise the judges adjudicating that law increasingly reach consensus about its meaning. Coincidentally, similar to the contradictory influence judicial annotations present for the likelihood of sincere voting, they also substantially decrease the likelihood of unanimous decisions on the Supreme Court. Consequently, while detailed statutes substantially increase the number of unanimous decisions, if those statutes have been frequently adjudicated before the Supreme Court the additional annotations significantly decrease the likelihood of unanimity.

Second, our results pertaining to state supreme courts identify an important corollary concerning statute length and judicial elections. The empirical evidence in Chapter 5 indicates that states with direct and complete control over the composition of their supreme courts (i.e., through judicial appointments) are significantly more likely to pass vague and ambiguous statutes. However, as state legislatures lose control over the makeup of their courts—as they move to retention elections and then to partisan/non-partisan direct elections—they respond by passing more detailed legislation (which in turn significantly affect judicial behavior). This finding highlights an important intervening variable that has heretofore been excluded in existing research. The scholarly consensus agrees that state court judges facing electoral pressures are more likely to deviate from voting according to their ideological preferences. Our corollary analysis suggests that future research should explore the potentially mediating effects of legislation on the impact of electoral pressures. It is possible that judges in states with judicial elections are not simply encountering direct electoral pressure as the previous research indicates. Rather, these judges may face competing pressures—from both the electorate and from the state legislature that is attempting to make elected supreme court judges more accountable to the legislative branch.

These findings support the validity of our measure, showing that it has broader influence than merely those we initially anticipated or hypothesized. They are further evidence that factors relevant to the model of contingent discretion exert other, predictable secondary effects on judicial decision making. While better, more sophisticated measures of statutory language may be developed in the future, in the short term our measure has passed a series of important validity tests.

Theoretical and Substantive Implications

It is quite remarkable that these primary empirical results remain consistent across judicial institutions (i.e., appeals courts, state courts, and Supreme Court) and legislative type (i.e., federal and state legislatures). This general conclusion is important because many previous studies of the legal model have not been able to provide empirical support for legal influences (especially across multiple institutions). As we argue earlier, continuous and more dynamic measures of legal factors are required to test accurately and rigorously the precise relationship between these aspects and ideological preferences.

Given this ability to better measure the influence of certain legal factors, our results suggest an important new theoretical direction for conceptualizing the attitudinal and legal models. To illustrate this new direction, in Figure 7.1 we offer an initial depiction of judicial behavior under these multiple influences. In this figure, X_1 represents a judge's ideal point and the solid arc represents the range of his or her ideological preferences. According to a purist interpretation of the attitudinal model any vote within the solid arc is considered consistent with ideological voting (what we label sincere voting in our analyses), though the judge ultimately prefers legal policy set as close to his or her ideal point as possible. Our model of contingent discretion indicates that detailed statutory provisions (represented by the dashed line) can facilitate sincere voting by allowing the judge to vote closer to his or her ideal point (and presumably use the language of the statute as justification for this vote). This result occurs when the statute generally prescribes outcomes ideologically congruent with the judge's ideology (as in Figure 7.1).[1]

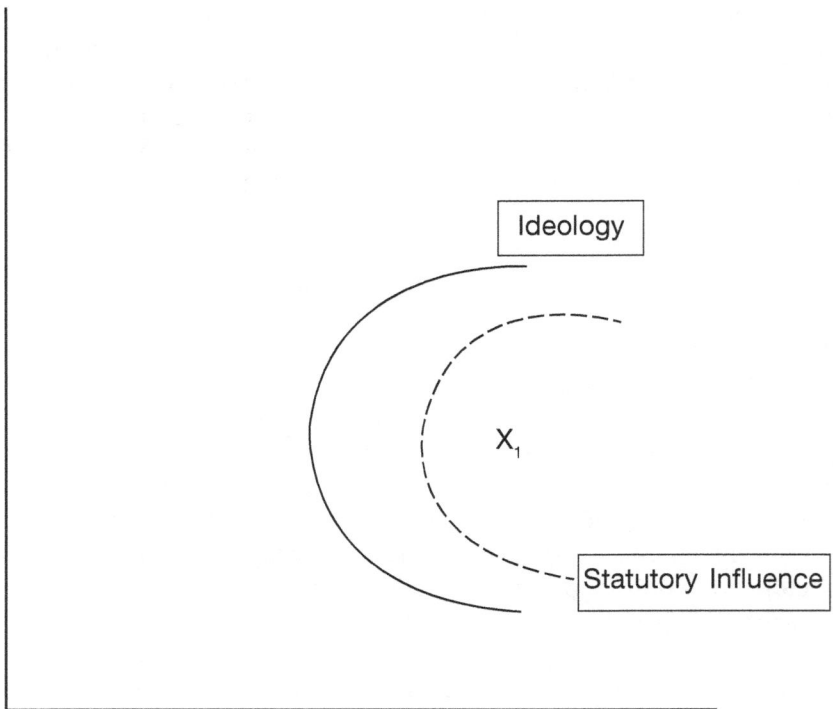

Figure 7.1. Individual Decision Making Under Multiple Influence Scenario A

Yet, when detailed statutes prescribe outcomes opposite a judge's ideological preferences (as depicted in Figure 7.2), our model demonstrates that a constraining influence emerges. In Figure 7.2 the judge's ideological preferences (represented by the solid arc) are contrary to the statutory language (represented by the dashed arc). According to a purist interpretation of the attitudinal model, we should expect to see a vote either at or near X_1 because no other influence matters beyond personal ideological preferences. However, our results repeatedly demonstrate that the presence of detailed statutory language can constrain judges from voting ideologically. Consequently, our model predicts that the judge will vote at X_2—in contrast to his or her ideological preference.

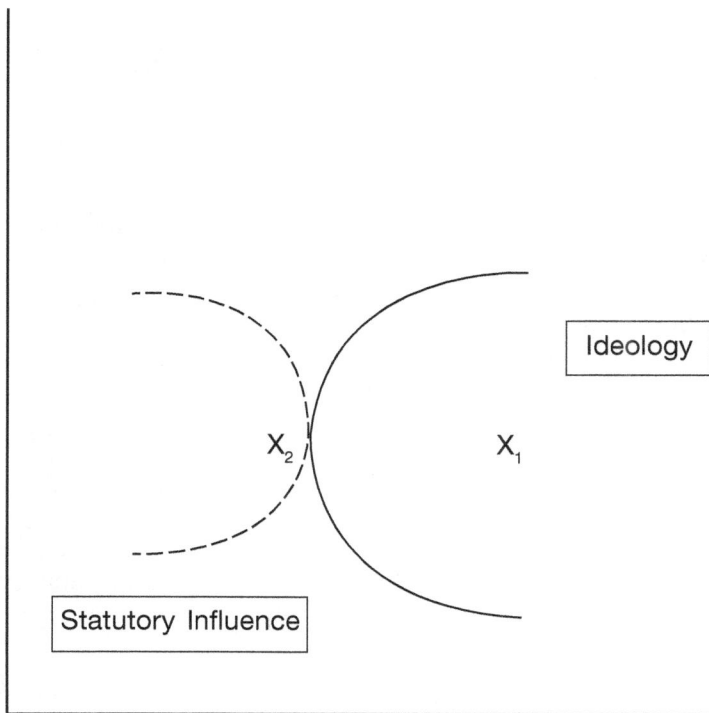

Figure 7.2. Individual Decision Making Under Multiple Influence Scenario B

But we must also be able to account for the influence of judicial annotations among statutes that receive frequent interpretations by the courts. If we reexamine the scenario (from Figure 7.1) in which the statutory language reflects the judge's ideological preferences and then factor in judicial annotations, we see a different pattern of behavior emerge—represented by Figure 7.3. In this figure, though the judge prefers to vote at X_1 and this is reinforced by the language of the legislative statute, the judicial annotations may nonetheless dictate a vote at X_2. Conversely, in situations where the statutory language contradicts a judge's ideological preferences—such as the scenario depicted in Figure 7.4—the judicial annotations may provide an opportunity to cast a sincere vote. As Figure 7.4 indicates, while a judge may prefer an outcome at X_1 he or she is constrained from voting sincerely because of the statute; thus forcing the judge to vote

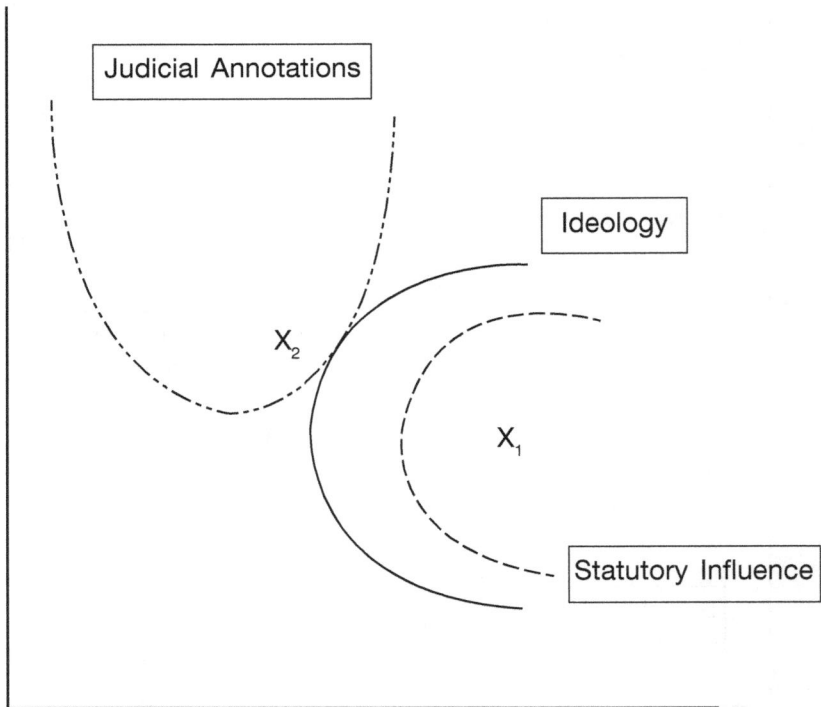

Figure 7.3. Individual Decision Making Under Multiple Influence Scenario C

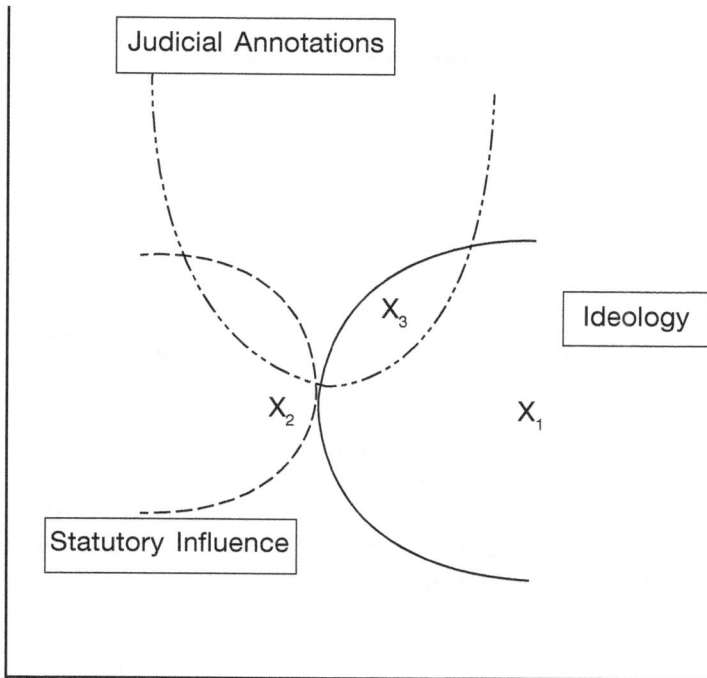

Figure 7.4. Individual Decision Making Under Multiple Influence Scenario D

at X_2. Yet, for those statutes frequently adjudicated by the courts that possess numerous judicial annotations, the annotations may allow the judge to vote at X_3, within the range of his or her sincere preferences.

What does all of this mean for the collective voting of courts? Again our model of contingent discretion offers an innovative refinement to the attitudinal model by incorporating specific legal factors into the decision calculus. To see how these multiple influences affect the collective decision making process of courts, let us begin with an illustration of the attitudinal model in its purest form (see Figure 7.5). Here we offer a hypothetical court with three judges (J_1, J_2, and J_3) who are arrayed in a unidimensional space according to their ideological preferences. If we locate a case in this space at X_1 and use the tenets of the attitudinal model, we can predict a 2–1 vote with judges J_2 and J_3 joining together. Additionally, we can likely expect a policy outcome at J_2's ideal point. This leaves J_1 as a dissenting judge.

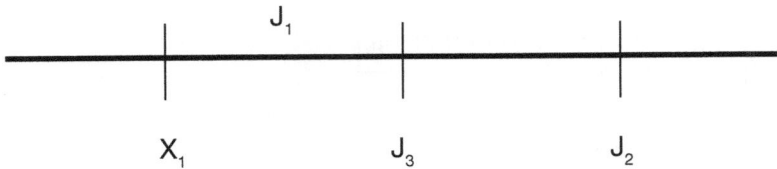

Figure 7.5. Ideological Decision Making.

If, however, we incorporate our model of contingent discretion and include the relevant statutory language (as illustrated in Figure 7.6) a different conclusion emerges. Note, the same array of judges and their ideal points (J_1, J_2, and J_3), and the same set of case facts (X_1) are in force. Thus, the attitudinal model would continue to predict a 2–1 vote with the policy outcome set at J_2's ideal point. However, if the legislative statute contains relatively detailed language (represented by the narrow ellipse) then we expect a unanimous decision (a result for which the attitudinal model fails to account), or a 2–1 vote in the opposite direction, with the policy outcome set either at or near J_1's ideal point.

For the vast majority of legislative statutes, Figure 7.6 accurately illustrates the multiple influences facing judges (at least for the justices of the Supreme Court, as our results from Chapter 6 indicate). Yet, there are some statutes that receive frequent interpretations by courts at all levels. These interpretations often produce additional annotations that become part of the "official record" pertaining to that statute. As these judicial annotations increase, they provide an additional influence for judges. Figure 7.7 illustrates this new dynam-

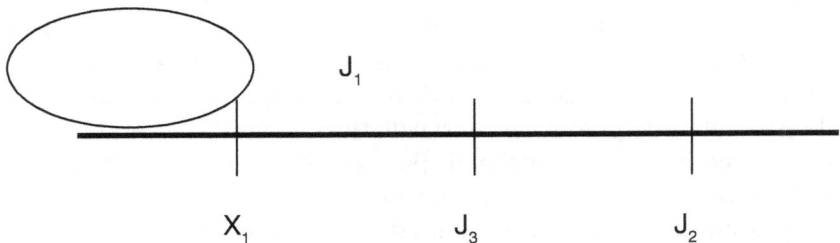

Figure 7.6. Ideological Decision Making with Statutory Influences.

ic—judges are arrayed according to their ideal points (J_1, J_2, and J_3) and the statutory details are depicted by the solid ellipse. The judicial annotations are therefore represented by the dashed ellipse. Here we would expect either a 2-1 vote (with J_2 and J_3 voting together) or possibly a unanimous decision (with J_1 joining) and a policy outcome at or near J_2's ideal point.

In sum, our model offers a new and more dynamic paradigm to conceptualize the influences of law and ideology on judicial behavior. Rather than continue to treat these influences as mutually exclusive (and contradictory), scholars should view them as dynamic and interactive. If everything else is held equal, the justices will render decisions according to their ideological preferences. Yet, all things are not equal and the presence of legal factors, such as statutory language, limits the ability of some justices to rule ideologically. Additionally, it is important to recognize that not all justices are affected in the same manner. Thus, while some justices experience significant constraint from the presence of detailed statutory language, others experience support for their ideological positions and are more likely to vote according to those preferences. This conclusion is vitally important for principal-agents models because they generally assume that all agents react to the principal in the same manner. Our findings demonstrate that they do not. Once one delves into the "black box" it is apparent that the same stimuli from the principal (i.e., statutes from Congress or state legislatures) can affect judges in different ways. Whereas one agent is constrained, another's behavior is facilitated or enhanced. These findings suggest that scholars need to develop

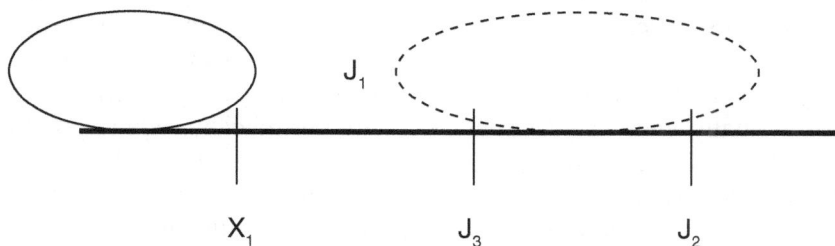

Figure 7.7. Ideological Decision Making with Statutory and Temporal Influences.

more robust and dynamic models of principal-agent interactions in other settings.

Importantly, based on this dynamic interaction between political attitudes and statutory influences, one should not think of the legal model only as a set of forces that operates in contrast to ideological attitudes. Legal factors can simultaneously constrain and facilitate judicial behavior. Consequently a more complete model of judicial decision making should include measures of both political preferences and statutory influences, and account for the differential impact of these measures.

Important Caveats

While the empirical results for our model of contingent discretion present new and interesting ways to conceptualize the myriad of influences affecting judicial behavior, there are three important caveats for which we would be remiss in not discussing. The first involves the potential impact of precedent. Our model does not directly account for, nor measure, precedent. However, the inclusion of a measure tracking judicial annotations allows us to control for the judicial history related to specific statutes. While this is not an application of *stare decisis*, it does allow for additional judicial influences related to statutory interpretation. Yet, we concede that a more direct measure of precedent would be useful. Such efforts will eventually move us all toward a more complete and robust model of judicial behavior.

The second important caveat involves the measure of statutory language that we incorporate in these models. As we admit in Chapter 2, our analysis does not focus on the substantive meaning of any particular statute. That is, we do not control for, nor measure, the substantive policies of statutes. We recognize that the substantive meaning of the law is more closely related to the concept of plain meaning. Additionally, we recognize that courts are periodically called upon to adjudicate the substantive meaning of single words or small phrases. Unfortunately, conducting large-N empirical studies on the substantive meaning of statutes is extremely difficult. While we believe our proxy measure concerning discretion is a reasonable and legitimate focus of study, hopefully the continued advances in content-analysis software will someday allow for a systematic analysis on the substantive meaning of statutes.

Finally, we recognize that the Executive Branch (including federal agencies) plays an important role in the decision calculus of judges. Scigliano (1971, vii) argues that the presidency and the Supreme Court "were intended by the framers of the Constitution to act, for certain purposes, as an informal and limited alliance against Congress. . . ." Additionally, several scholars (e.g., Lindquist, Yalof, and Clark 2000; Segal, Timpone, and Howard 2000) demonstrate the influence exerted on courts by the Executive, mostly through the appointment process. We therefore invite future research to further explore the dynamic relationships (especially from a principal-agent perspective) among all three branches of government.

Despite these three caveats, we believe our measure of statutory detail possesses important advantages. First, its creation is extremely transparent (i.e., a simple word count) and can be used in a wide variety of situations and institutional contexts. Second, the connection between statute length and discretion is plausible from a theoretical perspective. Thus, there is a direct connection between our theoretical argument and the empirical measure used to test that argument (a connection that is often lacking in research). Finally, the empirical results demonstrate the measure's robustness and validity.

Remaining Questions

As is often the case with empirical research, the results obtained and conclusions drawn raise additional questions. This is certainly true with the conclusions generated from our analyses on the effects of statutory language for judicial behavior. In particular we identify two questions for which further research is needed. The first involves the motivations of legislatures when they pass statutes. Our results demonstrate that the language of these statutes substantially affects the discretion of judges at all levels of the judiciary. Thus, the obvious "follow up" question is whether legislatures intentionally seek to affect judicial behavior or whether our results are coincidental. Stated another way, do legislatures pass statutes with the intent to affect judicial behavior? Moreover, if there is an identifiable "legislative intent" to the passage of laws, under what conditions does this intent manifest? We know that some statutes are deliberately vague and others contain more detailed language, but we are less clear about why this variation exists—especially if we assume that legislatures care about making good policy. Perhaps in some cases, legislatures merely wish to take positions on certain salient issues by passing legislation knowing (and perhaps even hoping) that courts will strike down these statutes. In other cases, legislatures pass statutes aimed at reversing decisions made by courts. Determining the conditions under which legislatures write detailed statutes is therefore an important consideration for future research.

The second question involves whether similar statutory effects exist in other countries. With the United States possessing arguably one of the most politicized judiciaries in the world, it is somewhat surprising to see empirical support for statutory language. Presumably judges in this country are most likely to operate according to the tenets of the attitudinal model. Yet, given the robustness of empirical evidence for statutory influence in the United States the next question should be whether similar patterns exist in other countries. And, in particular, what effects exist for civil law courts—such as those in mainland Europe? We would expect even more pronounced evidence to exist given the profound influence legislative statutes exert in civil law courts. However, it is also quite plausible that the prominence of legislatures means that longer statutes are not as necessary to determine outcomes. Thus, European legislatures may be able to effectively influence courts using shorter (and more ambiguous) legislation.

Appendix

Word Count of Federal Statutes

Code	Section §	Word Count	Year Passed
2	192	112	1938
2	431	3792	1972
2	437	152	1972
4	105	141	1947
4	111	266	1966
5	301	61	1966
5	501	41	1966
5	504	1472	1980
5	551	651	1966
5	552	4922	1966
5	553	387	1966
5	554	555	1966
5	556	676	1966
5	559	141	1966
5	701	190	1966
5	702	213	1966
5	704	112	1966
5	706	204	1966
5	1101	45	1966
5	2302	1837	1978
5	5596	813	1967
5	7101	195	1978
5	7102	123	1978
5	7114	705	1978
5	7117	952	1978
5	7501	78	1978
5	7511	616	1978
5	7703	583	1978
5	8101	1517	1966
5	8102	363	1966
5	8116	631	1966
5	8128	136	1966
5	8132	259	1966

Code	Section §	Word Count	Year Passed
5	8337	1580	1966
7	6	1457	1922
7	21	5398	1922
7	136	4199	1947
7	241	291	1916
7	291	189	1922
7	601	58	1933
7	602	428	1933
7	1921	44	1961
7	1925	239	1961
7	1961	1241	1961
7	2011	146	1964
7	2012	3023	1964
7	2015	7607	1964
7	2543	178	1970
7	7256	508	1996
8	1101	11784	1952
8	1105	545	1952
8	1151	1678	1952
8	1152	1958	1952
8	1155	49	1952
8	1158	2403	1952
8	1160	3226	1952
8	1182	24420	1952
8	1185	567	1952
8	1189	1727	1952
8	1225	2305	1952
8	1226	748	1952
8	1227	3136	1952
8	1231	4712	1952
8	1252	3112	1952
8	1253	830	1952
8	1255	3276	1952
8	1259	172	1952
8	1282	421	1952
8	1324	1624	1952
8	1326	648	1952
8	1357	1933	1952
8	1362	51	1952
8	1401	572	1952
8	1409	314	1952
8	1421	920	1952
8	1427	1219	1952
8	1440	860	1952

Code	Section §	Word Count	Year Passed
8	1451	1285	1952
8	1453	187	1952
8	1481	559	1952
8	1612	2692	1996
9	1	131	1947
9	2	84	1947
9	3	101	1947
9	4	387	1947
9	10	252	1947
9	16	186	1988
9	201	27	1970
10	802	812	1956
10	820	143	1956
10	826	414	1956
10	856	23	1956
10	876	125	1956
10	890	94	1956
10	934	82	1956
10	1089	877	1976
10	1408	5122	1982
10	1431	672	1956
10	1552	856	1956
10	2462	725	1988
10	2489	300	1998
10	2687	623	1977
10	5031	198	1986
11	101	7948	1978
11	104	306	1978
11	105	424	1978
11	106	381	1978
11	108	364	1978
11	109	1294	1978
11	110	1921	1994
11	307	37	1986
11	323	32	1978
11	329	175	1978
11	330	759	1978
11	362	6876	1978
11	365	3919	1978
11	501	209	1978
11	502	1653	1978
11	503	1291	1978
11	505	583	1978
11	506	436	1978

Code	Section §	Word Count	Year Passed
11	507	1681	1978
11	510	202	1978
11	522	4059	1978
11	523	2112	1978
11	541	1997	1978
11	542	395	1978
11	544	353	1978
11	547	1429	1978
11	548	1235	1978
11	552	333	1978
11	553	439	1978
11	554	152	1978
11	701	154	1978
11	707	2699	1978
11	727	1237	1978
11	761	1867	1978
11	1107	125	1978
11	1109	88	1978
11	1111	281	1978
11	1112	970	1978
11	1123	848	1978
11	1129	1994	1978
11	1322	1081	1978
12	24	2947	1922
12	81	43	1927
12	84	1138	1906
12	85	335	1933
12	90	443	1901
12	92	193	1913
12	321	562	1913
12	355	241	1913
12	1464	16295	1933
12	1759	1635	1934
12	1812	947	1950
12	1818	12862	1950
12	1819	738	1950
12	1821	26308	1950
12	1823	7810	1950
12	1842	3044	1956
12	1864	487	1962
12	1972	2000	1970
12	2607	1039	1974
12	4010	630	1987
13	141	842	1954

Code	Section §	Word Count	Year Passed
14	89	361	1949
15	1	96	1890
15	2	82	1890
15	4	141	1890
15	7	54	1890
15	10	72	1894
15	13	875	1914
15	14	156	1914
15	15	538	1914
15	16	1728	1914
15	17	95	1914
15	18	623	1914
15	19	517	1914
15	21	2243	1914
15	26	187	1914
15	44	345	1914
15	45	3415	1914
15	46	1305	1914
15	77	629	1916
15	261	254	1918
15	381	432	1959
15	631	1896	1958
15	636	21536	1958
15	717	439	1938
15	771	798	1974
15	1011	52	1945
15	1012	159	1945
15	1051	1504	1946
15	1114	1591	1946
15	1116	1904	1946
15	1125	2088	1946
15	1331	114	1965
15	1334	73	1965
15	1601	230	1968
15	1602	2049	1968
15	1604	888	1968
15	1635	1314	1968
15	1666	1087	1968
15	1681	199	1968
15	1692	187	1968
15	2301	712	1975
15	3301	2124	1978
15	3611	174	1980
15	7102	276	1988

Code	Section §	Word Count	Year Passed
16	1	221	1916
16	551	189	1897
16	703	423	1918
16	796	1646	1920
16	797	1362	1920
16	800	303	1920
16	814	383	1920
16	817	345	1920
16	824	954	1920
16	825	453	1920
16	1247	646	1968
16	1331	103	1971
16	1456	2024	1966
16	1531	407	1973
16	1533	3842	1973
16	1536	4714	1973
16	1537	461	1973
16	1540	2902	1973
16	1600	408	1974
16	2611	41	1978
16	3120	397	1980
16	3372	810	1981
16	3821	458	1985
16	5954	1303	1998
17	101	3020	1976
17	102	148	1976
17	106	160	1976
17	107	180	1976
17	109	992	1976
17	301	575	1976
17	504	754	1976
17	505	58	1976
17	802	1943	2004
18	2	55	1948
18	3	106	1948
18	6	90	1948
18	13	478	1948
18	17	85	1984
18	111	177	1948
18	113	311	1948
18	152	399	1948
18	201	1068	1962
18	209	584	1962
18	228	502	1992

Code	Section §	Word Count	Year Passed
18	232	479	1968
18	241	173	1948
18	242	202	1948
18	247	499	1988
18	248	1181	1994
18	291	95	1948
18	401	76	1948
18	472	63	1948
18	474	545	1948
18	500	505	1948
18	505	116	1948
18	542	229	1948
18	594	109	1948
18	608	102	1986
18	610	108	1993
18	641	175	1948
18	656	324	1948
18	657	262	1948
18	658	128	1948
18	659	632	1948
18	665	279	1973
18	666	502	1984
18	700	223	1968
18	702	69	1948
18	751	349	1948
18	752	291	1948
18	793	1128	1948
18	842	2277	1970
18	844	1801	1970
18	871	237	1948
18	875	224	1948
18	891	405	1968
18	892	441	1968
18	894	274	1968
18	912	61	1948
18	921	2922	1968
18	922	8895	1968
18	924	3367	1968
18	925	1172	1968
18	982	1016	1986
18	1001	259	1948
18	1005	398	1948
18	1006	315	1948
18	1010	164	1948

Code	Section §	Word Count	Year Passed
18	1014	333	1948
18	1028	1784	1982
18	1029	1495	1984
18	1072	33	1948
18	1084	397	1961
18	1111	317	1948
18	1112	118	1948
18	1114	114	1948
18	1151	199	1948
18	1152	111	1948
18	1153	174	1948
18	1154	340	1948
18	1162	361	1953
18	1165	107	1960
18	1201	708	1948
18	1202	167	1948
18	1302	229	1948
18	1304	113	1948
18	1307	395	1975
18	1341	229	1948
18	1343	104	1952
18	1344	73	1984
18	1365	835	1983
18	1382	87	1948
18	1461	391	1948
18	1462	245	1948
18	1464	28	1948
18	1465	157	1955
18	1503	329	1948
18	1510	532	1967
18	1512	1171	1982
18	1621	159	1948
18	1623	395	1970
18	1693	33	1948
18	1701	35	1948
18	1702	100	1948
18	1708	211	1948
18	1715	266	1948
18	1791	546	1948
18	1905	225	1948
18	1951	292	1948
18	1952	300	1961
18	1955	517	1970
18	1956	3092	1986

Code	Section §	Word Count	Year Passed
18	1957	470	1989
18	1958	224	1984
18	1959	347	1984
18	1961	1204	1970
18	1962	341	1970
18	1963	2527	1970
18	1964	323	1970
18	1965	254	1970
18	2113	736	1948
18	2114	189	1948
18	2117	170	1948
18	2119	148	1992
18	2152	121	1948
18	2199	188	1948
18	2241	522	1986
18	2252	818	1978
18	2256	562	1978
18	2262	356	1994
18	2312	34	1948
18	2314	328	1948
18	2315	374	1948
18	2320	1020	1984
18	2385	321	1948
18	2421	64	1948
18	2510	1213	1968
18	2511	2382	1968
18	2515	75	1968
18	2516	1498	1968
18	2518	2924	1968
18	2520	716	1968
18	3005	159	1948
18	3006	25	1948
18	3013	249	1984
18	3061	218	1968
18	3109	58	1948
18	3141	94	1984
18	3142	2824	1984
18	3144	138	1984
18	3146	398	1984
18	3153	474	1975
18	3161	2483	1975
18	3162	600	1975
18	3182	163	1948
18	3184	304	1948

Code	Section §	Word Count	Year Passed
18	3237	248	1948
18	3238	110	1948
18	3243	84	1948
18	3282	179	1948
18	3481	58	1948
18	3486	1349	1996
18	3500	564	1957
18	3501	577	1968
18	3505	357	1984
18	3509	3759	1990
18	3551	267	1984
18	3553	1826	1984
18	3559	2061	1984
18	3561	219	1984
18	3563	1518	1984
18	3565	307	1984
18	3572	852	1984
18	3581	144	1984
18	3582	668	1984
18	3583	1752	1984
18	3584	203	1984
18	3585	132	1984
18	3591	472	1994
18	3601	64	1984
18	3603	460	1984
18	3626	2287	1994
18	3663	1151	1982
18	3664	1942	1982
18	3731	266	1948
18	3742	1352	1984
18	4007	50	1948
18	4042	944	1948
18	4083	54	1948
18	4102	509	1977
18	4126	371	1948
18	4241	661	1948
18	4244	556	1949
18	4246	1237	1949
18	5032	1334	1948
18	5037	1556	1948
18	6002	153	1970
19	1305	1494	1930
19	1526	886	1930
19	1581	726	1930

Code	Section §	Word Count	Year Passed
19	1607	268	1930
20	954	4100	1965
20	1001	363	1965
20	1070	177	1965
20	1072	5100	1965
20	1400	1373	1970
20	1401	3135	1970
20	1412	7568	1970
20	1415	6936	1970
20	1681	956	1972
20	4071	495	1984
20	7301	346	1965
21	321	4655	1938
21	331	1911	1938
21	333	2675	1938
21	334	2817	1938
21	346	234	1938
21	355	14971	1938
21	360	3789	1938
21	811	3307	1970
21	841	3260	1970
21	846	39	1970
21	848	4509	1970
21	851	772	1970
21	853	2901	1970
21	856	309	1970
21	860	811	1970
21	861	536	1970
21	862	953	1970
21	881	2013	1970
21	963	39	1970
22	288	225	1945
22	611	1342	1938
25	163	128	1919
25	396	199	1909
25	461	39	1934
25	472	68	1934
25	677	78	1954
25	1911	306	1978
25	2206	8944	1983
26	22	910	1954
26	23	1468	1996
26	41	5409	1981
26	48	1238	1962

Code	Section §	Word Count	Year Passed
26	56	4702	1986
26	57	1125	1986
26	61	158	1954
26	83	1159	1969
26	101	3185	1954
26	102	226	1954
26	103	148	1954
26	104	894	1954
26	108	3933	1954
26	112	774	1954
26	117	548	1954
26	119	973	1954
26	125	1208	1978
26	145	1178	1986
26	162	4605	1954
26	163	6968	1954
26	165	2436	1954
26	166	324	1954
26	167	2672	1954
26	170	11589	1954
26	172	4583	1954
26	174	718	1954
26	179	1746	1958
26	183	657	Not available
26	212	65	1954
26	213	1519	1954
26	272	122	1954
26	275	243	1964
26	301	694	1954
26	302	1562	1954
26	311	220	1954
26	316	510	1954
26	336	775	1986
26	337	495	1986
26	351	1643	1954
26	354	654	1954
26	356	810	1954
26	404	6186	1954
26	411	7695	1969
26	446	318	1954
26	448	1294	1986
26	453	3346	1980
26	456	980	1961
26	469	4753	1986

Code	Section §	Word Count	Year Passed
26	482	128	1954
26	501	9577	1954
26	511	500	1954
26	531	47	1954
26	561	102	1954
26	611	348	1954
26	642	1919	1954
26	703	1414	1954
26	752	194	1954
26	801	297	1984
26	811	637	1984
26	812	984	1984
26	846	2114	1986
26	902	1211	1954
26	936	9954	1976
26	1012	69	1954
26	1041	279	1984
26	1221	928	1954
26	1231	1110	1954
26	1402	4863	1954
26	1563	3347	1964
26	2002	12	1954
26	2010	218	1976
26	2031	1418	1954
26	2036	363	1954
26	2042	281	1954
26	2056	2757	1954
26	2057	2755	1997
26	2501	752	1954
26	3101	335	1954
26	3111	347	1954
26	3301	88	1954
26	3304	2861	1954
26	3401	1824	1954
26	3402	6501	1954
26	3405	1604	1982
26	4371	190	1954
26	4401	263	1954
26	4411	109	1954
26	4412	200	1954
26	4461	119	1986
26	4462	1312	1986
26	4971	901	1974
26	4975	4629	1974

Code	Section §	Word Count	Year Passed
26	5601	904	1958
26	5812	233	1968
26	5821	76	1968
26	5861	281	1968
26	6012	1364	1954
26	6013	2726	1954
26	6103	18601	1954
26	6303	134	1954
26	6321	65	1954
26	6323	4126	1954
26	6331	1984	1954
26	6332	795	1954
26	6501	3387	1954
26	6511	2830	1954
26	6512	1088	1954
26	6513	617	1954
26	6651	1203	1954
26	6672	1018	1954
26	6851	706	1954
26	6861	705	1954
26	7121	155	1954
26	7201	69	1954
26	7203	195	1954
26	7206	421	1954
26	7402	352	1954
26	7403	352	1954
26	7421	163	1954
26	7422	1681	1954
26	7454	259	1954
26	7482	1050	1954
26	7602	830	1954
26	7605	167	1954
26	7609	1823	1976
26	7805	755	1954
26	9011	225	1971
26	9701	989	1992
26	9706	1286	1992
27	205	2774	1935
28	46	415	1948
28	49	351	1978
28	129	134	1948
28	157	797	1984
28	293	61	1948
28	455	730	1948

Code	Section §	Word Count	Year Passed
28	473	845	1990
28	516	46	1966
28	593	1103	1978
28	621	237	1967
28	636	2287	1948
28	994	3001	1984
28	1251	81	1948
28	1253	54	1948
28	1254	101	1948
28	1257	135	1948
28	1291	101	1948
28	1292	975	1948
28	1294	115	1948
28	1295	885	1982
28	1330	142	1976
28	1331	22	1948
28	1332	1865	1948
28	1333	60	1948
28	1334	422	1948
28	1335	304	1948
28	1336	160	1948
28	1341	36	1948
28	1343	234	1948
28	1345	42	1948
28	1346	602	1948
28	1361	37	1962
28	1362	46	1966
28	1367	364	1990
28	1400	78	1948
28	1404	183	1948
28	1407	1005	1968
28	1408	131	1984
28	1441	864	1948
28	1442	275	1948
28	1446	770	1948
28	1447	283	1948
28	1491	565	1948
28	1500	77	1948
28	1602	117	1976
28	1604	52	1976
28	1605	1929	1976
28	1607	120	1976
28	1651	56	1948
28	1653	15	1948

Code	Section §	Word Count	Year Passed
28	1732	205	1948
28	1738	155	1948
28	1782	273	1948
28	1783	249	1948
28	1821	739	1948
28	1826	290	1970
28	1865	301	1948
28	1915	1038	1948
28	1920	129	1948
28	1961	323	1948
28	2072	98	1988
28	2106	63	1948
28	2107	246	1948
28	2201	166	1948
28	2202	32	1948
28	2241	676	1948
28	2244	832	1948
28	2253	211	1948
28	2254	833	1948
28	2255	642	1948
28	2283	41	1948
28	2341	152	1966
28	2401	130	1948
28	2409	131	1949
28	2410	1003	1948
28	2412	1781	1948
28	2463	47	1948
28	2465	525	1948
28	2501	142	1948
28	2671	218	1948
28	2674	253	1948
28	2675	252	1948
28	2676	46	1948
28	2679	986	1948
28	2680	613	1948
29	52	314	1914
29	101	68	1932
29	104	302	1932
29	106	68	1931
29	113	347	1932
29	141	201	1947
29	151	456	1935
29	152	889	1935
29	153	694	1935

Code	Section §	Word Count	Year Passed
29	157	90	1935
29	158	3048	1935
29	159	1126	1935
29	160	2657	1935
29	161	700	1935
29	164	287	1935
29	173	602	1947
29	178	211	1947
29	182	36	1947
29	185	362	1947
29	186	1973	1947
29	187	120	1947
29	203	2587	1938
29	206	1549	1938
29	207	4553	1938
29	211	433	1938
29	213	5355	1938
29	215	456	1938
29	216	1410	1938
29	254	562	1947
29	255	360	1947
29	259	279	1947
29	260	118	1947
29	401	392	1959
29	411	734	1959
29	412	79	1959
29	481	1105	1959
29	482	558	1959
29	501	517	1959
29	504	898	1959
29	621	183	1967
29	623	3270	1967
29	626	1279	1967
29	633	227	1967
29	651	541	1970
29	652	465	1970
29	654	86	1970
29	655	2451	1970
29	657	1371	1970
29	667	1204	1970
29	794	551	1973
29	1001	552	1974
29	1002	5177	1974
29	1055	3184	1974

Code	Section §	Word Count	Year Passed
29	1056	2992	1974
29	1101	1213	1974
29	1102	357	1974
29	1104	921	1974
29	1106	392	1974
29	1109	145	1974
29	1113	132	1974
29	1132	2829	1974
29	1133	87	1974
29	1140	153	1974
29	1144	1227	1974
29	1162	1094	1974
29	1301	1710	1974
29	1344	1740	1974
29	1347	201	1974
29	1381	178	1974
29	1399	1530	1974
29	1441	795	1948
29	1451	436	1974
29	1802	627	1983
29	1854	1155	1983
29	2101	650	1988
29	2102	580	1988
29	2601	361	1993
29	2611	753	1993
29	2614	938	1993
29	2615	168	1993
30	81	300	1909
30	813	2087	1969
30	901	156	1969
30	902	1218	1969
30	921	969	1969
30	932	1587	1969
30	1260	1525	1977
31	1304	394	1982
31	3124	213	1982
31	3701	739	1982
31	3713	151	1982
31	3729	675	1982
31	3730	2149	1982
31	5322	283	1982
33	403	174	1899
33	902	1379	1927
33	903	460	1927

Code	Section §	Word Count	Year Passed
33	904	109	1927
33	905	597	1927
33	906	311	1927
33	908	2733	1927
33	909	819	1927
33	920	89	1927
33	921	1034	1927
33	922	262	1927
33	933	1080	1927
33	941	1204	1927
33	1251	800	1948
33	1268	4134	1948
33	1285	3498	1948
33	1311	6526	1948
33	1319	4763	1948
33	1321	10981	1948
33	1341	1567	1948
33	1342	4640	1948
33	1344	3988	1948
33	1365	929	1948
33	1369	811	1948
35	102	427	1952
35	255	111	1952
35	271	1445	1952
37	401	615	1962
38	1151	578	1958
38	7252	138	1988
39	410	707	1970
40	3131	478	2002
41	351	615	1965
42	254	74	1944
42	300	440	1944
42	402	21603	1935
42	404	1454	1935
42	405	14447	1935
42	406	2491	1935
42	407	167	1935
42	408	1657	1935
42	416	6671	1935
42	418	6765	1935
42	421	3415	1935
42	423	5714	1935
42	503	4291	1935
42	602	1249	1935

Code	Section §	Word Count	Year Passed
42	606	298	1935
42	607	2586	1935
42	608	4787	1935
42	620	147	1935
42	651	98	1935
42	664	1537	1935
42	701	929	1935
42	1302	365	1935
42	1381	38	1935
42	1382	4802	1935
42	1395	74	1935
42	1396	123	1935
42	1437	534	1937
42	1971	2878	1957
42	1973	211	1965
42	1981	149	1991
42	1982	35	1866
42	1983	145	1979
42	1985	590	1861
42	1986	205	1981
42	1987	111	1982
42	1988	387	1976
42	1996	68	1978
42	1997	401	1980
42	2002	270	1954
42	2018	71	1946
42	2134	431	1946
42	2201	3749	1946
42	2210	8047	1946
42	2235	79	1946
42	2996	186	1964
42	3601	7247	1968
42	3604	1150	1968
42	3610	1985	1968
42	3612	2202	1968
42	4001	799	1968
42	4321	68	1970
42	4332	687	1970
42	5851	1704	1974
42	6903	1846	1965
42	6921	3190	1965
42	6926	1148	1965
42	6928	1771	1965
42	6972	1587	1965

Code	Section §	Word Count	Year Passed
42	7401	313	1955
42	7407	2881	1955
42	7409	725	1955
42	7410	5590	1955
42	7411	3279	1955
42	7412	22336	1955
42	7413	4574	1955
42	7414	1077	1955
42	7502	1430	1955
42	7545	14209	1955
42	7604	1499	1955
42	7607	3216	1955
42	9601	7247	1980
42	9607	8151	1980
42	10601	1238	1984
42	11046	1111	1986
42	11101	137	1986
42	11601	285	1988
42	12101	486	1990
42	12102	171	1990
42	12111	768	1990
42	12112	1123	1990
42	12114	745	1990
42	12131	133	1990
42	12132	48	1990
42	12181	797	1990
42	12182	1389	1990
42	12201	377	1990
42	12203	162	1990
42	12205	53	1990
42	13981	566	1994
43	423	160	1926
43	641	617	1894
43	666	271	1952
43	1301	671	1953
43	1312	193	1953
43	1313	223	1953
43	1331	1239	1953
43	1344	2207	1953
43	2101	56	1988
43	2105	280	1988
44	3303	181	1968
44	3501	388	1995
45	51	248	1908

Code	Section §	Word Count	Year Passed
45	151	679	1926
45	152	2052	1926
45	153	3692	1926
45	154	998	1926
45	156	173	1926
45	231	4333	1935
45	354	1398	1938
45	701	389	1974
45	1005	364	1980
46	8501	207	1983
46	10313	550	1983
46	12104	62	1983
46	31342	83	1988
47	153		1934
47	160	445	1934
47	203	571	1934
47	223	2171	1934
47	224	1333	1934
47	227	4655	1934
47	230	886	1934
47	251	2031	1934
47	253	379	1934
47	271	2688	1934
47	301	328	1934
47	304	52	1934
47	305	385	1934
47	308	583	1934
47	309	7289	1934
47	311	711	1934
47	312	856	1934
47	315	1127	1934
47	332	2385	1934
47	338	3323	1934
47	401	300	1934
47	403	148	1934
47	501	156	1934
47	521	151	1934
47	522	835	1934
47	531	397	1934
47	532	2063	1934
47	534	3175	1934
47	605	1768	1934
47	1001	430	1994
49	304	119	1983

Code	Section §	Word Count	Year Passed
49	305	330	1983
49	309	1757	1991
49	322	404	1983
49	323	54	1983
49	521	2263	1983
49	10501	542	1995
49	10702	60	1995
49	10706	1912	1995
49	10903	776	1995
49	11101	392	1995
49	11347	77	1978
49	11702	105	1995
49	11705	372	1995
49	11706	834	1995
49	14706	1433	1995
49	20101	21	1994
49	24301	1178	1994
49	31105	750	1994
49	31139	1250	1994
49	40101	1317	1994
49	41713	396	1994
49	46101	357	1994
50	841	351	1954
50	1701	140	1977

Notes

Chapter 1

1. In crafting this particular phrase, Corwin examined the struggle between Congress and the President over the right to control foreign policy. The Constitution, however, also invites other struggles including ones between Congress and the courts over the issue of statutory interpretation. Additionally, we believe this logic also applies to state constitutions, state legislatures, and state courts.

2. 5 U.S. (1 Cranch) 137 (1803).

3. *Marbury v. Madison* (1803) at 178.

4. Reported in *The Washington Post* on September 13, 2005.

5. Reported in *The Washington Post* on September 13, 2005.

6. Reported in *The Washington Post* on July 13, 2009.

7. Reported in the *New York Times* on July 15, 2009.

8. Reported in the *New York Times* on July 15, 2009.

9. 524 U.S. 742 (1998).

10. 490 U.S. 581 (1989).

11. *Mansell v. Mansell* (1989) at 594.

12. 493 U.S. 365 (1990).

13. *Guidry* (1990) at 376.

14. 466 Mich. 879; 645 N.W. 654 (2002).

15. Emphasis in the original. Quoted in 645 N.W. at 655.

16. 645 N.W. at 656.

17. Since there are too many analyses to mention here, please refer to Segal and Cover 1989 or Martin and Quinn 2002 for descriptions of ideological measurements and their effects.

18. But, see Hansford and Spriggs (2006); Bailey and Maltzman (2011); and Lax (2012).

Chapter 2

1. Quoting from Hart and Sacks (1994, 1169).

2. *Heydon's Case*, 76 Eng. Rep. 637 (K.B. 1584) at 638.

3. Llewellyn (1950).

4. See, for example, Bates (1992), Macey and Miller (1992), Shapiro (1992), Stevens (1992), Martineau (1993), Mank (1993), Popkin (1999), Manning (2002), O'Connor (2003), and Cross (2009).

5. Quoted in Starr 1987, 378.

6. 242 U.S. 470.

7. It is important to recognize that judges rely on multiple methods to adjudicate disputes. Though we reference particular individuals, such as Justice Scalia, as advocates of one method, we do not claim that other methods are not used by these individuals.

8. 465 U.S. 555 (1984).

9. From here the models diverge along many aspects: whether to model the legislature as a single chamber or bicamerally; whether to include gatekeeping committee preferences or multiple veto points (such as the President); whether to model policy preferences unidimensionally or multidimensionally; whether to include uncertainty or model the game with perfect information; and, whether to include transaction costs for the various actors (see Segal 1997, 1998)

10. Quoted from *Mansell v. Mansell* 490 U.S. 581 (1989) at 594.

11. For examples, see Segal and Spaeth 1993, 2002; and Spaeth and Segal 1999.

12. But see Lax and Rader (2010).

13. See Appendix A for a list of federal statutes and word counts.

14. In addition to the text of the actual statute the LexisNexis entries for many laws include references to previous judicial decisions interpreting a given statute as well as any cross-references to other relevant statutes. Our measure of a statute's word count includes the full LexisNexis entry thereby allowing us to capture all information available to judges when they interpret a particular statute.

15. It is possible that statutory constraint may possess a quadratic relationship with judicial discretion. Similar to the effects identified by Lindquist and Cross (2005) regarding precedent, it is possible that more detailed statutes have a constraining effect up to a certain level at which time they begin to afford greater discretion by allowing judges to pick and choose the specific language upon which to base their decisions. Yet, because statutes are unified documents rather than a set of separate and disparate decisions (similar to a set of precedents) our contention is that a linear specification is more accurate.

16. These datasets can be reached through the University of South Carolina's Judicial Research Initiative (JuRI) website: <http://artsandsciences. sc.edu/poli/juri/>.

17. The calculations of the dummy variables are discussed in later chapters, based on specific measures of ideology relevant to the court under consideration.

18. Since our empirical models contain different dependent variables, the particular sign of the interaction term (and its subsequent test of statistical significance) will change. These details are discussed more specifically in later chapters.

Chapter 3

1. We also recognize that while the appellate panels have no formal docket control authority, they can (and do) engage in extensive screening of cases to determine which ones receive full review (including attorneys' briefs and oral arguments), and also which decisions receive published opinions.

2. The Federal Circuit was created through consolidation of the Court of Claims and the Court of Customs and Patent Appeals.

3. With the current caseloads, this number has dropped to approximately one-tenth of 1 percent in terms of Supreme Court review of appellate decisions.

4. For an alternative approach to statutory interpretation see Posner (1983).

5. 856 F.2d 1457 (1988).

6. These datasets are archived at the University of South Carolina's Judicial Research Initiative (JuRI) at <http://artsandsciences.sc.edu/poli/juri/>.

7. Techincally, the Songer database is a stratified random sample, stratified across circuits by year, and random within each circuit year.

8. We also exclude cases before 1961 because the Songer database reduces the random sample to 15 cases per circuit per year from 1925–1960, and we wish to keep the sample size consistent throughout our analysis.

9. Since we are not testing a strategic model, we hesitate to use the term sincere. However, this is the most straightforward connotation to determine the influence of ideology and constraint.

10. The directionality of each judge vote is recorded in the Appeals Court Database and follows a specific coding scheme determined by Donald Songer and stated explicitly in the documentation.

11. To identify the relevant statute, we relied on the USC1 variable in the Songer database, which records the section of the U.S. Code most frequently cited in a case's headnotes. Relying on this variable ensures we capture those cases where the appellate courts interpret a federal statute (where the FED-

LAW variable is recorded) as well as those cases where the courts examine the constitutionality of a statute (where the CONST variable is recorded). We acknowledge that our procedure may include references to statutes that are not necessarily interpreted by the courts. However, inclusion of these potentially irrelevant statutes should hinder our ability to discover significant levels of constraint, thus providing a more conservative test. This potential outcome is preferable to searching only on the FEDLAW variable, which risks excluding relevant statutes and consequently introduces substantial bias into the analysis.

12. In our article published in the *Journal of Politics* (Randazzo, Waterman, and Fine (2006)), we ran separate models for liberal (Democratic appointees) and conservative judges (Republican appointees). Consequently, we only tested for a constraining effect on judicial behavior. Including interaction terms in a pooled sample provides greater flexibility to identify both a potential constraining and facilitating effect.

13. See Pinello (1999) for a survey of research relying on this surrogate.

14. The folding is accomplished simply by taking the absolute value of the Giles, Hettinger, and Peppers' score for each individual judge.

15. Additionally, using the lincom command in Stata reveals that the interaction term possesses a coefficient of –.862 with a standard error of .308 and a significant t-statistic of –2.80.

16. It is important to note that these results differ from the original findings reported in an earlier article (Randazzo, Waterman, and Fine 2006). One of the primary reasons is that these models are based on expanded and updated data.

17. Though the table reports a statistically significant coefficient for the interaction term in Model 2, an examination of the conditional effect using the lincom command in Stata reveals that the interaction term possesses a coefficient of –.083 with a standard error of .322 and a non-significant t-statistic of –0.26.

Chapter 4

1. Although there are other mechanisms by which the Supreme Court can review cases, such as on appeal or certification, the *certiorari* process is the primary avenue through which cases come before the justices.

2. Before the capitol of the United States moved to Washington, DC (in the early nineteenth century) the Supreme Court met in unused spaces within buildings in New York City and Philadelphia.

3. *Scott v. Sandford* 19 Howard 393 (1857).

4. 7 Wall (74 U.S.) 506 (1869).

5. For a list of specific statutes related to the size of the Supreme Court, see Table 1-2 of Epstein, Segal, Spaeth, and Walker (1996).

6. For a description of accounts leading to FDR's Court-Packing Plan and the subsequent "switch in time that saved nine" see Epstein and Walker 2010, 428–432.

7. But, see Spaeth (1964) for an analysis of Frankfurter's voting behavior where he demonstrates that the Justice voted according to his ideological preferences despite proclaiming a philosophy of judicial restraint.

8. 529 U.S. 120 (2000).

9. 526 U.S. 865 (1999).

10. 467 U.S. 837 (1984).

11. The original Supreme Court database was coded by Harold J. Spaeth. Each of the justice-centered databases (Warren Court, 1953–1969; Burger Court, 1969–1985; and Rehnquist Court, 1986–1998) was transformed by Sara C. Benesh. These data are archived at the University of South Carolina's Judicial Research Initiative (JuRI) website: <http://artsandsciences.sc.edu/poli/juri/>.

12. This is accomplished by setting the variable ANALU = 0 and DEC_TYPE = 1, 6 or 7.

13. Since we examine subsets of cases based on issue area, the total number of observations in each statistical model will fluctuate.

14. Coded "1" if a liberal justice casts a liberal vote and "0" if that justice votes conservatively. Similarly, the variable is coded "1" if a conservative justice votes conservatively and "0" if that judge casts a liberal vote

15. To identify the relevant statute, we relied on the LAW variable in the Spaeth dataset. This provides information about the sections of the U.S. Code interpreted by the Supreme Court. In some instances, Spaeth lists frequently litigated statutes by acronym (for example, NLRA refers to the National Labor Relations Act). For all cases in which an acronym occurs we recoded the specific statute in question.

16. The folding is accomplished simply by taking the absolute value of the Martin and Quinn score for each individual justice.

17. These cases are identified in the Spaeth dataset by setting the variable CRIM_DUM = 1.

18. These cases are identified in the Spaeth dataset by setting the variables CIVRTS_D, FIRSTA_D, DP_DUM, and PRIV_DUM equal to 1.

19. These cases are identified in the Spaeth dataset by setting the variables UNION_DU, ECON_DU, FED_DUM, and TAX_DUM equal to 1.

20. Due to the inclusion of the interaction term, the variable *Statutory Detail* effectively measures the influence of congressional statutes on conservative justices only (i.e., when *Liberal Justices* = 0).

21. This conditional effect is measured using the lincom command in Stata to examine the *Statutory Detail * Liberal Justice Interaction* term and its two base constituent terms, *Statutory Detail* and *Liberal Justice*. When all three components are examined the resulting coefficient is –.708 with a standard error of .248 and a significant t-statistic of –2.85.

22. Relying on the lincom command in Stata reveals that the conditional effect of the interaction term and its two constituent terms is 1.283 with a standard error of .179 and a significant t-statistic of 7.14.

23. Relying on the lincom command in Stata reveals that the conditional effect of the interaction term and its two constituent terms is .029 with a standard error of .132 and a non-significant t-statistic of 0.22.

24. These cases are identified in the Spaeth dataset by setting the variable CIVRTS_D = 1.

25. These cases are identified in the Spaeth dataset by setting the variables FIRSTA_D, DP_DUM, and PRIV_DUM equal to 1.

26. These cases are identified in the Spaeth dataset by setting the variable FED_DUM = 1.

27. Relying on the lincom command in Stata reveals that the conditional effect of the interaction term and its two constituent terms is .626 with a standard error of .220 and a significant t-statistic of 2.85.

28. These cases are identified in the Spaeth dataset by setting the variables FIRSTA_D, DP_DUM, and PRIV_DUM equal to 1.

29. Relying on the lincom command in Stata reveals that the conditional effect of the interaction term and its two constituent terms is 2.387 with a standard error of .339 and a significant t-statistic of 7.03.

30. The graphs are constructed holding all other influences (i.e., variables in the statistical model) constant.

31. The graphical relationships in Figure 4.1 correspond to the statistical results included in Table 4.5, Model 5.

32. For graphical purposes we "unfold" the Martin and Quinn measure of ideology. Consequently, the axis labeled IDEOLOGY represents the entire ideological continuum, with scores ranging from the most extreme liberal justices to the most extreme conservative justices.

33. This result is observed by focusing on the "left edge" of the hyperplane—when statutory constraint is at its lowest level.

34. The graphs represent voting patterns for all justices in the time period, with the exclusion of Justices Goldberg and Burton due to a lack of sufficient observations.

35. Since the analysis is conducted per Court term, we take the average statute length per term as the independent variable.

36. This movement represents a statistically significant difference.

Chapter 5

1. A large portion of this chapter comes from Randazzo, Kirk A., Richard W. Waterman, and Michael P. Fix. 2011. "State Supreme Courts and the Effects of Statutory Constraint: A Test of the Model of Contingent Discretion" *Political Research Quarterly.*

2. *Arkansas Department of Human Services v. Collier* 95 S.W.3d 772 (2003, at 778).

3. 24 Cal. 4th 1057 (2001).

4. 835 N.E.2d 526 (2005).

5. 95 S.W.3d 772 (2003).

6. 665 N.W.2d 729 (2003).

7. In addition to the text of the actual statute the LexisNexis entries for many laws include references to previous judicial decisions interpreting a given statute as well as any cross-references to other relevant statutes. Our measure of a statute's word count includes the full LexisNexis entry thereby allowing us to capture all information available to judges when they interpret a particular statute.

8. This includes all fifty-two state supreme courts since Texas and Oklahoma possess separate courts of last resort for civil and criminal cases.

9. Since we examine subsets of cases, the total number of observations in each statistical model will fluctuate.

10. The folding is accomplished by subtracting 50 from the PAJID score for each individual judge and taking the absolute value of that result.

11. This is calculated by subtracting the year in which the legislation was passed from the year in which the specific case came to the state supreme court.

12. Previous versions of this analysis also included measures of state ideology developed by Wright, Erickson, and McIver (1987) and Berry et al. (1998). The substantive results with these alternative measures are consistent with the analyses presented here.

13. We define criminal cases as the set of cases in the original Brace and Hall dataset where the variable *genissue* = 1.

14. We define civil liberties cases as the set of cases in the original Brace and Hall dataset where either *gen_frst* = 1 or *gen_priv* = 1.

15. Additionally, the defeat of California Chief Justice Rose Bird in her recall election of 1986 serves as a primary example of the pressures state judges encounter during retention elections.

16. As measured by Wright, Erickson, and McIver (1987).

17. For example, future models should examine factors pertaining to legislative intent when passing detailed statutes. In particular scholars should focus on the ideological influences of state legislatures, the costs associated with such behavior, and whether the preferences of sitting legislatures affect judicial behavior.

Chapter 6

1. A large portion of this chapter comes from Randazzo, Kirk A., Richard W. Waterman, and S. Andrew Martin. 2009. "The Evolution of Legal

Constraint and the U.S. Supreme Court." Paper presented at the annual meeting of the American Political Science Association in Toronto, Canada. Our sincere thanks to Andrew Martin for his work on developing this research.

2. 494 U.S. 872 (1990).

3. 521 U.S. 507 (1997).

4. Often amendments to existing statutes are minor in nature. Statutory amendments generally rework a couple of sentences or paragraphs. Drastic changes to the law generally mean a repeal of an existing statute and subsequent replacement with new legislation.

5. These interpretations are recorded in the U.S. Code as judicial annotations and are available through services such as Westlaw and LexisNexis.

6. For an analogous argument pertaining to the effects of precedent, see Lindquist and Cross (2005).

7. 865 F. 2d 1566.

8. 630 F. Supp. 551.

9. Specifically, the graph represents all public laws passed by Congress that were subsequently interpreted by the Supreme Court.

10. More research is necessary to precisely identify the causes of this progression.

11. The original Supreme Court database was coded by Harold J. Spaeth. Each of the justice-centered databases (Warren Court, 1953–1969; Burger Court, 1969–1985; and Rehnquist Court, 1986–1998) was transformed by Sara C. Benesh. These data are archived at the University of South Carolina's Judicial Research Initiative (JuRI) website: <http://artsandsciences.sc.edu/poli/juri/>.

12. This is accomplished by setting the variable ANALU = 0 and DEC_TYPE = 1, 6 or 7.

13. Since we examine subsets of cases based on issue area, the total number of observations in each statistical model will fluctuate.

14. Since we are not testing a strategic model, we hesitate to use the term sincere. However, this is the most straightforward connotation to determine the influence of ideology and constraint.

15. We rely on the Martin and Quinn (2002) measure of Supreme Court ideology to determine whether a justice is considered "liberal" or "conservative."

16. Similar to our operationalization of *Statutory Detail* we take the natural log of this raw word count for our actual measure.

17. Due to the inclusion of this interaction term, the original variable *Judicial Annotations* actually measures the effects of annotations on conservative justices only.

18. See Model 1 in Table 4.4.

Chapter 7

1. Additionally, our model indicates that vague or ambiguous statutes exert no effect on judicial behavior. Thus, the judge is free to vote based solely on his or her ideological preferences.

References

Allison, Garland W. 1996. "Delay in the Senate Confirmation of Federal Judicial Nominees." *Judicature* 80: 8–15.

Bailey, Michael A., and Forrest Maltzman. 2011. *The Constrained Court: Law, Politics, and the Decisions Justices Make*. Princeton, NJ: Princeton University Press.

Baird, Vanessa A. 2004. "The Effect of Politically Salient Decisions on the U.S. Supreme Court's Agenda." *Journal of Politics* 66 (August): 755–772.

———. 2007. *Answering the Call of the Court: How Justices and Litigants Set the Supreme Court Agenda*. Charlottesville, VA: University of Virginia Press.

Barrow, Deborah J., Gary Zuk, and Gerald Gryski. 1996. *The Federal Judiciary and Institutional Change*. Ann Arbor: University of Michigan Press.

Bates, Joseph H. 1992. "Symposium: A Reevaluation of the Canons of Statutory Interpretation." 45 *Vanderbilt University Law Review* 529.

Baum, Lawrence. 1997. *The Puzzle of Judicial Behavior*. Ann Arbor: University of Michigan Press.

Black, Ryan C., and Ryan J. Owens. 2009 "Agenda Setting in the Supreme Court: The Collision of Policy and Jurisprudence," *Journal of Politics* 71: 1062–1075.

Brace, Paul, and Melinda Gann Hall. 1995. "Studying Courts Comparatively: The View from the American States." *Political Research Quarterly* 48 (March): 5–29.

———. 1997. "The Interplay of Preferences, Case Facts, Context, and Rules in the Politics of Judicial Choice." *Journal of Politics* 59 (November): 1206–1231.

Brace, Paul, Melinda Gann Hall, and Laura Langer. 2000. "Measuring the Preferences of State Supreme Court Justices." *Journal of Politics* 62 (May): 387–413.

———. 2001. "Placing Courts in State Politics." *State Politics and Policy Quarterly* 1 (Spring): 81–108

Boucher, Robert L., and Jeffrey A. Segal. 1995. "Supreme Court Justices as Strategic Decision Makers: Aggressive Grants and Defensive Denials on the Vinson Court." *Journal of Politics* 57 (August): 824–837.

Breger, Marshall J. 1987. "Introductory Remarks." In the *Symposium on the Use of Legislative History. Duke Law Journal* 1987 (June): 361–386.

Brennan, William J., Jr. 1989. "Why Have a Bill of Rights?" *Oxford Journal of Legal Studies* 9 (Winter): 425–440.

Brenner, Saul. 1979. "The New *Certiorari* Game." *Journal of Politics* 41 (May): 649–655.

Brenner, Saul and John F. Krol. 1989. "Strategies in *Certiorari* Voting on the United States Supreme Court." *Journal of Politics* 51 (November): 828–840.

Brisbin, Richard A., Jr. 1996. "Slaying the Dragon: Segal, Spaeth and the Function of Law in Supreme Court Decision Making." *American Journal of Political Science* 40 (November): 1004–1017.

Caldeira, Gregory A. 1986. "Neither the Purse nor the Sword: Dynamics of Public Confidence in the Supreme Court." *American Political Science Review* 80 (December): 1209–1226.

Caldeira, Gregory A. and John R. Wright. 1988. "Organized Interests and Agenda Setting in the Supreme Court." *American Political Science Review* 82: 1109–1127.

———. 1990. "*Amici Curiae* before the Supreme Court: Who Participates, When, and How Much?" *Journal of Politics* 52 (August): 782–806.

Caldeira, Gregory A., John R. Wright, and Christopher J.W. Zorn. 1999. "Sophisticated Voting and Gate-Keeping in the Supreme Court." *Journal of Law, Economics, and Organization* 15 (Number 3): 549–572.

Cameron, Charles M., Jeffrey A. Segal, and Donald R. Songer. 2000. "Strategic Auditing in a Political Hierarchy: An Informational Model of the Supreme Court's *Certiorari* Decisions." *American Political Science Review* 94 (March): 101–116.

Campbell, Colton C. and John F. Stack, Jr., editors. 2001. *Congress Confronts the Court: The Struggle for Legitimacy and Authority in Lawmaking.* Lanham, MD: Rowman & Littlefield Publishers.

Carp, Robert A., and Ronald Stidham. 2001. *Judicial Process in America, Fifth Edition.* Washington, DC: CQ Press.

Clark, Tom S. 2009. "The Separation of Powers, Court Curbing, and Judicial Legitimacy." *American Journal of Political Science* 53 (October): 971–989.

Corley, Pamela A., Amy Steigerwalt, and Artemus Ward. 2013. *The Puzzle of Unanimity: Consensus on the U.S. Supreme Court.* Palo Alto, CA: Stanford University Press.

Corwin, Edward S. 1957. *The President: Office and Powers, 1787–1984, 5th Revised Edition.* New York: New York University Press.

Cross, Frank B. 2009. *The Theory and Practice of Statutory Interpretation.* Palo Alto, CA: Stanford University Press.

Easterbrook, Frank H. 2004. "What Does Legislative History Tell Us?" In *Judges on Judging: Views from the Bench, Second Edition*. David M. O'Brien, editor. Washington, DC: CQ Press

Epstein, David, and Sharyn O'Halloran. 1999. *Delegating Powers: A Transaction Cost Politics Approach to Public Policy Making Under Separate Powers*. Cambridge: Cambridge University Press.

Epstein, Lee, Jeffrey A. Segal, Harold J. Spaeth, and Thomas G. Walker. 1996. *The Supreme Court Compendium: Data, Decisions, and Developments*. Washington, DC: CQ Press.

Esptein, Lee, and Thomas G. Walker. 2010. *Constitutional Law for a Changing America: Institutional Powers and Constraints*. Washington, DC: CQ Press.

Eskridge, William N., Jr. 1987. "Dynamic Statutory Interpretation." *University of Pennsylvania Law Review* 135 (July): 1479–1555.

———. 1991a. "Overriding Supreme Court Statutory Decisions." *Yale Law Journal* 101 (November): 331–455.

———. 1991b. "Reneging on History? Playing the Court/Congress/President Civil Rights Game." *California Law Review* 79 (May): 613–684.

———. 1999. "Norms, Empiricism, and Canons in Statutory Interpretation." *University of Chicago Law Review* 66 (Summer): 671–684.

Ferejohn, John, and Barry R. Weingast. 1992. "Limitation of Statutes: Strategic Statutory Interpretation." *Georgetown Law Journal* 80 (February): 565–582.

Fisher, Louis. 2001. "Congressional Checks on the Judiciary." In *Congress Confronts the Court: The Struggle for Legitimacy and Authority in Lawmaking*. Colton C. Campbell and John F. Stack, editors. Lanham, MD: Rowman & Littlefield Publishers.

———. 2011. *Defending Congress and the Constitution*. Lawrence, KS: University Press of Kansas.

Flemming, Roy B., and B. Dan Wood. 1997. "The Public and the Supreme Court: Individual Justice Responsiveness to American Policy Moods." *American Journal of Political Science* 41 (April): 468–498.

Franck, Matthew J. 1996. *Against the Imperial Judiciary: The Supreme Court vs. the Sovereignty of the People*. Lawrence, KS: University Press of Kansas.

Frankfurter, Felix. 2004. "Some Reflections on the Reading of Statutes." In *Judges on Judging: Views from the Bench, Second Edition*, David M. O'Brien, editor. Washington, DC: CQ Press.

Friedman, Barry. 2006. "Taking Law Seriously." *Perspectives on Politics* 4 (June): 261–276.

George, Tracy E., and Lee Epstein. 1992. "On the Nature of Supreme Court Decision Making." *American Political Science Review* 86 (June): 323–337.

George, Tracy E., and Michael E. Solimine. 2001. "Supreme Court Monitoring of the United States Courts of Appeals *En Banc.*" *Supreme Court Economic Review* 9 (November): 171–204.

Geyh, Charles Gardner. 2006. *When Courts & Congress Collide: The Struggle for Control of America's Judicial System.* Ann Arbor, MI: University of Michigan Press.

———, ed. 2011. *What's Law Got to Do With It? What Judges Do, Why They Do It, and What's at Stake.* Palo Alto, CA: Stanford University Press.

Giles, Micheal W., Virginia A. Hettinger, and Todd Peppers. 2001. "Picking Federal Judges: A Note on Policy and Partisan Selection Agendas." *Political Research Quarterly* 54 (September): 623–641.

Gillman, Howard. 1994. "Preferred Freedoms: The Progressive Expansion of State Power and the Rise of Modern Civil Liberties Jurisprudence." *Political Research Quarterly* 3 (September): 623–653.

———. 2001. "Review: What's Law Got to Do With It? Judicial Behavioralists Test the 'Legal Model' of Judicial Decision Making" *Law and Social Inquiry* 26: 465–504.

Gillman, Howard, and Cornell Clayton, editors. 1999. *The Supreme Court in American Politics: New Institutionalist Interpretations.* Lawrence, KS: University Press of Kansas.

Goldman, Sheldon. 1997. *Picking Federal Court Judges: Lower Court Selection from Roosevelt through Reagan.* New Haven: Yale University Press.

Grundfest, Joseph A., and A. C. Pritchard. 2002. "Statutes with Multiple Personality Disorders: The Value of Ambiguity in Statutory Design and Interpretation." *Stanford Law Review* 54 (April): 627–736.

Hagle, Timothy M., and Glenn E. Mitchell, II. 1992. "Goodness-of-Fit Measures for Logit and Probit." *American Journal of Political Science* 36 (August): 762–784.

Hall, Melinda Gann, and Paul Brace. 1989. "Order in the Courts: A Neo-Institutional Approach to Judicial Consensus." *Western Political Quarterly* 42: 391–407.

Hall, Melinda Gann, and Paul Brace. 1992. "Toward an Integrated Model of Judicial Voting Behavior." *American Politics Quarterly* 20 (April): 147–168.

Hansford, Thomas G., and James F. Spriggs, II. 2006. *The Politics of Precedent on the U.S. Supreme Court.* Princeton, NJ: Princeton University Press.

Henschen, Beth M. 1983. "Statutory Interpretations of the Supreme Court." *American Politics Quarterly* 11: 441–458.

Hausegger, Lori, and Lawrence Baum. 1999. "Inviting Congressional Action: A Study of Supreme Court Motivations in Statutory Interpretation." *American Journal of Political Science* 43 (January): 162–185.

Hettinger, Virginia A., and Christopher J. W. Zorn. 1999. "Signals, Models and Congressional Overrides of the Supreme Court." Paper presented at the Annual Meeting of the Midwest Political Science Association, Chicago, IL.

Howard, J. Woodford, Jr. 1977. "Role Perceptions and Behavior in Three U.S. Courts of Appeals." *Journal of Politics* 39 (November): 916–938.

Howard, Robert M., and Jeffrey A. Segal. 2004. "A Preference for Deference? The Supreme Court and Judicial Review." *Political Research Quarterly* 57 (March): 131–143.

Huber, John D., and Charles R. Shipan. 2002. *Deliberate Discretion? The Institutional Foundations of Bureaucratic Autonomy.* New York: Cambridge University Press.

Huber, John D., Charles R. Shipan, and Madelaine Pfahler. 2001. "Legislatures and Statutory Control of Bureaucracy." *American Journal of Political Science* 45 (April): 330–345.

Kahn, Ronald, and Ken I. Kersch, editors. 2006. *The Supreme Court and American Political Development.* Lawrence, KS: University Press of Kansas.

Katzmann, Robert A. 1992. "Bridging the Statutory Gulf Between Courts and Congress: A Challenge for Positive Political Theory." *Georgetown Law Journal* 80 (February): 653–669.

Keck, Thomas M. 2002. "Activism and Restraint on the Rehnquist Court: Timing, Sequence, and Conjuncture in Constitutional Development." *Polity* 35 (Autumn): 121–152.

———. 2004. *The Most Activist Supreme Court in History: The Road to Modern Judicial Conservatism.* Chicago, IL: University of Chicago Press.

Kozinski, Alex. 2005. "What I Ate for Breakfast and Other Mysteries of Judicial Decision Making." In *Judges on Judging: Views from the Bench, Second Edition.* David M. O'Brien, editor. Washington, DC: CQ Press.

Kritzer, Herbert M., and Mark J. Richards. 2003. "Jurisprudential Regimes and Supreme Court Decisionmaking: The *Lemon* Regime and Establishment Clause Cases." *Law & Society Review* 37 (December): 827–840.

Langer, Laura. 2002. *Judicial Review in State Supreme Courts.* Albany: State University of New York Press.

Lax, Jeffrey R. 2012. "Political Constraints on Legal Doctrine: How Hierarchy Shapes the Law." *Journal of Politics* 74 (July): 765–781.

Lax, Jeffrey R., and Kelly T. Rader. 2010. "Legal Constraints on Supreme Court Decision Making: Do Jurisprudential Regimes Exist?" *Journal of Politics* 72 (April): 273–284.

Lindquist, Stefanie A., and Frank B. Cross. 2005. "Empirically Testing Dworkin's Chain Novel Theory: Studying the Path of Precedent." *New York University Law Review* 80 (October): 1156–1206.

Lindquist, Stefanie A., and David E. Klein. 2006. "The Influence of Jurisprudential Considerations on Supreme Court Decisionmaking: A Study of Conflict Cases." *Law & Society Review* 40 (1): 135–162.

Lindquist, Stefanie A., David A. Yalof, and John A. Clark. 2000. "The Impact of Presidential Appointments of the U.S. Supreme Court: Cohesive and Divisive Voting within Presidential Blocs." *Political Research Quarterly* 53: 795–814.

Llewellyn, Karl N. 1950. "Remarks on the Theory of Appellate Decision and the Rules or Canons About How Statutes are to be Construed." 3 *Vanderbilt Law Review* 395.

Macey, Jonathan R., and Geoffrey P. Miller. 1992. "The Canons of Statutory Construction and Judicial Preferences." 45 *Vanderbilt University Law Review* 647.

Mank, Bradford C. 1997. "Textualism's Selective Canons of Statutory Construction: Reinvigorating Individual Liberties, Legislative Authority, and Deference to Executive Agencies." 86 *Kentucky Law Journal* 527.

Manning, John F. 2002. "Legal Realism & the Canons' Revival." 5 *Green Bag 2d* 283.

Marks, Brian A. 1988. "A Model of Judicial Influence on Congressional Policymaking: *Grove City College v. Bell*." Unpublished manuscript, working papers in Political Science, P-88-7, Hoover Institution, Stanford University.

Martin, Andrew D. 2001. "Congressional Decision Making and the Separation of Powers." *American Political Science Review* 95 (June): 361–378.

Martin, Andrew D., and Kevin M. Quinn. 2002. "Dynamic Ideal Point Estimation via Markov Chain Monte Carlo for the U.S. Supreme Court, 1953-1999." *Political Analysis* 10 (Number 2): 134–153.

Martineau, Robert J. 1993. "Craft and Technique, Not Canons and Grand Theories: A Neo-Realist View of Statutory Construction." 62 *George Washington Law Review* 1.

McGuire, Kevin T., and Gregory A. Caldeira. 1993. "Lawyers, Organized Interests, and the Law of Obscenity: Agenda Setting in the Supreme Court." *American Political Science Review* 87: 717–726.

McNollgast. 1995. "Politics and the Courts: A Positive Theory of Judicial Doctrine and the Rule of Law." *Southern California Law Review* 68 (September): 1631–1689.

Mikva, Abner J. 1987. "A Reply to Judge Starr's Observations." *Duke Law Journal* 1987 (June): 380–386.

Mishler, William, and Reginald S. Sheehan. 1993. "The Supreme Court as a Countermajoritarian Institution." *American Political Science Review* 87 (March): 87–101.

Moraski, Bryon J., and Charles R. Shipan. 1999. "The Politics of Supreme Court Nominations: A Theory of Institutional Constraints and Choices." *American Journal of Political Science* 43 (October): 1069–1095.

Murphy, Walter F., C. Herman Pritchett, and Lee Epstein. 2002. *Courts, Judges, and Politics: An Introduction to the Judicial Process.* Boston: McGraw-Hill.

O'Brien, David M. 2005. *Storm Center: The Supreme Court in American Politics, Seventh Edition.* New York, NY: W.W. Norton & Company.

O'Connor, Gary E. 2003. "Restatement (First) of Statutory Interpretation." 7 *New York University Journal of Legislation and Public Policy* 333.

Paschal, Richard A. 1992. "The Continuing Colloquy: Congress and the Finality of the Supreme Court." *Journal of Law and Politics* 8: 142–226.

Perry, H. W., Jr. 1991. *Deciding to Decide: Agenda Setting in the United States Supreme Court.* Cambridge, MA: Harvard University Press.

Pinello, Daniel R. 1999. "Linking Party to Judicial Ideology in American Courts: A Meta-Analysis." *Justice System Journal* 20 (November): 219–254.

Popkin, William D. 1999. *Statutes in the Court: The History and Theory of Statutory Interpretation.* Durham, NC: Duke University Press.

Posner, Richard A. 1983. "Statutory Interpretation: In the Classroom and in the Courtroom." *University of Chicago Law Review* 50 (Spring): 800–822.

———. 2001. *Frontiers of Legal Theory.* Cambridge, MA: Harvard University Press.

Randazzo, Kirk A., Richard W. Waterman, and Jeffrey A. Fine. 2006. "Checking the Federal Courts: The Impact of Congressional Statutes on Judicial Behavior." *Journal of Politics* 68 (November): 1003–1014.

Rehnquist, William H. 2001. *The Supreme Court, New Edition.* New York, NY: Alfred A. Knopf.

Richards, Mark J., and Herbert M. Kritzer. 2002. "Jurisprudential Regimes in Supreme Court Decision Making." *American Political Science Review* 96 (June): 305–320.

Rivers, Christina R. n.d. *The Congressional Black Caucus, Minority Voting Rights, and the U.S. Supreme Court.* Ann Arbor, MI: University of Michigan Press Forthcoming.

Rogers, James R. 2001. "Information and Judicial Review: A Signaling Game of Legislative-Judicial Interaction." *American Journal of Political Science* 45 (January): 84–99.

Rogers, James R., Roy B. Flemming, and Jon R. Bond, editors. 2006. *Institutional Games and the U.S. Supreme Court.* Charlottesville, VA: University of Virginia Press.

Rosenkranz, Nicholas Quinn. 2002. "Federal Rules of Statutory Interpreta-
    tion." *Harvard Law Review* 115 (June): 2085–2157.
Rowland, C. K., and Robert A. Carp. 1980. "A Longitudinal Study of Party
    Effects on Federal District Court Policy Propensities." *American Journal
    of Political Science* 24 (May): 291–305.
Sala, Brian R., and James F. Spriggs. 2004. "Designing Tests of the Supreme
    Court and the Separation of Powers." *Political Research Quarterly* 57
    (June): 197–208.
Scalia, Antonin. 1997. *A Matter of Interpretation: Federal Courts and the Law.*
    Princeton, NJ: Princeton University Press.
Segal, Jeffrey A. 1984. "Predicting Supreme Court Cases Probabilistically:
    Search and Seizure Cases, 1962–1981." *American Political Science
    Review* 78 (February): 891–900.
———. 1997. "Separation-of-Powers Games in the Positive Theory of Con-
    gress and Courts." *American Political Science Review* 91 (March): 28–44.
———. 1998. "Correction to 'Separation-of-Powers Games in the Positive
    Theory of Congress and Courts." *American Political Science Review* 92
    (December): 923–926.
Segal, Jeffrey A., Charles M. Cameron, and Albert D. Cover. 1992. "A Spatial
    Model of Roll Call Voting: Senators, Constituents, and Interest Groups
    in Supreme Court Confirmations." *American Journal of Political Science*
    36 (February): 96–121.
Segal, Jeffrey A., and Albert D. Cover. 1989. "Ideological Values and the Votes
    of the U.S. Supreme Court Justices." *American Political Science Review*
    83 (June): 557–565.
Segal, Jeffrey A., and Harold J. Spaeth. 2002. *The Supreme Court and the Atti-
    tudinal Model, Revisited.* Cambridge: Cambridge University Press.
Segal, Jeffrey A., Richard J. Timpone, and Robert M. Howard. 2000. "Buyer
    Beware? Presidential Success Through Supreme Court Appointments."
    Political Research Quarterly 53 (September): 557–595.
Shapiro, David L. 1992. "Continuity and Change in Statutory Interpretation."
    67 *New York University Law Review* 921.
Shepsle, Kenneth A. 1992. "Congress is a 'They' not an 'It': Legislative Intent
    as Oxymoron." *International Review of Law and Economics* 12: 239–256.
Shipan, Charles R. 1997. *Designing Judicial Review: Interest Groups, Congress,
    and Communications Policy.* Ann Arbor: University of Michigan Press.
Songer, Donald R. 1979. "Concern for Policy Outputs as a Cue for Supreme
    Court Decisions on *Certiorari*." *Journal of Politics* 41 (November):
    1185–1194.
———. 1991. "The Circuit Courts of Appeals" in *The American Courts: A
    Critical Assessment*, John B. Gates and Charles A. Johnson, eds. Wash-
    ington, DC: CQ Press.

Songer, Donald R., and Susan B. Haire. 1992. "Integrating Alternative Approaches to the Study of Judicial Voting: Obscenity Cases in the U.S. Courts of Appeals." *American Journal of Political Science* 36 (November): 963–982.

Songer, Donald R., Jeffrey A. Segal, and Charles M. Cameron. 1994. "The Hierarchy of Justice: Testing a Principal-Agent Model of Supreme Court-Circuit Court Interactions." *American Journal of Political Science* 38 (August): 673–696.

Songer, Donald R., and Reginald S. Sheehan. 1990. "Supreme Court Impact on Compliance and Outcomes: *Miranda* and *New York Times* in the United States Courts of Appeals." *Western Political Quarterly* 43 (June): 297–316.

Songer, Donald R., and Reginald S. Sheehan. 1992. "Who Wins on Appeal? Upperdogs and Underdogs in the United States Courts of Appeals." *American Journal of Political Science* 36 (February): 235–258.

Songer, Donald R., Reginald S. Sheehan, and Susan B. Haire. 2000. *Change and Continuity on the United States Courts of Appeals.* Ann Arbor, MI: University of Michigan Press.

Spaeth, Harold J. 1964. "The Judicial Restraint of Mr. Justice Frankfurter—Myth or Reality." *Midwest Journal of Political Science* 8 (February): 22–38.

Spaeth, Harold J., and Jeffrey A. Segal. 1999. *Majority Rule or Minority Will: Adherence to Precedent on the U.S. Supreme Court.* Cambridge: Cambridge University Press.

Spiller, Pablo T., and Rafael Gely. 1992. "Congressional Control or Judicial Independence: The Determinants of U.S. Supreme Court Labor-Relations Decisions, 1949—1988." *RAND Journal of Economics* 23 (Winter): 463–492.

Spiller, Pablo T., and Emerson H. Tiller. 1997. "Decision Costs and the Strategic Design of Administrative Process and Judicial Review." *Journal of Legal Studies* 26 (June): 347–370.

Spriggs, James F., II, and Thomas G. Hansford. 2000. "Measuring Legal Change: The Reliability and Validity of Shepard's Citations." *Political Research Quarterly* 53 (June): 327–341.

———. 2001. "Explaining the Overruling of U.S. Supreme Court Precedent." *Journal of Politics* 63 (November): 1091–1111.

———. 2002. "The U.S. Supreme Court's Incorporation and Interpretation of Precedent." *Law & Society Review* 36 (Number 1): 139–160.

Starr, Kenneth W. 1987. "Observations About the Use of Legislative History." *Duke Law Journal* 1987 (June): 371–379.

Stevens, John Paul. 1992. "The Shakespeare Canon of Statutory Interpretation." 140 *University of Pennsylvania Law Review* 1373.

Stock, Arthur. 1990. "Justice Scalia's Use of Sources in Statutory and Constitutional Interpretation: How Congress Always Loses." *Duke Law Journal* 1990 (February): 160–192.

Stumpf, Harry P. 1965. "Congressional Response to Supreme Court Rulings: The Interaction of Law and Politics." *Journal of Public Law* 14: 377–395.

Tanenhaus, Joseph, Marvin Schick, Matthew Muraskin, and Daniel Rosen. 1989. "The Supreme Court's *Certiorari* Jurisdiction: Cue Theory." In *American Court Systems: Readings in Judicial Process and Behavior, Second Edition*. Sheldon Goldman and Austin Sarat, editors. New York, NY: Longman Publishers.

Teger, Stuart H., and Douglas Kosinski. 1980. "The Cue Theory of Supreme Court *Certiorari* Jurisdiction: A Reconsideration." *Journal of Politics* 42 (August): 834–846.

Ulmer, S. Sidney. 1972. "The Decision to Grant *Certiorari* as an Indicator to the Decision 'On the Merits.'" *Polity* 4: 429–447.

———. 1984. "The Supreme Court's *Certiorari* Decisions: Conflict as a Predictive Variable." *American Political Science Review* 78 (December): 901–911.

Wald, Patricia M. 1987. "Some Thoughts on Judging as Gleaned from One Hundred Years of the 'Harvard Law Review' and Other Great Books." *Harvard Law Review* 100 (February): 887–908.

Whittington, Keith E. 2005. "'Interpose Your Friendly Hand': Political Supports for the Exercise of Judicial Review by the United States Supreme Court." *American Political Science Review* 99 (November): 583–596.

———. 2007. *Political Foundations of Judicial Supremacy: The Presidency, the Supreme Court, and Constitutional Leadership in U.S. History*. Princeton, NJ: Princeton University Press.

Wood, B. Dan, and Richard W. Waterman. 1994. *Bureaucratic Dynamics: The Role of a Bureaucracy in a Democracy*. Boulder, CO: Westview Press.

Zorn, Christopher J. W. 2002. "U.S. Government Litigation Strategies in the Federal Appellate Courts." *Political Research Quarterly* 55 (March): 145–166.

Index

abortion, 40, 58
adjudicated, 33, 81, 106, 123, 147, 156
administrative, 75, 132
ambiguity, 12, 15, 24, 42, 71, 73, 101
ambiguous statutes, 44, 116, 144, 148, 191
amendments, 121, 190
annotation, 137
appeals, 45, 41, 43, 45, 5, 64, 82, 149
appeals courts, 45, 149
appellate court, 41, 59, 63, 65, 71, 73, 96, 97, 101, 112, 123, 181
appellate courts, 41, 59, 63, 65, 71, 123, 181
appellate jurisdiction, 44, 45, 69
appointed, 33, 57, 110
appointees, 69, 183
appointment, 155
attitudinal, 7, 9, 11, 13, 15, 23, 28, 40, 57, 75, 92, 93, 98, 99, 101, 102, 113, 127, 142, 141, 143, 147, 150, 151, 152, 156, 158, 157
attitudinal model, 7, 9, 28, 57, 75, 92, 93, 98, 101, 102, 113, 142, 143, 147, 151, 152, 156, 158, 157
attitudinally, 15, 35, 44, 54, 144

bureaucracy, 132
bureaucratic, 16, 30, 32, 37, 41
bureaucrats, 9, 13, 33, 35, 121, 143

censorship, 36, 37
certiorari process, 63, 65, 82, 183
circuit courts, 43, 44, 45
circuits, 17, 45, 61, 5, 63, 67, 123, 181
civil, 4, 5, 40, 41, 43, 55, 59, 55, 57, 58, 64, 71, 80, 83, 86, 88, 81, 82, 84, 86, 89, 87, 90, 92, 91, 108, 112, 115, 119, 121, 129, 132, 133, 138, 157, 188
civil liberties, 40, 41, 55, 59, 55, 57, 58, 64, 80, 83, 86, 81, 108, 112, 115, 119, 129, 188
civil rights, 4, 40, 58, 64, 71, 81, 82, 86, 89, 87, 92, 91, 121, 133, 138
common law, 13, 18, 49
concurring opinion, 7, 16
confirmation, 3, 4, 9, 121, 143
confirmation hearing, 3, 4
congressional influence, 69
congressional overrides, 9, 143
congressional statute, 7, 35, 55, 59, 67, 69, 85, 87, 82, 84, 96, 13, 121, 124, 125, 135, 133, 134, 136, 138, 140, 142, 143, 144, 146, 185
congressional statutes, 7, 59, 69, 85, 87, 82, 84, 96, 135, 133, 134, 136, 138, 140, 142, 144, 146, 185
conservative judges, 36, 38, 39, 40, 57, 52, 54, 55, 58, 59, 5, 62, 81, 108, 113, 117, 113, 121, 183

conservative justices, 38, 73, 85, 87, 81, 84, 86, 88, 87, 91, 98, 135, 132, 133, 134, 136, 187

conservative outcomes, 23, 38, 58, 84, 85, 108, 118

constitution, 1, 90

constitutional, 4, 13, 19, 28, 35, 53, 65, 92, 141

constitutionalism, 4

constitutionality, 58, 65, 75, 85, 87, 92, 109, 136, 183

constrain judges, 35, 33, 44, 54, 152

constraining effects, 38, 44, 54, 58, 64, 84, 87, 91, 92, 96, 145

constraint hypothesis, 55

contingent discretion, 4, 15, 18, 35, 33, 44, 41, 43, 46, 55, 64, 63, 66, 71, 88, 94, 96, 98, 103, 143, 145, 147, 149, 156, 158, 153

court, 3, 6, 16, 20, 21, 31, 33, 43, 45, 47, 49, 51, 69, 71, 73, 75, 71, 72, 75, 85, 87, 88, 101, 103, 104, 106, 109, 110, 126, 137, 142, 156, 181

court decision, 20, 31, 75, 85, 87, 88, 106, 137

court of appeals, 51

court opinions, 47, 71

criminal, 37, 31, 38, 39, 40, 41, 44, 43, 50, 51, 55, 56, 59, 52, 53, 54, 55, 59, 5, 62, 64, 71, 73, 77, 80, 81, 82, 85, 88, 90, 92, 91, 106, 108, 112, 115, 117, 115, 119, 129, 132, 137, 132, 133, 188

criminal cases, 39, 44, 56, 52, 55, 59, 64, 73, 81, 88, 112, 117, 115, 188

criminal law, 40, 55, 71, 112, 129

criminal statute, 37, 31, 38, 39, 50, 51, 59, 52, 53, 54, 5, 62, 64, 77, 80, 81, 85, 90, 106, 137, 132, 133

criminal statutes, 37, 31, 38, 39, 51, 52, 53, 54, 5, 62, 64, 80, 81, 85, 90, 106, 137, 132, 133

death penalty, 101, 117, 119

detailed language, 6, 11, 31, 37, 33, 84, 117, 119, 157, 158

detailed legislation, 21, 117, 121, 129, 132, 149

discretion, 11, 13, 15, 16, 19, 22, 24, 26, 28, 29, 31, 33, 35, 37, 32, 33, 38, 44, 53, 52, 64, 65, 71, 80, 81, 86, 92, 102, 104, 106, 117, 119, 121, 143, 144, 151, 154, 155, 18

discretionary control, 17, 45, 71, 80

discrimination cases, 81, 113

dissenting opinion, 35, 37, 103, 123, 134

district court, 43, 44, 45, 52

economic disputes, 40, 82, 87, 88

economic statutes, 52, 80, 87

electoral, 101, 103, 115, 119, 149

facilitating effect, 65, 66, 81, 85, 89, 90, 91, 183

facilitation, 35, 38, 57, 52, 58, 5, 60, 64, 81, 96, 98, 121

facilitation hypothesis, 60

federal courts, 9, 19, 43, 98, 99, 123, 134, 143

federal judges, 63, 72, 97, 99

federal judiciary, 99

federal statutes, 40, 128, 18

federalism, 81, 84, 85

firearms, 38, 31

ideal point, 21, 22, 24, 21, 151, 156, 158, 151

ideological influences, 21, 57, 75, 113, 189

ideological preferences, 15, 14, 21, 26, 28, 35, 36, 35, 39, 40, 44, 41, 53, 54, 57, 73, 75, 76, 87, 81, 84, 85, 99, 115, 121, 122, 127, 135, 137, 142, 144, 145, 149, 150, 151, 152, 151, 191 ideological voting, 11, 17, 38, 39, 40, 44, 54, 57, 73, 84, 86, 87, 97, 108, 113, 117, 118, 113, 119, 11, 132, 145, 151

ideologically, 35, 36, 37, 34, 38, 60, 62, 96, 101, 113, 151

ideology, 4, 8, 15, 19, 35, 38, 44, 54, 57, 64, 65, 75, 85, 86, 96, 101, 102, 103, 108, 113, 135, 136, 138, 141, 145, 147, 151, 181, 187, 188, 190

implementation, 13, 33, 31, 41

individual ideology, 81, 86, 123

individual liberties, 58, 59

individual liberty, 40, 64

intent, 3, 4, 7, 13, 15, 17, 21, 23, 24, 31, 48, 49, 51, 53, 72, 75, 71, 101, 103, 121, 156, 157, 189

judges, 1, 3, 4, 6, 7, 8, 9, 11, 13, 15, 17, 19, 13, 14, 15, 17, 18, 20, 22, 21, 22, 23, 26, 27, 28, 29, 31, 33, 35, 36, 37, 31, 32, 33, 35, 38, 39, 40, 43, 44, 41, 46, 47, 49, 53, 54, 55, 57, 58, 52, 53, 55, 57, 58, 60, 61, 5, 60, 64, 63, 66, 69, 71, 72, 75, 71, 73, 85, 87, 96, 97, 99, 100, 101, 102, 103, 104, 106, 108, 109, 110, 112, 117, 112, 113, 114, 115, 119, 120, 11, 13, 121, 122, 123, 125, 126, 142, 141, 143, 144, 145, 147, 149, 156, 158, 151, 155, 157, 18, 188

judicial annotations, 125, 127, 134, 135, 133, 136, 138, 140, 142, 144, 145, 147, 154, 156, 158, 153

judicial appointments, 115, 148

judicial behavior, 4, 7, 9, 10, 15, 19, 22, 21, 24, 28, 33, 38, 44, 41, 49, 56, 57, 52, 57, 5, 65, 63, 71, 73, 82, 88, 98, 99, 101, 102, 110, 115, 113, 117, 119, 11, 13, 123, 135, 132, 142, 143, 145, 147, 149, 151, 153, 155, 156, 183, 189, 191

judicial decisions, 9, 32, 106, 143, 18, 188

judicial discretion, 21, 23, 39, 40, 41, 42, 49, 92, 11, 18

judicial elections, 119, 149

judicial ideology, 10, 21, 57, 97, 11

judicial institutions, 65, 96, 98, 149

judicial review, 1, 65, 67, 90, 92, 112

jurisdiction, 45, 41, 43, 45, 64, 63, 65, 69, 73

law, 4, 1, 3, 4, 7, 8, 9, 11, 13, 15, 16, 17, 19, 12, 15, 16, 17, 18, 20, 22, 24, 21, 23, 24, 25, 26, 28, 29, 30, 31, 33, 35, 36, 31, 32, 33, 37, 40, 42, 44, 45, 46, 47, 49, 53, 54, 52, 60, 64, 65, 63, 67, 69, 72, 71, 81, 85, 84, 86, 87, 92, 94, 96, 98, 101,102, 103, 101, 103, 104, 106, 110, 113, 11, 13, 121, 122, 123, 124, 125, 127, 134, 140, 142, 141, 143, 145, 147, 151, 153, 157, 190

lawmakers, 9, 143

lawmaking, 4, 18, 141

laws, 1, 4, 7, 13, 12, 20, 23, 28, 29, 31, 33, 35, 36, 33, 38, 40, 52, 58, 80, 90, 92, 104, 123, 125, 127, 129, 142, 145, 157, 18, 188, 190

legal factors, 4, 7, 10, 11, 15, 23, 13, 142, 141, 147, 156, 151

legal model, 9, 11, 24, 26, 57, 113, 143, 149, 150, 153

legislative history, 6, 16, 18, 49, 51, 72

legislative statute, 1, 4, 7, 9, 13, 12, 18, 24, 25, 28, 33, 38, 40, 42, 44, 49, 55, 73, 88, 99, 104, 117, 119, 140, 141, 143, 145, 147, 154, 158, 157

legislative statutes, 4, 7, 9, 13, 12, 18, 24, 25, 28, 33, 40, 42, 49, 55, 88, 99, 104, 117, 119, 140, 141, 143, 145, 147, 158, 157

legislators, 28, 37, 31, 72
liberal judge, 36, 38, 40, 55, 58, 60,
  5, 60, 62, 90, 108, 117, 118, 113,
  119, 121
liberal justice, 73, 85, 87, 81, 82,
  84, 85, 88, 89, 87, 90, 96, 127,
  132, 135, 132, 133, 134, 136, 142,
  185
liberal outcomes, 23, 58, 84, 113,
  121
lower courts, 45, 64, 65, 76, 13, 123,
  134

majority opinion, 16, 18, 35, 37, 73
monitoring, 30

opinions, 1, 3, 15, 18, 23, 42, 49, 53,
  69, 73, 75, 103, 104, 123, 127, 134,
  142, 181
override, 16, 22, 21
overriding, 51
overturning, 24, 92

plain language, 6, 24, 51
plain meaning, 9, 11, 13, 15, 23, 25,
  26, 53, 87, 101, 103, 13, 123, 127,
  143, 147, 153
policy preferences, 9, 21, 23, 99,
  100, 141, 143, 18
policymaking, 33
precedent, 13, 23, 24, 101, 11, 13,
  153, 18, 190
presidency, 155
president, 5, 6, 57
progeny, 13, 24

regulations, 41, 47, 55, 72, 73, 132
regulatory, 41, 73
retention, 115, 117, 120, 149, 188

sincere vote, 58, 54, 55, 57, 58, 59,
  60, 75, 76, 84, 85, 87, 88, 81, 82,
  83, 84, 86, 88, 87, 91, 108, 109,
  110, 112, 114, 117, 118, 111, 112,
  137, 131, 132, 133, 134, 135, 154
state authority, 40, 85
state constitutions, 19, 17
state court, 17, 19, 43, 44, 99, 101,
  102, 103, 104, 106, 108, 109, 110,
  115, 117, 112, 115, 119, 149, 17
state ideology, 101, 112
state judge, 13, 17, 103, 104, 108,
  110, 117
state legislature, 117, 119, 149, 151,
  189
state statute, 31, 40, 46, 99, 103, 101,
  104, 108, 115, 119
state supreme court, 7, 17, 45, 98,
  99, 112, 113, 115, 119, 11, 145,
  148, 188
statute, 6, 7, 15, 16, 17, 18, 22, 24,
  21, 26, 35, 36, 37, 31, 32, 33, 35,
  37, 38, 42, 49, 51, 53, 55, 58, 59,
  52, 54, 55, 58, 59, 5, 60, 71, 72,
  73, 75, 73, 75, 77, 80, 81, 84, 89,
  87, 92, 94, 97, 101, 103, 105, 106,
  109, 117, 13, 121, 122, 123, 125,
  127, 129, 132, 135, 136, 137, 132,
  138, 142, 145, 148, 151, 154, 158,
  153, 155, 18, 181, 183, 185, 187,
  188, 190
statute length, 31, 59, 54, 55, 58, 59,
  77, 80, 87, 92, 94, 105, 127, 129,
  132, 138, 148, 155, 187
statutory, 4, 7, 9, 17, 18, 19, 13, 15,
  16, 17, 18, 20, 21, 22, 24, 28, 33,
  36, 37, 33, 35, 38, 40, 41, 42, 43,
  44, 46, 41, 43, 47, 49, 51, 53, 55,
  56, 57, 52, 55, 57, 58, 60, 61, 5, 60,
  62, 64, 63, 65, 66, 67, 69, 71, 72,
  73, 75, 71, 73, 75, 82, 81, 82, 84,
  85, 86, 88, 89, 87, 90, 92, 97, 103,
  104, 101, 103, 104, 106, 108, 112,
  113, 115, 117, 113, 114, 115, 119,

121, 11, 13, 121, 123, 126, 135, 132, 140, 142, 144, 143, 145, 147, 149, 151, 152, 154, 158, 151, 153, 155, 157, 17, 18, 181, 187

statutory constraint, 37, 57, 60, 62, 75, 82, 81, 86, 88, 108, 18, 187

statutory construction, 13, 16, 49, 51, 72, 73, 101, 103

statutory detail, 38, 42, 43, 44, 55, 56, 55, 58, 60, 73, 86, 108, 115, 119, 11, 147, 151

statutory facilitation, 55, 62, 132

statutory influence, 9, 17, 18, 33, 49, 61, 67, 82, 97, 103, 121, 11, 135, 143, 147, 153, 157

statutory interpretation, 7, 19, 13, 15, 17, 18, 20, 28, 33, 35, 65, 72, 73, 75, 90, 97, 103, 104, 11, 121, 123, 142, 153, 17, 181

statutory language, 17, 19, 16, 22, 36, 37, 38, 40, 41, 43, 47, 51, 53, 52, 55, 57, 5, 60, 65, 63, 71, 82, 88, 89, 87, 92, 103, 104, 101, 104, 106, 108, 113, 115, 117, 113, 114, 13, 123, 135, 132, 145, 149, 152, 154, 158, 151, 155, 157

substantive meaning, 26, 121, 153

supreme court, 17, 43, 103, 117, 119, 149, 188

tax, 52

textualism, 15, 18, 47, 87

textualist, 15, 16, 53, 72, 71

textualist approach, 16, 72

unanimous decisions, 92, 94, 96, 138, 140, 144, 147

unconstitutional, 33, 11, 125

vague statutes, 24, 127

vague terms, 6, 22

validity tests, 37, 31, 104, 149

veto, 16, 18

word count, 37, 31, 33, 42, 94, 104, 105, 138, 155, 18, 188, 190